EARL H. FRY

THE POLITICS OF INTERNATIONAL INVESTMENT

McGRAW-HILL BOOK COMPANY

New York   St. Louis   San Francisco   Auckland   Bogotá
Hamburg   Johannesburg   London   Madrid   Mexico
Montreal   New Delhi   Panama   Paris   São Paulo
Singapore   Sydney   Tokyo   Toronto

Library of Congress Cataloging in Publication Data

Fry, Earl H.
  The politics of international investment.

  Includes index.
  1. Investments, Foreign—Political aspects. I. Title.
HG4538.F78   1983   332.6'73   82-18004
ISBN 0-07-022610-5

1 2 3 4 5 6 7 8 9 0 DOC/DOC 8 9 8 7 6 5 4 3

ISBN 0-07-022610-5

The editors for this book were William Sabin and Christine
Ulwick, the designer was Riverside Studios, and the production
supervisor was Thomas G. Kowalczyk. It was set in Melior by
Bi-Comp.

Printed and bound by R. R. Donnelley & Sons, Inc.

To Elaine, Chris, Lisa, Anna, and Kimberly

ABOUT THE AUTHOR

EARL H. FRY is associate professor of political science
and program coordinator for the Center for International and Area Studies at Brigham Young University. A former Fulbright lecturer at the Sorbonne,
he has also lectured on international investment before
audiences in Europe, Asia, Africa, and Latin America.
He is frequently asked by committees of the U.S.
Congress to testify on issues of international trade
and investment.

   Dr. Fry is the author of *Financial Invasion of the
USA: A Threat to American Society?*, which was
selected by the *Library Journal* as one of 1980's top
business books. A Ph.D. from the University of California, Dr. Fry has authored *Canadian Government and
Politics in Comparative Perspective* and coauthored
*The Other Western Europe: A Political Analysis of
the Smaller Democracies.*

|CONTENTS

PREFACE

Back in what many people considered to be the good old days, residents of the United States took great comfort in the notion of "Fortress America." According to this concept, the United States was immune from the ravages of war and economic strife, which might occur elsewhere in the world, because of the protection afforded by two mammoth oceans to the east and the west and the presence of friendly and weaker nations to the north and the south.

The era of Fortress America is, of course, a remnant of the past, both in strategic military and economic terms. The United States now has at least a fifty percent dependence on overseas suppliers for almost three-quarters of the strategic minerals deemed necessary for maintaining national security standards and the current level of economic prosperity. In recent years, overseas trade has also become a much larger component of America's overall gross national product. In the investment arena, the United States is now the number one host nation for direct investment in the world, and the rate of investment coming into the country has far surpassed that going out over the past decade. Almost two million Americans now labor for foreign-controlled enterprises on American soil, and many communities in the United States are now dependent on foreign companies for safeguarding the economic well-being of their citizens. Indeed, foreign-controlled businesses and industries in the United States now produce more goods and services than the vast majority of all the sovereign nations in the world.

As will be documented in the text, American firms in banking and in a dozen key industrial sectors have lost much of their competitive edge over the past twenty years. Because of this growing overseas competition and the increasing interdependence of the global economy, many American companies which have been perfectly content to service regional markets in the United States must now expand abroad simply to survive.

There is a strong possibility that we are entering an age of unprecedented direct investment activity worldwide, and there will be tremendous opportunities available for business expansion. On the other hand, political risks will increase. For example, over the past few years, many businesses and individual investors have been adversely affected by sudden currency devaluations in Mexico and Argentina, the imposition of economic nationalist measures in Canada, revolution in Iran, martial law in Poland, the Soviet incursion in Afghanistan, and the battle for the Falkland Islands. Similar disruptions linked to war, strife, and political machinations will continue to afflict international investors in the years ahead. Indeed, a monumental challenge facing both governments and businesses over the next two decades will be how to reconcile increasing global and resource interdependency with the parochial pressures of political nationalism and subnationalism.

This book indicates the specific ways in which political and governmental decisions will impact upon the future investment strategies of international businesses. It will also show why international firms must sensitize themselves to political changes at the international, national, and subnational levels and will illustrate why political risk forecasting must become an indispensable part of the corporate decision-making process. To be quite frank, the political acumen manifested by corporate leaders will be just as important as financial wizardry in determining the future success of international investment projects.

Finally, the book also contains a special message for governments, whether they be at the national, regional, or municipal levels. Foreign direct investment, with all of its inherent advantages and drawbacks, will in the future be a far more important factor than bilateral and multilateral aid in modernizing and diversifying economic bases and in enhancing the material well-being of citizens. Through a questionnaire and archival research, I have gathered current data on the investment restriction and investment incentive policies of sixty governments scattered around the globe. Rather surprisingly, considering the checkered reputations which multinational corporations have acquired in various parts of the world, each and every one of these governments was actively seeking certain types of foreign direct investment, including governments in the Soviet Union and China. The appendices provide a list of the restriction and incentive policies pursued by these sixty governments and should furnish some very useful comparative data for political and governmental representatives interested in attracting new investment.

Earl H. Fry

ACKNOWLEDGMENTS

I would like to thank Brigham Young University's Department of Political Science and Center for International and Area Studies for providing time, encouragement, and research assistance for this project. Special thanks should especially go to Thayne Lowe, Susan Hubbard, Ken Stiles, Wendy Butler, Donna L. Parkinson, and Marilyn Webb for their invaluable assistance in preparing the manuscript. In addition, it has been a distinct pleasure working with Bill Sabin and Christine Ulwick of McGraw-Hill, who are true "professionals" in the finest sense of the word. I am also extremely indebted to my wife Elaine and my four children for their moral support and patience.

I have also had the opportunity over the past three years to lecture extensively on the impact which foreign direct investment and technology transfer are having on national political and economic development. During my lecture tours to the Middle East, Southeast Asia, Australia, Brazil, and West Africa, I have met with many representatives of businesses, governments, and academia. Their advice and comments have been extremely valuable and have certainly influenced many sections of this book. I would especially like to thank these people for their warm hospitality and for showing me on a firsthand basis how interdependent the contemporary world has become. Their observations have also convinced me that in this complex age of global interdependence, we must learn how to go beyond the borders of nation-states in seeking solutions to serious problem areas which now surpass the decision-making capabilities of national governments.

THE FUTURE OF INTERNATIONAL INVESTMENT: A GOLDEN AGE OR PERILOUS ERA?

1

THE HIGHLY COMPETITIVE INTERNATIONAL SETTING

The stake in the international trade and investment game is heading toward the three trillion (3,000,000,000,000) dollar mark, and competition among business enterprises to secure overseas markets has intensified dramatically. Within an increasingly competitive and interdependent global economic setting, more and more businesses will soon be repeating the refrain voiced by Mitsubishi of Japan: "We must become multinational, otherwise we cannot survive."[1]

The 1980s and 1990s may well be decades of unprecedented international trade and investment activity, with direct investment levels easily dwarfing those of any other period in the post-World War II era. These decades will offer tremendous opportunities for business expansion, but political risks will also be magnified. Indeed, the great challenge facing both governments and international businesses through the remainder of the twentieth century is to reconcile the phenomenon of increasing global economic and resource interdependency with the incessant parochial pressures of political fragmentation and nationalism.[2]

For the first time in modern history, it is quite conceivable that all of the nations on earth will experience significant foreign direct investment activity. As a concrete example of the growing linkages in the economic and business spheres, China, which is home to one-fourth of the world's population, has finally opened its borders to selected foreign investment. Furthermore, there is little doubt that the Soviet Union and the Eastern European nations, which had already accumulated 80.4 billion dollars in debts to the West by the end of 1981 and which face severe economic structural problems and mounting consumer demands, will become progressively more receptive to international investment overtures.[3]

The Soviet Union, of course, is a classic example of the paradox which exists when a nation continues to emphasize the safeguarding of national political, ideological, and strategic priorities in a new era of internationalized and interdependent economic relationships. The U.S.S.R. remains very suspicious of Western intentions and possesses the capacity to literally decimate life on earth, while at the same time it pleads for access to Western technology and allows such clearly capitalist enterprises as Pepsi Cola and Pizza Hut to establish franchises on Russian soil.

In a golden age of international investment, the multinational corporation will continue to be the main initiator of direct investment activity and will be the most visible actor involved in the internationalization of the world economic system. Consequently, the multinationals will be the major institutions rendering decisions linked to the allocation of international production and the resulting patterns of global trade.

On the other hand, the golden age will definitely not be dominated by U.S.-based multinationals to the same extent as occurred immediately after World War II, when the United States singlehandedly provided more than 40 percent of the world's production. As will be documented in the next chapter, the number of U.S.-based multinationals among the world's largest corporations has decreased dramatically over the past two decades. In 1963, for example, U.S. multinationals accounted for almost two-thirds of the world's 100 largest enterprises and for approximately three-fifths of the top 500. By the end of the 1970s, the U.S. share had dropped below one-half in both categories. America's share of the world's total product also declined to 25 percent in 1970 and to 23 percent in 1980, and the U.S. portion of foreign direct investment attributable to the thirteen largest OECD (Organization for Economic Cooperation and Development) nations has decreased from a peak of 60 percent in the mid-1960s to less than 35 percent in the 1980s.[4] In the future, European- and Japanese-based multinational corporations will certainly continue to expand their international activities, and some of the OPEC (Organization of Petroleum Exporting Countries) nations, which are registering multibillion-dollar surpluses annually from worldwide oil sales, are already forces to be reckoned with in investment markets. In addition, enterprises in Third World countries have also made surprising progress in recent years, and the number of multinational businesses headquartered in the Soviet bloc nations has increased from 40 in the early 1960s to more than 500 two decades later.[5] Furthermore, powerful state-owned enterprises, such as Renault, British Petroleum, and Volkswagen, have boldly expanded their investments abroad and now are major actors in many foreign economies.[6] In the mid-1970s, 59 of the largest 500 industrial firms outside the United States were state-owned, and these corporations accounted for almost 21 percent of the total sales of the top 500 and 15 percent of total world trade.[7]

The heavy hand of politics will be easily discernible in international investment and trade activity through the duration of the next two decades. Indeed, in the thermonuclear age, economic tactics have in many ways become much more effective weapons in government arsenals than military hardware.[8] Furthermore, the growing vulnerability of national units to events which transpire outside their borders, whether it be oil pricing, resource availability, or other pertinent issue areas, frequently triggers domestic demands for protectionism. Therefore, businesses which dare to venture abroad must become acutely aware of the ways in which public bureaucracies or organized political movements can impact upon their operations. As a concrete example, in the current era of export-credit wars and increasing similarities in the price, quality, and availability of many product lines, government financing arrangements, both in the form of inducements and impediments, might well be the determining factor in the success or failure of overseas business pursuits. Whenever feasible, national governments will generally attempt to further the interests of their own home-grown enterprises, even when such actions run counter to the spirit of free trade or the free movement of capital. In his own inimitable way, the late George Meany summed up the feelings of many Americans when he surmised that "foreign trade is the guerrilla war of economics, and right now the U.S. is being ambushed."[9]

On the other hand, business enterprises can expect at times to be used as pawns in a national government's quest to achieve certain domestic or international goals. As a classic illustration, France was vehemently opposed to Libya's 1981 incursion into Chad, a former French protectorate. To underline this displeasure, the French government under President Giscard d'Estaing announced that it was cancelling an oil-exploration contract between Elf-Aquitaine and Libya, even though the oil company at that time was only partially owned by the French state and had worked arduously for more than a year to secure Libyan approval for this profitable venture.[10] Several U.S.-based multinational firms and their overseas subsidiaries were also used as pawns by governments in the United States and Western Europe during the height of the Siberian natural gas pipeline controversy.

Above all, businesses established on foreign soil must face up to the fact that even the tiniest of governments or subunits of governments wield potential authority which can dramatically impact upon their firm's activities. The exercise of the authority to tax, screen foreign investment proposals, establish exchange and repatriation-of-profit controls, set local participation levels, erect import and export barriers, or nationalize and expropriate foreign enterprises might well doom the subsidiaries of even the most powerful multinational corporations. Even in such a mature and stable market as the United States, astute foreign investors must first pave the way with extensive research and planning. Otherwise, they might find that some obscure bureaucratic unit, in its zeal to protect the snail darter fish, the Furbish lousewort, the Virginia fringed mountain snail, or perhaps even the orange-bellied mouse, has effectively thwarted the investment strategy of an overseas firm. As asinine as these examples might seem to be, the functional equivalents to the snail darter and Furbish lousewort episodes are to be found lurking in political systems throughout the world, waiting to wreak havoc with the plans of unsuspecting international investors.

American multinationals can thus expect to face stiff competition and many potential pitfalls throughout the 1980s and 1990s in international trade and investment markets. For those corporate and individual investors who are adroit enough to adjust to the new rules of the game in an economically interdependent but politically fragmented world, growth opportunities will be superb. On the other hand, a significant number of existing businesses will fold altogether because of increasing competition or will be absorbed by the large international conglomerates. Furthermore, political risks for businesses will be accentuated, and a proliferation of investment disasters similar to what occurred in post-Shah Iran and in the early days of the "opening" of China must be expected.

A POLITICAL PRIMER FOR INTERNATIONAL INVESTORS

This book will provide fundamental guidelines on the ways in which the political and governmental sectors will affect international direct investment and will represent a much-needed political primer for international investors. For example, how can international businesses begin to comprehend the intricacies and idiosyncrasies of national political systems and learn to reconcile the priorities of the business enterprise with the policy pursuits of the host government?[11] What opportunities and hazards will international businesses face as a result of the growing power base of subnational governments, such as the Canadian provinces, the American states, and the German Länder, or separatist organizations, such as the Parti Québécois, the Basque ETA (*Euzkadi ta Azkatasuna,* Basque Homeland and Freedom), or Ireland's IRA (Irish Republican Army)? What will be the repercussions of the accelerated activity of the OPEC, Eastern bloc, and Third World nations in international investment markets? Can state-owned enterprises which are now investing heavily overseas segregate purely business decisions from the political priorities of their home governments? What will be the implications for business of the North-South dialogue and the movement to create a New International Economic Order? Will a code of conduct for both multinationals and host governments be worked out in the near future, or will international investors face a new round of nationalization and expropriation policies? How can international businesses sensitize themselves to changes in subnational, national, and international political systems and why should multinational enterprises be involved in developing political risk forecasting strategies? Above all, as we move rapidly toward the dawning of a new century, which nations will offer the best political and governmental opportunities for business expansion and which will offer the most uncertainties and perils?

In terms of the development of the text, Chapter 2 will examine the political dimension of international economics in an age of complex interdependence and illustrate how profoundly American society in general and the business community in particular have already been impacted by direct investment activity. Chapter 3 will look at the rewards and perils of international investment from an historical standpoint and deal with the perceptions of investment which multinationals will currently find among citizens and governments in many nations. Chapter 4 then illustrates how political risk forecasting is emerging as an indispensable tool for international investors in an age of global economic interdependency and political fragmentation. Next, Chapter 5 provides a case study of direct investment in a host country, Canada, and shows how politics has dramatically influenced this activity. Chapter 6 proceeds to scrutinize the challenges facing investors at both the national and subnational government levels and indicates how the solidifying of contacts in local and regional governmental echelons may be the key to a successful investment project. Chapters 7 and 8 respectively look at the politics of investment restrictions and investment incentives. They are supplemented by appendices showing specific restriction and incentive policies in approximately sixty nations accounting for well over 90 percent of the world's trade and investment activity. The information contained in the appendices was obtained through questionnaires sent to pertinent ministries and departments in each of these nations. The final chapter then summarizes the lessons which will have to be learned about political and governmental processes and idiosyncrasies in order for businesses to expand globally with relative impunity during the 1980s and 1990s.

REFERENCES

[1] *Business Week,* June 16, 1980, p. 102.

[2] Peter F. Drucker, in *Managing in Turbulent Times* (New York: Harper and Row, 1980, p. 170), has observed that "an integrated world economy and a splintered world polity can co-exist only in tension, conflict, and mutual misunderstanding."

[3] At the end of 1980, when the Soviet bloc debt stood at 77 billion dollars, it was estimated that the U.S.S.R. had amassed 15.2 billion dollars in debts to the West, Bulgaria 4.3 billion, Czechoslovakia 5.0 billion, East Germany 12.0 billion, Hungary 7.6 billion, Poland 24.0 billion, and Romania 9.0 billion. See *Business Week,* February 16, 1981, p. 86.

[4] Herbert Block, *The Planetary Product in 1980—A Creative Pause?* (Washington, D.C.: U.S. Department of State, 1981, pp. 30–31), and Robert D. Hormats, "New Challenges in International Investment Policy," paper presented at the plenary session of the Economic Policy Council of the United Nations Association, September 18, 1981.

[5] "The Rise of Eastern Bloc Multinationals," *International Management,* December, 1980, p. 19; and David A. Heenan and Warren J. Keegan, "The Rise of Third World Multinationals," *Atlantic Community Quarterly,* Spring 1979, 108–121.

[6] For two contrasting views of the international activities of state-owned enterprises, see Douglas F. Lamont, *Foreign State Enterprises* (New York: Basic Books, 1979); and Yair Aharoni, "The State Owned Enterprise as a Competitor in International Markets," *Columbia Journal of World Business,* Spring 1980, 14–21.

[7] Aharoni, p. 16.

[8] The increasingly interdependent complexion of global affairs substantially contributes to the obsolescence of military options. As James Rosenau points out in his book, *The Study of Global Interdependence* (London: Frances Pinter, 1980, p. 41), "The more societies, cultures, economies, and polities become interdependent, the less do the resulting conflicts lend themselves to resolution through military threats and actions."

[9] Quoted in Martin Kupferman and Maurice D. Levi, *Slowth* (New York: Wiley, 1980, p. 120).

[10] *New York Times,* January 9, 1981, p. A2.

[11] Americans, for example, consider that some of the government-business cooperative ties so long identified with "Japan, Inc." should be adopted in the United States. In a recent survey, 55 percent of Americans who were interviewed stated that the United States should imitate some of the Japanese practices designed to help businesses develop new products and processes and then market them abroad. Sixty-three percent felt it would be a good idea to relax antitrust laws to permit companies to work together in developing new products and overseas markets. Seventy-one percent also want the government and businesses to work together to foster greater growth, with only 18 percent stating that the government and business sectors should work individually. See Cambridge Reports, *Adversaries or Allies? American Attitudes on Business, Government and Growth* (New York: Union Carbide, 1980, pp. 71, 108–110).

2 | INTERDEPENDENCE AND THE NEW CHALLENGES FACING THE UNITED STATES

THE IMPACT OF FOREIGN INVESTMENT ON THE UNITED STATES

Multinational corporations based in the United States have long been perceived as the dominant investors in the postwar period. Indeed, Servan-Schreiber's famous book entitled *The American Challenge* warned in the mid-1960s that if European industry did not wake up, the third great industrial power in the world after the United States and the Soviet Union would be American industry in Western Europe.[1]

With more than 227 billion dollars in direct investment abroad at the end of 1981, the United States continues by far to be the number one foreign investor in the world. The repatriation of profits from these investments overseas has recently permitted the United States to be one of the few major Western nations to enjoy a healthy current accounts balance, in spite of a string of years when spiraling oil-import prices have precipitated major trade deficits. Current accounts statistics measure trade in goods and services as well as aid outflows and investment income. During the 1980 to 1981 period, the U.S. current accounts ledger showed a surplus of approximately 10 billion dollars, whereas Germany and several other major developed countries suffered significant deficits.

Thus the United States continues to be an active investor abroad, and U.S.-based multinationals continue to be perceived as the major international investors. However, times are definitely changing.

In addition to being the number one investor abroad, the United States has recently passed Canada as the number one host country for foreign investment. Direct investment, which the U.S. Department of Commerce defines as providing a controlling interest in an enterprise, has skyrocketed from 13 billion dollars in 1970 to more than 89 billion dollars at the end of 1981. Because the U.S.-based enterprises were involved in international investment activity much earlier in the post-World War II era, U.S. investment abroad is still 2½ times higher than foreign investment in the United States. Figures 2-1 through 2-3 illustrate the levels of both U.S. direct investment abroad and foreign direct investment in the United States over the past three decades. During the past few years, however, the rate of investment coming into the United States from foreign sources has been substantially higher than that going out of the country.[2] For example, foreign investment in the United States increased by 25.5 percent in 1980 and a record 31.1 percent in 1981, whereas U.S. investment abroad went up 14.8 percent in 1980 and only 5.5 percent in 1981. It is expected that this trend will continue for the foreseeable future.

Americans are generally aware that Toyota, Volkswagen, Sony, and Shell Oil have foreign origins, but few realize that some of the products which they may use on a daily basis have recently been acquired by

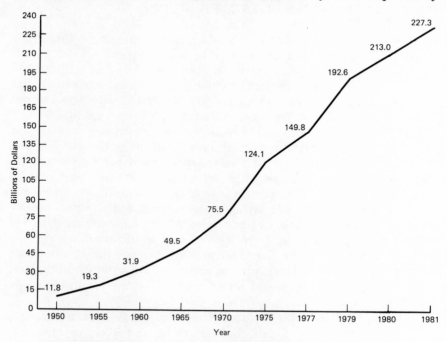

Figure 2-1   U.S. direct investment abroad, 1950 to 1981.

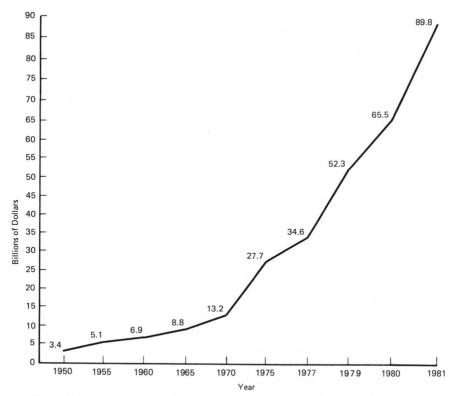

Figure 2-2 Foreign direct investment in the United States, 1950 to 1981.

foreign investors, including Alka-Seltzer, Clorox, Borax, Lipton tea, Pepsodent toothpaste, Kool cigarettes, Beechnut baby food, Girl Scout cookies, Libby fruits and vegetables, J & B scotch, Good Humor and Baskin-Robbins ice cream, Capitol records, Timex watches, Hills Bros. coffee, SOS soap pads, and Geritol.

Overseas concerns have also acquired a controlling interest in such well-known corporations as Standard Oil of Ohio, American Motors, Kennecott Copper, Howard Johnson's, International House of Pancakes, Stouffer Hotels, A & P and Grand Union supermarkets, Gimbels, and Saks Fifth Avenue. Foreign firms also control more than one-third of America's truck-manufacturing industry. In the publishing arena, foreign control has been extended to Bantam books, Viking books, the *New York Post, The Village Voice, Parents Magazine, Look, Esquire, New York, Geo,* and *The Star.* Marine Midland, the National Bank of North America, Union Bancorp, and Crocker Bank, four of America's top 40 banks, have also recently been purchased by foreign institutions. Quite clearly, a vast majority of the 150 largest banks outside of the

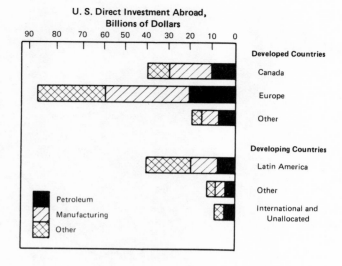

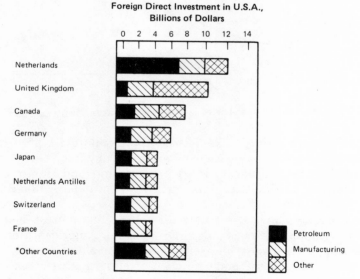

*Eight largest positions among the other countries

Figure 2-3 Geographic distribution of U.S. direct investment abroad and foreign direct investment in the United States. (U.S. Department of Commerce, Bureau of Economic Analysis—based on 1979 data.)

United States have established operations on American soil and are capturing a significant percentage of the overall banking market. As a concrete example, among the large banks which the U.S. Federal Reserve monitors, more than 20 percent of all commercial loans currently being made in the United States are attributable to foreign-controlled banks, which also account for 40 percent of the banking business in New York and more than 30 percent in California, America's two major financial centers. Overall, foreign-based banks doubled their market share of business loans made in the United States during the 1973 to 1980 period. Figure 2-4 lists some of the foreign-controlled products and enterprises in the United States.[3]

The overseas financial penetration of the U.S. market extends to most other economic sectors as well. In certain areas of the United States, such as sections of California's Central Valley and the Mississippi Delta, foreign buyers may have purchased at least 25 percent of all farmland which has come on the open market over the past five years. Ranch and timber land and other property rich in natural resources have also attracted strong foreign interest. For example, America's largest silver mine is now controlled by a Middle Eastern investment group. Preliminary data also indicate that perhaps one-quarter or more of all major commercial property transactions completed during the past few years in New York City, Miami, San Francisco, Houston, Portland, and certain other major cities have involved buyers from abroad. Foreign pension funds alone pumped 1.5 to 2.3 billion dollars into U.S. real estate in 1979 alone. The pension fund of Great Britain's National Coal Board, for example, has acquired a substantial interest in Washington, D.C.'s celebrated Watergate complex.[4] The largest residential home builder in the United States, U.S. Home, has also attracted significant foreign investment. Moreover, foreign involvement in the U.S. stock market has trebled over the past decade and foreign investors accounted for a startling 40 percent share of net equity purchases in the United States in 1980. Trading in U.S. equities by foreign institutions totaled 75 billion dollars in 1980, and foreign investors currently account for as much as 15 percent of the daily trading on the floor of the New York Stock Exchange.[5] Overseas residents are also among the major purchasers of government securities. As an illustration, the number one buyer of Fannie Maes, which generate funds for home mortgages, is Saudi Arabia.

WHY INVEST IN THE UNITED STATES?

The United States has the largest, most affluent market in the world, and in an increasingly interdependent global setting, it is natural that the giant foreign-based multinationals would want to acquire a piece of

Aim
Alka-Seltzer
All
Alpo
Aqua Velva
Aurora toys
Baskin-Robbins ice cream
Beechnut baby food
Bic pens
Borax
Bulova
Capitol records
Clorox
Close-up
Dove
Geritol
Girl Scout cookies
Good Humor ice cream
J & B scotch

Keebler cookies
KitchenAid
Kool cigarettes
Lawry's Foods
Libby fruits and vegetables
Lifebuoy
Lipton tea
Lux
Marx toys
Mrs. Butterworth's pancake mix
Nestle chocolates
Ovaltine
Pepsodent
Philco
Ronson
Sylvania
Timex
Wisk

Bantam books
Coles Book Stores
New West
New York
New York Post

Parents Magazine
The Star
Viking books
The Village Voice
Wadsworth books

A & P supermarkets
American Motors
BASF
Budd Co.
Colonial stores
Fairchild Camera
Fed-Mart
Ferguson Oil
Foster Grant
Gimbels
W. R. Grace

Hardee's restaurants
Howard Johnson's
International House of Pancakes
Kennecott
Lum's restaurants
Pic 'N Pay stores
Pop Shoppes of America
Mack Trucks
Marshall Field
Northrup King
Saks Fifth Avenue
Standard Oil of Ohio
Stouffer hotels

Bache
Crocker Bank
First Boston Corp.

Marine Midland Bank
National Bank of North America
Union Bancorp

Figure 2-4 Foreign-controlled products and enterprises.

the action. However, one cannot overemphasize the point that the rapid upsurge in foreign investment activity is largely predicated on the stability of America's economic and political systems. The Europeans in particular are fond of saying that the last capitalist on earth will die in America, and foreign investors in general appreciate the middle-of-the-road predictability of the U.S. governmental system. At a time when many regions of the world are suffering through major political turmoil and uncertainty, the United States is perceived more and more by overseas residents as a safe, attractive, investment haven.

Tax rates in the United States are among the lowest in the advanced industrial world, and when one takes into account fringe benefits, U.S. wage rates are also appreciably below those in several Western European nations. In spite of widespread publicity to the contrary, American production rates are also very competitive. As an example, Michelin, the giant French tire maker, has recently opened three plants in the state of South Carolina. These plants remain open for more than 340 days a year, whereas Michelin's facilities in Europe are open for less than 300 days annually. Furthermore, access to a secure supply of natural resources and energy within a stable political environment has prompted many foreign firms to establish operations in the United States.

The declining value of the U.S. dollar vis-à-vis many major currencies during the late 1960s and the 1970s and the rather static performance of the stock market during this period have also spurred on foreign interest in acquiring existing U.S. businesses. From January 2, 1970, to January 2, 1980, the value of the French franc increased by more than one-third in relationship to the U.S. dollar, the Japanese yen by one-half, and the values of the German mark and Swiss franc more than doubled in comparison to the American currency. As for the stock market's performance, the Dow average stood at 809.20 on January 2, 1970, and at 824.57 exactly one decade later. When one takes into account inflation, the stock value of an average American firm was actually cut in half during the ten-year period, whereas the value of the assets controlled by the firm doubled in value simply because of inflationary tendencies. Although the American dollar has recently made a remarkable recovery, foreign investors continue their frenzied activity in the United States, hoping to take advantage of the relative weakness of the stock market in order to acquire assets at what they consider to be bargain-basement prices.[6] Indeed, because of their eagerness to acquire existing U.S. firms, foreign investors may have helped to contribute to the astronomical interest rates of the late 1970s and early 1980s by maintaining a high demand for loans in order to finance acquisitions.

The relative weakness of the U.S. stock market and of the U.S. dollar before its robust recovery during the early 1980s should in no way be construed as indications of the demise of American economic prosperity. Even though several nations currently have an average per capita income higher than that of the United States, American consumers still enjoy the most clout when it comes to purchasing power, a fact which has not been overlooked by astute overseas investors looking for an affluent market. In its survey to ascertain purchasing power in forty-five major metropolitan areas in the non-Communist world, the Union Bank of Switzerland determined that Chicago, San Francisco, and Los Angeles ranked numbers one, two, and three in terms of their citizens' purchasing power and that New York, the only other American city included, ranked number six.[7] A Purchasing Power Parity (PPP) Index developed by three University of Pennsylvania professors also indicates that the relative prosperity of citizens in the United States vis-à-vis nations in Western Europe actually changed very little from 1970 through 1980, even though there were major currency fluctuations during this period. For example, the PPP of West Germany was 78 percent of that of the United States in 1970 and had increased slightly to 81 percent by the end of the decade. By 1980, Sweden's Purchasing Power Parity was 78 percent of that of the United States, Belgium's 78 percent, the Netherlands' 70 percent, and Switzerland's 70 percent, to give just a few illustrations. Overall, on an annual basis, the average European has about 3500 dollars less in real goods and services available for investment or consumption purposes than the average American, with per family differences being at least twice as great.[8]

The bargain-basement motivation also partially explains the almost insatiable appetite which foreigners have for U.S. farm, ranch, and timber land. Geographically, the United States is one of the largest nations in the world, and it has been blessed with hundreds of millions of acres of fertile land. Keeping dimensions in perspective, one should remember that the entire nation of Great Britain is only the size of Oregon, with 3 million people settled in the Northwestern state, whereas 60 million are cloistered in the European island nation. Japan is approximately the size of Montana, with Montana having less than one million inhabitants and Japan 120 million. Because choice land is at a premium in Europe and Japan, investors from these regions can acquire property in the United States for perhaps one-tenth the price it would cost them in their own home countries. Furthermore, since the value of U.S. farmland has traditionally kept pace with inflation, foreigners are making a very safe and secure investment at a price which is comparatively dirt cheap. The Japanese, for example, who import one-quarter of all the timber grown in the U.S. Pacific Northwest, have begun to buy tree farms in this region to ensure a steady supply of this U.S. natural resource.

Even though the U.S. government is officially neutral toward foreign investment activity, many state governments are presently offering huge incentive packages to overseas investors. During the past few years, approximately two-thirds of the American states have opened offices abroad for the expressed purpose of attracting foreign investment. When Volkswagen announced it was searching for a plant location in the United States, thirty-five states tendered offers. Pennsylvania finally landed VW, but the bidding war among the states became so intense that the Pennsylvania State government had to muster together a 100-million-dollar incentive package for the German-based multinational, with a fair share of the money coming out of the pockets of that state's taxpayers.

Even local communities are becoming very actively involved in the chase for foreign money. Over the past fifteen years, the city government and chamber of commerce in Spartanburg, South Carolina, have waged a concerted campaign to attract foreign investment. This effort has thus far paid big dividends, with more than forty foreign firms investing well over a billion dollars in the city, thereby creating thousands of new jobs. Spartanburg has been dubbed "Euroville" by some residents because 1500 European executives now live there and Bastille Day, Oktoberfest, and other well-known European holidays are celebrated hand in hand with the Fourth of July.

Some U.S. real estate firms and investment banking establishments have also begun to cater almost exclusively to the foreign clientele. Through the use of computers, satellite technology, and periodic "Market Days," a San Francisco-based corporation is advertising U.S. properties in London, Zurich, Tokyo, and other major overseas capitals, making it almost as easy for foreign investors to keep pace with what is transpiring in the U.S. real estate market as it is for American investors. On an annual basis, this corporation is arranging the sale of hundreds of millions of dollars worth of U.S. property to foreign buyers. Moreover, many of the new clients of Wall Street investment bankers are overseas investors seeking to acquire major U.S. businesses. Once again, millions of dollars in commissions are being made in this sector because of the avid foreign interest in the U.S. market.

THE PROS AND CONS OF FOREIGN INVESTMENT ACTIVITY

The dramatic increase in foreign investment activity in the United States has several benefits. For one thing, it helps to defuse criticism of

U.S. direct investment abroad, which, because of America's head start in the 1950s and early 1960s, is still far greater than foreign direct investment in the United States. The foreigners are catching up rapidly, however, and when one adds their investments in farm and commercial properties, government securities, and stock portfolios, they are now about even with total U.S. investment overseas.

More importantly, foreign investment is creating jobs for American workers, expanding tax revenues, diversifying the economic base, introducing new technology and marketing strategies, and creating more competition. For example, a company such as American Motors may not have been able to survive without the transfusion of funds from its new controlling partner, Renault of France. In spite of gibes that the name of American Motors should be changed to "Amnault" or "Franco-American Motors" and the inherent difficulties involved in bringing together people speaking different languages and from corporate "cultures" whose headquarters are 4500 miles apart, thousands of jobs may well have been preserved because of Renault's investment in this sector of the American economy. For the U.S. balance-of-payments picture, it is also preferable to buy a product manufactured by U.S. workers in a foreign-owned plant on American soil than to import that same product from the firm's overseas facilities.

The willingness of the foreign giants to compete head on with U.S. firms on America's own turf should also serve as a rallying cry for American industries. Quite frankly, some of the key industrial sectors in the United States have lost ground to their foreign competitors. The Big Three in Detroit have not produced the cars which the American consumers want, thus permitting the Japanese and European automakers to capture a very large chunk of the U.S. market. The Satra Corporation has even announced plans to assemble Russian-built Lada economy cars in the United States, hoping to cash in on the consumers' demand for smaller automobiles. Furthermore, the U.S. steel and chemical-dye industries have not remained competitive with foreign firms, and several foreign takeovers of key U.S. companies within these sectors have already occurred.

It is imperative, of course, that the American business community meet this foreign challenge head on and begin to show once again the innovation and panache which characterized U.S. business throughout the 1950s and 1960s and which is still evident in many of the high-technology sectors today. Through greater innovation and competitiveness, the U.S. industries can be revitalized, with the American consumer emerging as the ultimate winner.

Unfortunately, some trouble spots may be on the horizon insofar as foreign investment is concerned. Some farmers are complaining that foreign buyers are paying a premium price for land, making it virtually impossible for the sons and daughters of the farmers to acquire acreage. Because of loopholes in U.S. laws which have only partially been closed as a result of recent legislation, foreign residents may still be exempt from paying capital-gains taxes on land which they sell, thus permitting them to pay up to 15 percent more for land than American investors and still reap the same profit margin. In addition, as the value of the land escalates, so do the taxes, making the operating expenses on the family farm more prohibitive. Moreover, Americans take great pride in their country's being the breadbasket of the world, and some fear having foreign residents control strategically important food-producing acreage. Laws have recently been implemented in Iowa and Missouri which limit severely or prohibit altogether foreign access to farmland, and several other state legislatures are currently considering similar legislation.

The OPEC dimension is also a potentially explosive problem area. In 1979, the United States spent 60 billion dollars for OPEC oil. In 1980, the OPEC bill increased to 76 billion dollars, or 2 percent of America's gross national product. In spite of the recent leveling off of oil prices, selected OPEC countries should continue to enjoy huge dollar surpluses from worldwide sales of oil.

Billions of dollars are now being invested in the U.S. economy, either directly from the OPEC nations or through intermediate institutions in European and Caribbean tax havens such as Luxembourg and the Netherlands Antilles. Middle Eastern interests now control a group of mines, several banks, as well as a number of hotels, industrial development parks, and resorts, and OPEC investors are continuing to seek out solid investment opportunities in the United States. Moreover, within the past few years, such influential people as John Connally, Clark Clifford, Bert Lance, Richard Helms, Stuart Symington, William Simon, William P. Rogers, and J. William Fulbright have been retained at one time or another by Arab members of OPEC to represent their interests in the United States. It is certainly not inconceivable that the vast economic clout wielded by OPEC within the U.S. market could eventually be translated into substantial political influence on Capitol Hill or in the White House.

Furthermore, the OPEC nations could severely damage the U.S. economy by suddenly withdrawing their money *en masse*, perhaps in reaction to a U.S. policy stance toward the Middle East with which they vehemently disagree. This scenario is not without some substance in light of the Ayatollah Khomeini's efforts to quickly remove Iranian assets from the United States immediately after his ascension to power. In 1979, the Progressive Conservative government of Prime Minister

Joe Clark attempted to move Canada's embassy in Israel from Tel Aviv to Jerusalem but was warned by Arab diplomats of the investment and trade consequences of such an action. The Canadian government quickly reconsidered its policy stance and continues to have its embassy situated in Tel Aviv.

On the other hand, OPEC investors do not differ from their counterparts in Europe, Asia, Latin America, and other parts of the world in viewing the United States as a safe and secure haven for their money. Indeed, some of this OPEC money is flight capital which serves as a hedge against possible future unrest in the Middle East. For example, a typical Saudi investor would certainly be alarmed by what has recently transpired in Iran and is therefore salting away money in the United States in case militants one day seize control of the Saudi government. Furthermore, the threat of an oil embargo is still the major political weapon available to the OPEC nations, and OPEC investors recognize that a sudden and coordinated effort to withdraw their funds from the United States would probably force the President to freeze assets, such as occurred in the case of Iran, or even to expropriate them, a policy which was pursued during World War II.

A less ominous but nonetheless significant problem area is the cutthroat competition for foreign investment now being waged by state governments. In an effort to create new job opportunities, states are literally anteing up millions of dollars to entice foreign firms to their respective localities. Quite frankly, the investment climate in the United States is so attractive that these foreign enterprises are going to establish facilities on U.S. turf even without incentive packages. It is time for the state and federal governments to sit down together and work out an overall game plan so that a good chunk of the incentive money now being paid out can remain in the pockets of the taxpayers. If incentives are to be offered, they should be earmarked for use by foreign investors willing to set up plants in areas of endemically high unemployment.

U.S. officials must also look very closely at recent developments in the banking sector. Because of their traditional exemptions from reserve currency and geographical requirements, foreign banks have had a definite advantage over U.S. banks in conducting business in the United States. The 1978 International Banking Act will certainly help to remove some of these advantages, but sixty-three foreign banking organizations are exempt from the act's geographic provisions and will be allowed to continue multistate banking operations, a luxury not permitted to U.S. banks. Although the General Accounting Office's recommendation for an indefinite ban on foreign takeovers of large U.S. banks is premature, federal officials must nevertheless move quickly to ensure that foreign banks and American banks can compete fairly on U.S. soil and that competitive advantages do not accrue to the foreign firms.

Foreign direct investment linked to the defense sector and to the control of America's strategic natural resources will also be subjected to greater scrutiny in the future. For example, the California-based Santa Fe International Corporation was recently acquired by a wholly owned subsidiary of the Kuwait government. One of Santa Fe International's own subsidiaries, C. F. Braun, has been engaged for years in sensitive nuclear-processing plant research at the U.S. Energy Department's Hanford Reservation in the state of Washington. Although Braun was forced to withdraw from the Hanford project after the Kuwaiti acquisition, the company continues to employ people well-versed in nuclear-processing technology and in the specific activities carried out at the Energy Department's facility, a situation which has raised many eyebrows in Washington's regulatory circles.

In all, the U.S. federal government has to deal with more than 300 companies under foreign ownership, control, or influence that do classified defense work.[9] Some of these firms are allowed to participate in defense work by setting up quasi-independent agencies. For example, a few years ago Fujitsu made a direct investment in the Amdahl Corporation of Sunnyvale, California. For a time, high-technology-oriented Amdahl was prohibited from servicing computers in areas requiring security clearance. Currently, however, Amdahl is back in business in the security field because it has created a spin-off firm called the Amdahl Federal Service Corporation. This new enterprise is located on the third floor of a Washington office building, three floors below the office of the parent business. The U.S. government now requires seven days' notice in writing for representatives of one company to make "informational visits" to the other.[10] Such ad hoc solutions may work satisfactorily in the case of Amdahl and many other enterprises, but the U.S. government will most likely be forced in the future to come up with clearly defined guidelines and procedures to ensure that those personnel having access to sensitive defense-related information are adequately insulated from pressures which might be exerted by foreign owners.

In addition, the Committee on Foreign Investment in the United States, which was created by President Gerald Ford in 1975 to monitor inward direct investment, can be expected in the future to look much more closely at transactions involving state-controlled enterprises, particularly in the resource sector. This committee, which is an inter-agency group composed of the U.S. Trade Representative and officers from the Council of Economic Advisers and the Departments of Defense, State, Commerce, and Treasury, has reviewed such transactions as Renault's takeover of American Motors, Shell's acquisition of Belridge Oil, and Elf Aquitaine's purchase of Texasgulf. Elf Aquitaine has recently become a state-controlled petroleum company in France, and its takeover of Texasgulf will provide the French government with a significant share of U.S. phosphate and sulphur reserves. The Committee on Foreign Investment in the United States asked Elf Aquitaine to delay the purchase until a thorough study could be made of the ramifications of the acquisition, but Elf Aquitaine's management refused to comply with the request, prompting one Congressman to label the committee as a "doormat" for foreign investors.[11] In spite of the committee's reluctance to act in this particular instance, a new spate of foreign acquisitions of strategic resources in the United States might well prompt the U.S. federal government to postpone or annul future takeovers on a case-by-case basis.

THE FOREIGN INVESTMENT ISSUE IN PERSPECTIVE

This foreign investment surge into the United States illustrates quite conclusively the increasing interdependency of the global economy. More than 1.6 million Americans now labor for foreign-controlled enterprises on U.S. soil, and decisions rendered in faraway places such as Riyadh, Tokyo, and Amsterdam may have a substantial impact on the lifestyles of residents in Provo, Peoria, Plattsburgh, and countless other towns and cities which dot the American landscape. In strategic terms, the development of sophisticated delivery systems for weapons of unimaginable destructive capacity has rendered obsolete the once popular notion of a Fortress America, protected forever by two mammoth oceans and friendly but weaker nations to the north and south. The United States is also very dependent on other nations for raw materials, having at least a 50 percent dependency on overseas sources for twenty-four of thirty-two minerals deemed necessary for national survival, according to a recent congressional study.[12] And, of course, the archaic nature of the Fortress America concept is also in evidence in the economic, financial, and business spheres, as the international investment statistics clearly bear out.

With a pool of upwards of 800 billion U.S. dollars currrently held overseas and with the continued attractiveness of the United States as a safe and secure investment haven, it is quite possible that foreign investment activity in the United States will become even more frenetic over the next two decades. The steady growth in the number of foreign-based multinationals and banks should also provide greater competition for their American counterparts both on U.S. turf and abroad. In 1960, there were 175 U.S.-based companies among the top

275 industrial corporations in the world in terms of overall sales, 64 percent of the total number.[13] The company ranked as number 100 among the U.S. companies, Weyerhauser, had sales greater than the company ranked as number 51 among foreign-based corporations. In 1970, 167 U.S.-based industrials were still in the top 275 worldwide, representing 61 percent of the largest corporations. The company ranked as number 100 among the U.S.-based firms at that time, Whirlpool, had a greater sales volume than the enterprise ranked as number 61 on the foreign list.[14] But by the end of the 1970s, only 132 American companies were left among the world's top 275 industrial corporations, down to 48 percent of the total. Furthermore, the corporation which ranked as number 100 among U.S.-based firms, Textron, had sales below those of the enterprise which ranked as number 109 among foreign-based companies. Indeed, of the top 850 firms in the world in 1979, only 355 were headquartered in the United States. In addition, number 500 on the foreign-based company list, Associated Biscuit Manufacturing of Great Britain, would have ranked as number 359 among America's top 500 corporations.[15]

The relative decline in U.S. competitiveness is also borne out by the number of U.S. firms among the top dozen world leaders in each of thirteen major industrial groupings: aerospace, automotive, chemicals, electrical equipment, food products, general machinery, iron and steel, metal products, paper, petroleum, pharmaceuticals, textiles, and commercial banking. In 1959, a U.S.-based company was the world's largest in eleven of the thirteen categories and 111 U.S. companies were among the total of 156 in the thirteen groupings.[16] In 1979, U.S. firms were leading in only seven categories and a total of 72 American companies were left among the top dozen enterprises in each of the thirteen distinctive groupings. Figure 2-5 provides a clear illustration of the trends in these industrial sectors over the past two decades.

In the commercial banking sector, this trend toward stiffer foreign competition is also very evident. In 1960, twenty U.S. banks (33 percent) were to be found among the top sixty in the world. A decade later, among the sixty largest banks in the world in terms of assets, seventeen (28 percent) were American. That same year, the fifty largest commercial banks outside the United States controlled assets worth 382 billion dollars, whereas the top fifty U.S. banks had attracted 278 billion dollars in assets. At the beginning of the 1980s, the top fifty foreign banks controlled 2.5 trillion dollars in assets in comparison to the 882 billion dollars in America's top fifty banking institutions. Furthermore, only ten U.S. banks (17 percent) remained on the list of the top sixty banking enterprises in the world.[17]

Industry	1960	1970	1979
Aerospace	10	10	10
Automotive	6	5	4
Chemicals	9	7	6
Electrical equipment	10	8	6
Food products	9	9	9
General machinery	8	6	4
Iron and steel	6	4	2
Metal products	8	3	3
Paper products	10	11	8
Petroleum	10	10	8
Pharmaceuticals	11	7	6
Textiles	7	4	3
Commercial banking	7	7	3
Total	111	91	72

Figure 2-5 **Number of U.S. enterprises among world's top dozen in major industrial groupings.**

POLITICAL SOVEREIGNTY VERSUS INTERDEPENDENCE

The growing influence of foreign firms in the markets of other countries has also had a significant influence on the power capabilities of national governments. In effect, the events which triggered the demise of the Fortress America phenomenon have been repeated time and again in nations all over the world. In addition, for many years, political scientists considered that it was fairly easy to differentiate between what was domestic policy and what was foreign policy. However, with increasing global interdependence, events which transpire abroad may have a major impact at home and vice versa. Thus, the term "intermestic" politics has been developed to illustrate the close interrelationship between domestic and foreign policies. To explain the term, one should remember that issues such as food production, access to and pricing of raw materials, and movement of capital clearly have both domestic and foreign policy implications.[18]

Perhaps the first major intermestic political issue occurred in 1973 with the quadrupling of oil prices by OPEC. This international issue soon became a serious domestic concern with rapidly rising inflation and higher unemployment rates afflicting American society. The average American found that a decision rendered thousands of miles away by a consortium of foreign nations was costing him or her much more money for running the car or heating the house. In addition, some of these average Americans were forced to join the ranks of the unemployed as the U.S. economy tumbled into a recession. Alarmed by these developments, people placed intense pressure on Washington to find quick-fix solutions to these domestic ailments, but none was forthcoming. In essence, interdependence precipitates intermestic political issues and diminishes the national government's capacity to cope with what have traditionally been considered as strictly domestic concerns, such as inflation, unemployment, and monetary and fiscal policies. Unfortunately, citizens often wind up demanding protectionist policies in the hope that the nation will somehow be insulated from outside pressures, an aspiration which has little credence in this new era of complex interdependence.

Foreign direct investment, in particular, may often intensify social change in a host country and affect many other aspects of the host country's environment. Furthermore, one should not forget that multinational corporations, which are without a doubt the major institutions making decisions as to the allocation of international production and the resulting patterns of trade, are generally intent on maximizing their overall profit base, even if this quest necessitates scaling back commitments to particular subsidiaries. In contrast, governments are vigilant about safeguarding national sovereignty and attempt to maximize payoffs and opportunities for their own constituencies. Consequently, the objectives of multinationals and governments may periodically clash, at times to the detriment of the former group. Economic nationalism and the protection of indigenous businesses and jobs periodically swing the global pendulum away from interdependence and toward parochialism. For example, the U.S. General Accounting Office was very vocal in 1980 in advocating the imposition of a moratorium on foreign acquisitions of U.S. banks, fearing that the financial control of the home economy was slipping out of American hands. Canada has also mandated that at least 50 percent of its oil and natural-gas industry must be owned by the Canadian government or Canadian citizens by 1990. Nissan's proposal for a 45-million-dollar joint venture with state-owned Alfa-Romeo moved Fiat's chairman to warn of the destruction of Italy's auto industry by the Japanese "Trojan horse." Some French businesses have also sharply criticized Sony's plans for a tape-cassette plant in Bayonne, claiming unfair competition from Japan. Labor unions in Tennessee also carried on a raucous demonstration at the groundbreaking ceremony for a Datsun truck-assembly plant because of the use of nonunion labor in the construction of the plant. The political pressure placed on governments to preserve jobs, especially during times of recession, has also prompted the imposition of rules

which clearly place foreign-based multinationals at a competitive disadvantage vis-à-vis state-owned enterprises. Thus as a result of these
parochial concerns, periodic campaigns which at times verge on
xenophobia are still occurring, with the "ugly American" or "ugly
Japanese" or an investor from some other country depicted as malevo-
lently impacting on the local economy.

Furthermore, in what has often been referred to as the age of a
nuclear balance of terror, definite limits have been placed on the prudent use of military force. In order to bridge the gap left by this military
vacuum and in recognition of the growing importance of trade and
investment, economic restrictions and incentives have now become
important weapons in the arsenals of national governments. Restrictions on trade and investment are legendary, running from sporadic
toughening of customs standards to outright nationalization or expropriation. Incentives are also a vital policy prerogative of governments,
helping to create jobs in economically depressed regions or in popular
high-technology sectors. A growing number of nations are also offering
incentives for their own investors to establish facilities abroad, often to
lay claim to a secure source of raw materials or to remain internationally competitive in a wide array of industries. The Japanese government, for example, passed new laws in late 1979 which provided for
liberalized foreign-exchange rules, thus facilitating overseas ventures.
Japanese government investment guarantees and financing are also
very generous, with Tokyo's Export-Import Bank providing loans at
concessionary rates for as much as 30 percent of a project's costs. Other
government agencies insure against political and exchange-rate risks,
and no taxes are imposed on the earnings of Japanese employees
stationed abroad. In addition, Japan has forsaken laws which inhibit
"commissions" to host country officials, and companies are not obli-
gated to resist boycott clauses or to take into account the substantiated
or alleged human rights violations of host governments. With Japanese
foreign direct investment doubling from 1976 to 1980 and expected to
quadruple through the 1980s, it is clear that the political and governmental apparatus is working hand in hand with industry to foster
this financial onslaught overseas. For a nation which is so integrally
involved in international trade and investment and which with just 3
percent of the world's population buys one-quarter of the world's total
exports of raw materials and accounts for 84 percent of all foreign
investments in Asia, it is a matter of economic survival to be integrally
involved abroad.[19]

It is to be expected that more nations in the future will face up to this
reality of economic survival and begin to tailor-make government policies in order to facilitate investment overseas, once again leading to a

heady mixture of politics and economics. This new concoction of politics and economics will impact not only on the overseas strategies of U.S.-based multinationals but also on the activities of U.S. companies which must now face intensified competition from foreign enterprises within America's own home market. Consequently, this new epoch of complex global interdependence will not just impact on the large and medium-size U.S. firms which invest abroad but will also dramatically affect the future viability of an increasing number of small businesses which have traditionally been content to stay at home and carve out a comfortable niche in a local or regional market. The average American citizen will also be increasingly impacted by this drift toward interdependence, for it is certain that the 1.6 million U.S. workers now laboring for foreign-controlled enterprises will be augmented rapidly in the years ahead. Local communities such as Spartanburg, South Carolina, or San Diego, California, will also become increasingly dependent for their economic prosperity on foreign investment. American households will also use a growing number of product lines which are made by foreign-owned corporations.

How Americans react to this foreign presence at home and the treatment of U.S. firms abroad will largely determine whether the U.S. federal government will retain its traditional free-trade and investment stance or become progressively more protectionistic. The maintenance of a liberal free-trade policy on the part of Washington would go a long way toward ensuring that a golden age of international investment will reign supreme during the 1980s and 1990s. A drift toward protectionism, however, would provide the impetus for neomercantilism and make it politically much more difficult for international firms to prosper, in spite of the persistent drift toward global economic interdependence. It is the perception of the benefits and costs of international investment activity, as well as the reaction of national and regional governmental units to future investment strategies, which will be the subject of discussion in the next chapter.

REFERENCES

[1] J. J. Servan-Schreiber, *The American Challenge* (New York: Avon, 1968, p. 3).

[2] During the 1975 to 1979 period, foreign direct investment in the United States increased at an average annual rate of 17.8 percent, whereas U.S. direct investment abroad increased at a rate of 11.0 percent. During the 1978 to 1980 period, foreign direct investment in America was up more than 20 percent in each of those three years.

[3] For a detailed examination of foreign investment in the United States, see Earl H. Fry, *Financial Invasion of the U.S.A.: A Threat to American Society?* (New York: McGraw-Hill, 1980).

[4] *Business Week,* April 13, 1981, p. 163.

[5] *The Wall Street Journal,* April 29, 1981, p. 37. These estimates were made by the Securities Industry Association.

[6] As a concrete example of the currency exchange advantages which certain foreign investors have enjoyed, a U.S. company priced at 100 million dollars in 1970 would have cost a German investor 360 million marks at the prevailing exchange rate of 3.6 marks to a dollar. In 1980, when the exchange rate was 1.8 marks per dollar, the 100 million dollar purchase price would have set the German investor back only 180 million marks.

[7] Union Bank of Switzerland, *Prices and Earnings Around the Globe,* 1979/80 edition (Zurich: Economic Research Department of Union Bank of Switzerland, 1979, pp. 4–10). The purchasing power was determined by taking the ratio between the earnings level for the occupations selected and the price levels of the goods and services which were included in a "basket."

[8] Robin Marris, "Is EC Really Richer than U.S.?" *Europe,* March 1981, pp. 30–32; and *San Francisco Examiner,* April 26, 1981, p. D6. The three University of Pennsylvania professors are Irving Kravis, Alan Heston, and Robert Summers.

[9] *The Wall Street Journal,* January 8, 1982, p. 25.

[10] Ibid.

[11] Ibid., August 3, 1981, p. 27. The Congressman was Representative Benjamin Rosenthal of New York, the chairman of the U.S. House of Representatives Subcommittee on Commerce, Consumer, and Monetary Affairs.

[12] These estimates were contained in the Santini Report. See *The New York Times,* February 6, 1980, p. 11.

[13] Based on data appearing in *Fortune,* July 1961, pp. 168–175, and August 1961, pp. 130–131.

[14] Ibid., May 1971, pp. 172–179, and August 1971, pp. 150–155.

[15] Ibid., May 5, 1980, pp. 274–295, and August 11, 1980, pp. 190–199. Among the top 850 firms in the world, 355 were based in the United States, 128 in Japan, 86 in the United Kingdom, 63 in Germany, 39 in France, 30 in Canada, 28 in Sweden, 75 in other parts of Western Europe, 6 in other advanced industrial nations, and 40 in either the advanced development or the developing countries.

[16] Lawrence G. Franko, "Multinationals: The End of U.S. Dominance," *Atlantic Community Quarterly,* Summer 1979, 187–190.

[17] *Fortune,* May 1971, pp. 192–193; August 1971, pp. 156–157; July 14, 1980, pp. 148–149; and August 11, 1980, pp. 202–203; and *American Banker,* August 1, 1961, pp. 37–38.

[18] For additional information concerning the intermestic dimension, consult John Spanier, *Games Nations Play,* 3d ed. (New York: Holt, Rinehart and Winston, 1978, pp. 494–497).

[19] *Business Week,* June 16, 1980, pp. 92–94; and *Christian Science Monitor,* April 28, 1981, p. B2.

INTERNATIONAL INVESTMENT IN PERSPECTIVE: THE HISTORICAL AND IDEOLOGICAL DIMENSIONS

3

INTRODUCTION

Multinational corporations now account for the major portion of international investment, and their activities have occasionally been at odds with host governments, especially in the developing nations. This chapter will provide some insights into how various groups perceive international investment, with special attention given to the liberal, Marxist, dependency, and economic-nationalist points of view. These perspectives should be of special interest to potential investors, because as investment expands to all corners of the earth, individuals and companies will at times confront powerful proponents of these theories, regardless of whether or not the theories correspond with reality. As a result, it is important to understand the rationale for and the main tenets of each of these theoretical approaches.

The first section of the chapter will set the stage for the plunge into the murky waters of theory by showing how political considerations have always impacted on international investment. In addition, this section will document how such investment may return tremendous profits but is also fraught with occasional pitfalls.

HISTORY'S LESSONS

International investment may well date back thousands of years to the opening of trade routes in the Middle East and China, but the Hanseatic

League was the first institutionalized arrangement providing the necessary economic and political infrastructures for investment links to be established with some degree of permanency. The Hanseatic League was an association of North German towns which existed from the thirteenth through the seventeenth centuries and at its peak included almost 100 municipalities. The League's primary purpose was to protect mutual commercial interests, and it eventually secured lucrative trading and market privileges in England, Russia, Norway, the Netherlands, and other regions of Europe.[1] The League used what political power it could muster together to protect its dominant merchant class from the whims of foreign rulers, and for a time these merchants enjoyed a virtual monopoly in Northern Europe over East-West trade.

The few investment agreements which existed were generally in the form of partnerships involving two to four associates. Such partnerships made more capital available and spread out the financial risks. The partners frequently lived in different cities or even different countries in order to maximize their local and regional marketing expertise. An example was the Venetian Company, which was set up in 1407 with capitalization of 5000 marks divided between partners in Bruges and Venice. The Venetians used the partnership to export spices, cotton, and silk to the north and received in return cloth, amber, and furs. The venture eventually expanded into too many product lines and made too many risky investments, thus leading to its financial demise.[2] A much more elaborate multinational system was established in the fifteenth century by the Augsburg-based Fuggers. The Fuggers eventually established financial houses, trading facilities, mining operations, and processing plants in many parts of Europe.[3]

Because of the continual risk of war, the Hanseatic representatives inserted clauses into trading agreements which provided guarantees of security for people and property and which exempted the merchants from prosecution for delivering goods to either side during a period of hostility and insured them against material loss as a direct result of warfare. The league was also able to exempt its merchants from the laws concerning flotsam and jetsam on seashores and river banks, thus assisting them to maintain ownership rights to their cargo. The league also negotiated a significant reduction in customs duties and managed to procure the right in some foreign ports to reexport unsold merchandise without having to pay the customs levy, somewhat reminiscent of modern free-trade-zone regulations.[4]

With shifting trade routes and strong competition from France, Holland, England, and other countries and regions, the Hanseatic League eventually diminished in importance. The conquest of the seas by its formidable navy was soon to enable England to emerge as the dominant center for international investment activity. In effect, England became the home of enterprises daring enough to reach across the oceans for business gain and adventure, in that order. Just three years prior to Elizabeth's ascension to the throne in 1558, the Muscovy Company was chartered to seek out a northeast passage through Russian territory to Asia. The African Company was chartered in 1588 to develop the slave trade, the Levant Company was formed four years later to expand trade links in the Mediterranean, and the East India Company was set up in 1602 to find a secure sea route to Asia.

The thrust into North America was spearheaded by the Virginia Company (originally known as the London Company), which obtained a charter in 1606 authorizing it to form a new settlement in America and to monopolize trade between that settlement and England. Approximately 1700 investors bought shares in this joint stock company which established the Jamestown Colony in 1607.[5] The Jamestown venture took an especially heavy toll in terms of human life. The 105 people who set up the original colony were basically seeking quick riches, and more than half had perished before the end of the first year. In 1609, 800 new settlers were sent to Jamestown to replenish the ranks, but most of them also died within a very short period of time.

Commercially, Jamestown failed to discover a cash crop which would make the colony profitable. The leaders of the Virginia Company were oblivious to the fact that profitability in the North American settlement would have to be based on long-term economic development, in sharp contrast to some of the ventures in Asia which had resulted in quick and lucrative profits. Although instrumental in helping to open up a new continent, the Virginia Company was a dismal business failure, and none of the investment, which totaled 200,000 pounds by 1621, was ever repaid.[6] Once subscribers lost interest in the project because of the lack of dividends, company officials had to rely on a lottery to raise enough money to keep Jamestown going.

Thus, quite ironically, England's first settlement in America was prompted by visions of quick riches and partially financed by a gambling ploy! Indeed, almost every early stock-company venture in North America, including the New Plymouth, Massachusetts Bay, Providence Islands, and New Foundland Companies, proved to be financial disasters. Eventually, these company colonies, spurred on by the promise of trade monopolies, were replaced by proprietary colonies which gave the settlers a direct stake in the land and a voice in local governance.

International investment activity began to mushroom significantly after the conclusion of the Napoleonic Wars. Up until that time, overseas investment had actually had a minimal impact on both borrowing and lending countries, with the important exception of helping to consolidate control over colonial possessions. After 1815, investment surged as a result of the period of relative peace which prevailed in Europe, a general acceptance of economic liberalism, improved communications and transportation, a reliable international monetary yardstick provided by the gold standard, a vast increase in trade and human migration, and colonial expansion. Two billion dollars were invested abroad between 1815 and 1855. This figure had trebled by 1870, was up to 23 billion dollars in 1900, and had doubled again by 1914.[7]

The United States was significantly influenced by this foreign investment surge. Soon after the new Constitution was ratified, Dutch banks played a major role in floating the U.S. government's debt in 1791 and again in 1803. European money was also largely responsible for President Jefferson's successful bid to purchase the vast Louisiana Territory from France. By 1807, one-half of the entire debt of the U.S. federal government was held by Europeans. Investors in Great Britain and on the continent were also instrumental in funding the construction of the Erie Canal and other important transportation projects during the U.S. canal era which spanned the period from 1817 to 1844. At the end of the U.S. Civil War, Europeans were responsible for almost one-half of the entire war debt of the victorious North.

The railroad-building era in North America, which was vital to the continent's industrial expansion, was also heavily subsidized by the Europeans. Shareholders from overseas held one-fourth of all U.S. railroad securities in 1853 and as much as one-third by 1890.[8] In 1915, 63 percent of the shareholders of the Canadian Pacific Railway resided not in Canada but in the United Kingdom.[9] Europeans also provided technological and management expertise to help ensure the success of these massive continental projects. Later, the American cattle industry would be heavily influenced by British investors who provided the financial wherewithal for the development of almost forty major ranches in Texas, Wyoming, New Mexico, and a few other Western states. Municipalities such as Boston, Providence, and New York City also relied extensively on foreign borrowings just before and after the turn of the twentieth century.[10]

However, all was not rosy in terms of foreign investment in the rapidly expanding American marketplace. In order to finance public works projects, state governments began to act as financial intermediaries and issued their own bonds, which for a time were popular among European investors because the states were well-known entities and could always fall back on their taxing powers. However, nine states stopped paying interest on their debts during the depression period of the late 1830s and early 1840s, with Florida, Mississippi, and

Michigan actually going so far as to repudiate some or all of their debts.[11] Overseas residents were given a further jolt when the Bank of the United States defaulted in 1841 at a time when 60 percent of its 35 million dollars in stock was held by European investors.

Consequently, a fair number of investors either lost their capital through default or were forced to wait many years for the resumption of interest payments. For a time during the 1840s, the United States was understandably considered as a very poor credit risk by overseas investors. However, the discovery of gold in California brought a quick change of heart and overseas money once again began to stream into the nation, in spite of the ominous and growing threat of civil strife between the North and the South. Investment continued to pour into the country after the war between the Union and the Confederacy, and by the beginning of World War I, the United States ranked as the globe's number one debtor nation.

The occasional linkage between politics and investment was also quite evident, particularly in terms of British interests in both the North and the South during the American Civil War. After 1890, a fair share of the investment in Europe itself was also politically motivated as nations rushed to solidify military alliances. Thousands of French investors plunged billions of francs into Russian government securities prior to 1914, accounting for 25 percent of France's total foreign investment. The British also invested heavily in the Czarist regime, in part to keep the Russians firmly aligned against the Germans. However, with the success of the Bolshevik Revolution and Russia's subsequent withdrawal from the war, most of this investment was forfeited without any form of compensation whatsoever.

World War I devastated Europe and left millions of soldiers and civilians killed or maimed. Economically, because of the forfeiture of investments and the need to liquidate holdings in order to pay for armaments and provisions, European foreign investment in 1918 stood at less than one-half of its 1914 level. On the other hand, the war marked America's entry as a potent investor nation. The United States did not suffer territorial damage and was the main supplier to the Allied military forces, thus permitting industrial expansion. U.S. financial houses soon began to seek out new investment opportunities with reckless abandon, battling one another to negotiate loans for such entities as the Colombian government, the city governments of Budapest and Belgrade, and other municipal, regional, and national governments spread around the world. The campaign to lend money became so intense that several representatives of American investment firms reportedly raced one another to an isolated Bavarian hamlet which was seeking a modest loan of 125,000 dollars for civic improvements. By the time these representatives had browbeaten the small town's local officials, the amount of the loan had been pushed up to 3 million dollars.[12] This euphoria to invest in exotic and faraway places finally dimmed as the Great Depression set in, but quickly picked up steam again after World War II.

The U.S. government also mixed overseas investment with political pursuits, thus following faithfully in the footsteps of the earlier investment giants of Europe. In this case, however, the tables were turned on the Europeans who found themselves in desperate need of U.S. capital after World War I. Washington decided to use this demand for capital as a bargaining chip in an attempt to recoup the Allies' wartime debt, which stood at 9.5 billion dollars in 1919. French officials in particular were pushed into a corner and forced until 1927 to rely on indirect borrowing routes because of the U.S. government insistence on linking loans to debt repayments. In 1934, Congress pushed the linkage issue even further by passing the Johnson Act, which temporarily closed U.S. loan markets to foreign governments in default on wartime debt payments.[13]

In the Western Hemisphere, "gunboat diplomacy" left a clear imprint on U.S. investment policies. Teddy Roosevelt announced in 1904 the Roosevelt Corollary to the Monroe Doctrine, which stipulated that in flagrant cases of wrongdoing in Latin America, such as the nonpayment of loans, U.S. military forces might be forced to intervene. Repeatedly, the United States did dispatch troops ostensibly to protect U.S. citizens and to ensure the payment of debts to both U.S. and European investors. Direct military intervention occurred in the Dominican Republic in 1906 and 1916, Panama in 1908, 1912, and 1918, Nicaragua in 1912 and 1926, and Mexico in 1914, 1916, and 1917.[14] A typical case prompting intervention occurred after the National Bank of Nicaragua, a U.S.-controlled company, asked for help in 1912 because of domestic unrest. Nearly 3000 marines were dispatched to render assistance, and a small contingent of the original marine force remained in Nicaragua until 1933. Franklin D. Roosevelt's Good Neighbor Policy of 1933 officially relinquished the U.S. right of unilateral armed intervention, and a few years later the treaty rights to intervene in Cuba and Panama were stricken from the books.

The era of massive foreign direct investment, which provides a substantial or controlling interest in an overseas enterprise, began after World War II and has often pitted the investors, host nations, and parent nations against one another in bitter political and economic competition. The Germans, for example, had to wait until 1952 before gaining permission from the Allies to start rebuilding their foreign networks which had been confiscated by "enemy property custodians" in many countries. Until 1961, this rebuilding was strictly limited to projects which would provide clearly demonstrable foreign-exchange benefits. Many major German corporations had also forfeited their foreign assets, not once but twice, as a result of the two World Wars. For example, Bayer, the giant German chemical and pharmaceutical firm, not only lost its assets in the United States but has never regained the right to use its name on its aspirin. Consequently, "Bayer" aspirin is now sold by an American corporation.[15]

Parent nations have also taken steps to protect the interests of their foreign investors. In the United States, the Hickenlooper and the Gonzalez Amendments and provisions in the 1974 Trade Act are among the substantive actions taken by Washington to punish nations which treat American investors unfairly or nationalize U.S. property without adequate compensation. The Hickenlooper Amendment was passed by Congress in 1962 as a reaction to the 1960 Cuban nationalizations and to the expropriation of an ITT subsidiary in Brazil. The amendment mandates the termination of all U.S. aid to any country that nationalizes American-owned property and does not within six months take appropriate steps to offer just compensation. The Gonzalez Amendment was ratified in January 1972 and stipulates that if U.S. property is nationalized without proper remuneration, U.S. representatives at the World Bank and its affiliates must vote against any loan or any other utilization of funds earmarked for the offending nation. With the weighted voting formula utilized at the World Bank, a U.S. negative response would effectively veto the loan application of the nation involved in the dispute. In actuality, however, these provisions have rarely been invoked and have only had a minor impact on the policies pursued by host nations. Cuba, for example, has thus far successfully confiscated 1.8 billion dollars in U.S. assets without any compensation, and Allende's short-lived regime in Chile was able to seize 740 million dollars in U.S. holdings before being overthrown.

In its role as a parent government to multinational corporations investing around the world, the United States has traditionally supported the need for international investment as a means to develop the global economy. American foreign policymakers have also generally supported the notion that foreign direct investment is a major tool in the struggle against Communism, particularly in the developing world.[16] Washington has backed up this policy preference by offering limited insurance arrangements to protect U.S. investors in developing countries against the ravages of war, expropriation, and repatriation limitations.

On the other hand, domestic conditions will frequently have an overriding influence on the parent government's policy stance toward overseas investment activity. The cases of Germany in the 1950s, Japan in the 1950s and 1960s, and several other countries show conclusively that the foreign investment tap will be firmly closed if domestic economic circumstances seemingly warrant it. Even the United States once turned off the tap as a proposed remedy to chronic balance-of-payments deficits. On January 1, 1968, President Lyndon Johnson imposed for the first time in U.S. history mandatory controls on the outflow of all U.S. direct investment and placed strict limits on the reinvestment of U.S. profits earned abroad. These restrictions, which have since been removed, were predicated on the notion that the health and vitality of the U.S. economy took clear precedence over the unimpeded movement of international capital. Such a policy stance on the part of a parent government, which has been repeated time and again in many national capitals, remains as one of the strong political challenges to a world facing increased economic and resource interdependency.

Host nations have also sought recourse from the excesses of foreign direct investment and have attempted to weaken the links between foreign multinationals and their home governments. In the Western Hemisphere, Article 15 of the Charter of the Organization of American States (OAS) stresses the principle of nonintervention and was primarily aimed at avoiding a repeat of the spate of U.S. incursions which occurred up to 1930. However, the United States did send the marines into the Dominican Republic in 1965 and, depending on which political perspective one advocates, has had a greater or lesser degree of direct influence over economic and governmental development in many Latin American countries. Although articulated early in the twentieth century, the Drago Doctrine and Calvo Clause also continue to have numerous proponents among host nations in Latin America and other parts of the developing world. The Drago Doctrine was prompted by the British and German blockade of the Venezuela coast in 1902 and 1903 in an effort to force the settlement of the financial claims of their citizens against Venezuela. Drago, the Argentine Foreign Minister, argued forcefully that public debt was not an acceptable pretext for armed intervention nor for the material occupation of the soil of any Latin American nation by a European power. The Drago principle is now construed as including a prohibition on the armed intervention or occupation of a sovereign nation by any other nation. Calvo was also an Argentine diplomat, and he developed the point of view that foreigners in a given country were to be treated equally to the nationals of that country; thus, they should not have the right to lay claim to diplomatic protection or intervention by the governments of their home countries. Such intervention, he claimed, would violate the territorial sovereignty and judicial independence of the host nation. Even in a few modern-day investment contracts, the Calvo Clause is inserted and the foreign investor is requested to renounce any appeal beyond that of the national courts of the host country.

Many of the host nations in the developing world have complained to the United Nations that doctrines, clauses, and agreements which are designed to protect their interests have been ineffective and that they remain at the mercy of the advanced industrial world. Indeed, international investment over the past few centuries has been dominated by a few nations in the Northern Hemisphere blessed with surplus capital derived from industrial development, overseas trade, and the control of natural resources (often in distant lands). Moreover, in spite of the risks involved and the occasional losses, foreign investment has for the most part been quite profitable. Furthermore, the political linkage has been very evident as nation-states have used their overseas investments to secure new markets, sources of raw materials, and, not to be underestimated, diplomatic leverage.[17] In a later chapter we will look at the progress being made on the formulation and implementation of an international investment code of conduct which would govern the activities of foreign investors and host and parent governments alike. Such a code, if practical, would be to the world of investment what the General Agreements on Tariffs and Trade (GATT) is to international trade and the International Monetary Fund (IMF) is to global monetary policy. The next section will discuss various perceptions of the reasons for and utility of foreign investment and should illustrate quite vividly why it will be extremely difficult to come up with a comprehensive and universally accepted code of conduct.

THE IDEOLOGICAL AND PHILOSOPHICAL DIMENSIONS

Even in contemporary "free-market" economies, the state plays a primordial if not overbearing role in the economic sphere. Back in the early days of nation-states, the fostering of religions seems to have been the major concern of state leaders, but in recent generations the emphasis has shifted from the pursuit of heavenly salvation to earthly rewards. As one author surmises, "the rise of economics as state business is the concomitant of the decline of religion as state business; for as people feel less need to insure future salvation by the strongest social forces available, so they turned to that force to provide them with earthly welfare."[18]

With the growth in interdependency, the state's preoccupation with safeguarding national security has certainly gone beyond simply military concerns to include both economic and resource issue areas. A major problem arises, however, when the state frantically persists in its efforts to control and protect the home economy in an era when there are many pressures on economic development which clearly transcend national borders. Instead of cooperating with other states to solve areas of dispute within the interdependent setting, individual states have far too often decided to go it alone. As Peter Drucker has pessimistically observed, "an integrated world economy and a splintered world polity can co-exist only in tension, conflict, and mutual misunderstanding."[19]

International investment is a crucial component of the interdependent era, and how the elite and the general populace in host and parent countries perceive the investment issue will have a dramatic impact on future investment activity. Foreign direct investment is subject to a great deal of controversy because it involves not simply the transfer of capital, but also management, technology, products, processes, marketing, and financial expertise, and at times ideological and cultural values. Such investment permits an enterprise headquartered in one country to acquire a controlling interest in an enterprise in another country and to lay claim to labor, land, and markets in that host country. Foreign direct investment may often go where trade cannot and thus provides a way to penetrate tariff walls. Direct investments are also made in an effort to lower production costs (particularly labor costs), to avoid home country restrictions (such as antitrust regulations), to diversify product lines and markets, to exploit technological advantages, to secure steady sources of supply, and to forestall efforts by competitors to capture larger shares of foreign markets.[20]

Representatives of some nations have been very critical of foreign direct investment, claiming it is stacked entirely in favor of the advanced industrial societies and perpetuates the economic dependency of the Third World on the great Western industrial powers. These critics point out that three-quarters of the world population reside in the Third World but that the income levels of most of these people are forty to fifty times lower than that of a typical resident of the United States, Germany, Japan, or any other advanced industrial nation. Indeed, more than thirty developing nations have an annual per capita income of 250 dollars or less, with industrial production accounting for less than 10 percent of their total output. Only one in five citizens of these countries can read and write, and the average life expectancy is forty-five years, as compared to seventy years in the advanced industrial nations.

Furthermore, these critics claim that the great industrial powers have done very little to help solve the plight of the Third World and that the situation will deteriorate further unless drastic and immediate steps are taken to institute a new international economic order favorable to the developing nations. Demographers have predicted that during the 1980s the world population aged fifteen to twenty-nine will increase by at least 200 million, mostly in the poorer countries. By the year 2000, approximately 640 million new jobs must be created in the developing nations to forestall massive unemployment.[21] Thus, according to many observers, the Third World region represents a powder keg which is ready to explode and engulf the industrial nations in constant turmoil unless corrective measures are rapidly implemented.

The remainder of this chapter will compare and contrast various ideological and philosophical perspectives of international investment and look closely at this North-South dilemma. Once again, regardless of how closely these perspectives approximate reality, if governments perceive them as being accurate and act accordingly, investment opportunities will inevitably be affected.

LIBERALISM

Liberals have a deep and abiding faith in free-market forces and believe that humanity as a whole will best be served by an international system which provides for the free movement of goods, services, and capital. They want minimal national government interference in the international investment sphere and contend that if an investment code is ever formulated, it should be voluntary, should not discriminate against multinational enterprises in favor of "national" companies, and should be balanced to include reference to the responsibilities of governments as well as multinational firms and to all enterprises whether ownership is private, state-directed, or mixed.

Multinational corporations are viewed with favor by liberals, who consider that these firms are very well equipped to cope with the challenges of economic and resource interdependency. These corporations are not pressured by the parochial interests of individual states and can manage problems which transcend national boundaries. Multinationals already account for the great bulk of foreign direct investment, with the top 100 multinationals responsible for perhaps one-half of all direct investment in the manufacturing sector. Liberals also point out that the multinationals are the main purveyors of technology transfer, which for them is the key to modernizing developing countries. After all, contact lenses were first developed in Japan, computers in the United States, electrodialysis in Germany, and penicillin in Great Britain, but because of international investment and the accompanying technology transfer, these products and processes are now available to large segments of the human population. With the benefits of high technology, Third World nations may be able to quicken the process of economic development and provide the employment opportunities and necessities of life which their citizenry so desperately need. The developing nations should also be able to select from the international "supermarket" of products and processes that technology most suitable to their needs and to reject that which is inappropriate for their particular stage of economic development.

International direct investment is also perceived as providing substantial benefits for both host and parent countries. In the case of the host country, new jobs are created, tax revenues increase, the economic base is diversified and expanded, new technology, management, personnel, and marketing strategies are introduced, and competition is intensified, a condition which should definitely benefit the consumers. A fair share of this investment is also earmarked for economically depressed areas, even in advanced industrial societies. For example, one-third of U.S. investment in the United Kingdom is in specially designated depressed regions. Moreover, the balance-of-payments picture generally becomes much rosier for the host nation in spite of the specter of the repatriation of profits by foreign-controlled enterprises. In effect, as many Americans have been told in recent years, it is much better in terms of the U.S. balance-of-payments situation to have Americans buy Volkswagens and Hondas manufactured in the United States than to import them from Germany and Japan.

In spite of criticism by some observers in parent countries that overseas investment exports jobs, liberals do believe that even these nations benefit from such investment. Liberals refer to studies that indicate such investment helps to expand global market opportunities for the home-based corporation and therefore produces new jobs on the home front. Furthermore, these studies point out that the home-based companies would risk losing a lion's share of their overseas markets if they attempted to serve them simply through exports.[22] In essence, companies can only remain competitive in the interdependent global setting if they are involved in propitious investments abroad. In addition, as the American current accounts ledger has illustrated so conclusively, the repatriation of overseas profits by home-based firms can substantially improve the balance-of-payments picture of a parent nation.

The multinationals which account for the bulk of international investment are not viewed by liberals as a threat to national governments. In well-organized democratic societies, multinationals are only one voice among many and do not monopolize the agenda of national governments. Furthermore, even very weak states have the ability to thwart the investment strategies of the largest multinationals. Interdependence should also provide greater leverage for governments and their constituencies in their negotiations with multinational enterprises, because there are more competitors for markets to be found among indigenous firms, other multinational corporations, and the licensors of technology, thereby diluting the bargaining strength of any single multinational enterprise.[23]

Liberals worry that growing protectionism is endangering the gains already achieved in this modern age of interdependence. Some would prefer to see the return to world leadership of a single nation dedicated to free trade and investment flows, similar to the political and economic ascendancy of first Great Britain and then the United States in the period from 1815 to 1970. Others feel that all nation-states are antiquated and incapable of coping creatively with the problems and challenges which accompany interdependence. Therefore, either the multinationals must be given more freedom of latitude to strengthen trade and investment networks or a federalized world governmental structure must evolve to cope with international problems from a global, nonparochial perspective. The final vindication of the position favoring the unimpaired flow of direct investment, according to the liberals, is the fact that so many nations actively seek such investment today. Moreover, those developing nations which generally accept free-market principles and attributes, such as Taiwan, South Korea, Singapore, and Hong Kong, have shown that this approach to economic development can benefit their citizenry as a whole. Conversely, the liberals emphasize that the mercantilist, beggar-thy-neighbor spectacle of the 1930s has shown conclusively that such policies will fail miserably, especially in this complex age of interdependence.[24]

THE DEPENDENCY POINT OF VIEW

Dependency proponents are in strong disagreement with the liberals concerning the salutary effects of international investment. The Marxist strain of dependency considers that such investment is a method used by the capitalist class in the industrial societies to dominate the lesser developed nations. One should remember that Marx described capitalism as a dog-eat-dog creed culminating in a very few rich capitalists acting as overlords vis-à-vis a vast multitude of destitute workers (whom Marx referred to as the proletariat). According to Marx, the great attribute of humankind which differentiates it from the animal kingdom is the ability to perform creative work. An artisan, for example, can create a piece of furniture from start to finish and sell or barter the product for an amount which provides a comfortable standard of living. In the industrial age, however, workers are assigned to the drudgery of piecework on the assembly line and their labor is devoid of creativity. Moreover, the "surplus" that the worker produces, which is the difference between a subsistence and comfortable standard of living, is appropriated by the owners of the means of production, the capitalists. Because of their insatiable greed for profits, the capitalists force the small entrepreneurs out of business and then square off against one another for the domination of the economic sector. Governments in the capitalist nations are also considered by the Marxists as simple pawns in the hands of the owners of the means of production. Therefore, government policy is designed to entrench the power base of the capitalists. Eventually, however, the proletariat will recognize their common blight and by virtue of sheer numbers rise up to overthrow the very powerful but numerically inferior capitalist class. The revolt of the proletariat will then lead to a socialist society which will permit the workers to assume control of both the government and the means of production. The final stage of societal evolution will be Communism, which is only briefly and vaguely described by Marx. Under Communism, the state will have withered away and each person will be free to pursue his or her own creative desires.

Marx asserted that the proletarian revolution would first occur in the most industrialized nations, because that was where the repression and exploitation of the workers would be the most flagrant. When the revolution failed to occur in Great Britain, France, or Germany, second-generation Marxists attempted to piece together an explanation. Lenin finally came up with his very famous treatise that colonialism had allowed capitalism to survive for yet another season. According to Lenin, colonial possessions permitted the capitalists to secure a new source of cheap raw materials and new markets which would serve as dumping grounds for their finished products. Lenin added that imperialism would be the final stage of capitalism and that because of bitter warfare between the capitalist nations over control of colonies and because of socialist revolutions in both the industrial and colonial countries, capitalist ascendancy would soon end.

The Marxist version of dependency is thus fairly clear-cut. International investment is a tool of the capitalist nations used to maintain economic dominance over the Third World, and the way to remedy the situation is to establish socialist regimes in the developing nations and rupture the umbilical cord leading to the capitalist countries.[25]

On the other hand, there is a non-Marxist school of dependency theorists which does not buy Marx's thesis but does consider that structural characteristics make it very difficult for the Third World nations to get a fair shake in the international investment game. Raul Prebisch, former director of the U.N. Economic Commission for Latin America, has been one of the most articulate representatives of this school. Prebisch argues that the Third World nations will continue to lose ground so long as they import industrial products and export commodities.

Because of relatively high wage and other production cost increases in the advanced industrial societies, the price for developing nations to acquire these goods will continue to escalate in terms of what these countries can receive for their raw materials. Consequently, the system of trade and investment is structurally biased against the economic advancement of the developing nations.[26] At the 1980 meeting of the Commonwealth heads of government held in Melbourne, Australia, President Nyerere of Tanzania provided a concrete example of what he considered to be the structural problems in the current international economic system. He stated that because of price increases in the advanced industrial world and the volatility of price levels for Third World commodities, a truck which cost the equivalent of 7 tons of Tanzanian cotton in 1972 would have to be purchased with 28 tons of cotton in 1980. He added that as long as the North controls both the prices for manufactured goods and the markets where developing nations must sell their commodities, gross inequities would continue to exist.

There is a rather extensive litany of complaints lodged by dependency advocates against multinational investment activities in the Third World. Foreign direct investment is viewed as leeching off local capital sources and thereby making it difficult to provide local financing for the establishment of indigenous businesses. A U.S. Senate Committee report is often cited to support this point of contention. This report estimates that 85 percent of the financial needs of U.S. subsidiaries abroad are financed by sources in the host nations.[27] Multinational corporations are also accused of maintaining monopolistic advantages in Third World markets, stifling local competition, stripping developing countries of their precious resource base, and creating a technology dependence in these poorer nations because of the stringent strings attached to technology transfer and the lack of research and development performed by their subsidiaries.[28] Moreover, the technology which is transferred is often considered inappropriate, and multinationals are blamed for creating distorted consumer tastes. For example, why should Third World citizens be asked to buy Coca-Cola when they have a great need for milk and nutritious juices or to use Nestle's baby formula when the water which must be added to the formula is often contaminated?

Because the multinationals are mobile and states are not, dependency proponents claim these firms often play one state against another, threatening to move their facilities elsewhere unless concessions are granted by these already impoverished nations. Through the repatriation of profits, multinationals are blamed for draining desperately needed funds from these nations. Export figures are also viewed as suspect because so much export activity is simply an intrafirm transfer.

Up to 30 percent of all Third World exports of manufactured goods to the United States may be intracorporation transactions, and between Mexico and the United States this figure may be as high as 75 percent.[29] Transfer pricing is also perceived as a tool for multinational enterprises to maximize their profits at the expense of host nations. Transfer pricing refers to the setting of prices on goods and services bought and sold between a parent company and its foreign subsidiaries. Parent firms may purposefully discriminate against their subsidiaries and reduce host country tax liability by charging high transfer prices, or they might move profits from one subsidiary to another in order to take advantage of lower tax rates or to avoid dividend repatriation restrictions. Multinationals may also overcharge subsidiaries for imports. It has been estimated by one source that subsidiaries of U.S. pharmaceutical companies in Colombia have been charged up to 150 percent above world prices for the importation of intermediate drugs from their parent firms.[30]

In addition, both the parent firms and parent governments are accused of interfering in the political and governmental affairs of the developing nations and of undermining their cultural and national identities. ITT's documented role in the Allende episode in Chile is mentioned time and again in dependency literature as firm proof of a trend to interfere in the internal affairs of sovereign nations. The sporadic attempts of the U.S. Justice Department to extend American antitrust laws to overseas subsidiaries and to insist that subsidiaries desist from trading with unfriendly nations have also been viewed as an unfair extraterritorial application of U.S. regulations. A classic example of this extraterritorial dimension occurred when the U.S. government ordered the subsidiaries of American multinationals operating in Canada to cease from shipping products to Cuba. At the time, the Canadian government was carrying on normalized relations with Cuba and considered the U.S. edict as a flagrant violation of Canadian sovereign rights. Parent governments may also attempt to exact concessions from host governments by employing subtle economic weapons such as threatening to reduce or to cut off altogether licensing and technology transfers, the shipment of spare parts, bilateral and multilateral loans and grants, credit lines, etc.[31]

If international investment in the Third World is so destructive, what should be done to rectify the problem? Some dependency advocates claim that the first step is to wrestle control of governmental and economic power from the host country elites which are so closely aligned with the multinational corporations. In contrast to the Marxists, however, revolution is not perceived as the only way to attain this goal. The second step is to transform the developing nation's agrarian structure, which is viewed as being primarily responsible for political and social inequality and economic stagnation. The third step is to revamp the export sector, which is the prime source of capital accumulation, in order to sustain industrial expansion. The final step is to reorient the industrial sector away from the conspicuous consumption patterns of the few toward the provision of basic needs for the many.[32] The advanced industrial nations can help the process along by channeling development assistance through the United Nations and other international and regional organizations, by accepting Third World exports at concessionary rates, and by not interfering when these developing nations place major restrictions on foreign direct investment activity. The establishment of a new international economic order which would gradually redistribute wealth and economic development opportunities from the North to the South is also touted as a necessary policy revision.[33] If these recommendations are implemented, the dependency advocates claim that the asymmetrical nature of international economic relations which makes Third World nations so dependent on the Western capitalist nations could finally be rectified.[34]

ECONOMIC NATIONALISM

Mercantilism, or economic nationalism, had its heyday in Europe in the seventeenth and eighteenth centuries. Under such a system, the financial and business sectors were to subordinate their activities to the collective good of the nation as a whole. Moreover, nations were to strive for military, political, and economic superiority over their European counterparts, and a favorable balance of trade was considered as an absolute necessity. These nations competed against one another to secure colonies, with these colonies providing the homeland with precious raw materials. In addition, the mother nation made sure that it maintained a trade monopoly with these colonial possessions.[35]

Even newly dependent nations were caught up in this mercantilist thrust. After having thrown off its colonial yoke through revolution, the United States embarked on a program of protecting and enhancing its own infant industrial base. For example, President Washington refused to come to the aid of France in the 1790s when that nation was threatened by several of its European neighbors. Thomas Jefferson insisted that America had a moral duty to assist a fellow democratic nation which at one time had played a pivotal role in America's own quest for independence. Although sympathizing with Jefferson's position, Washington contended that realistically the new nation could not afford politically or economically to become entangled in European intrigues. Washington's Secretary of Commerce, Alexander Hamilton, further argued that national security was closely linked to economic development; therefore, the state should naturally assume the principal role in guiding and protecting the economic sector.

As long as nation-states exist as the primary actors in the international system, mercantilism, or economic nationalism, will be present to a greater or lesser degree. The economic-nationalist perspective asserts that the main thrust of government is to protect the economic well-being of its own citizenry, even if this must be accomplished at the expense of people in other nations. In effect, economic nationalism is a policy which seeks to maintain a balance-of-payments surplus by reducing imports, stimulating home production, and promoting exports. The constituency of national governments continues to be their own citizens and incumbents in office are invariably afflicted with ballot-box fever. In other words, if they want to be reelected, they must attempt to satiate some of the major demands of the registered voters. High inflation, interest rates, and above all, unemployment, may be the kiss of death insofar as a politician's future is concerned.

Even though multinational corporations may have solid economic evidence that layoffs are warranted in some of their divisions, governments in nations where the layoffs are targeted may bitterly disagree and place intense pressure on these businesses to alter their policies. In 1962, Charles de Gaulle was incensed when General Motors and Remington Rand announced labor-force reductions in France without first having informed the government. De Gaulle retaliated by placing strict limitations for a time on the activities of foreign-owned subsidiaries in France, but his efforts were frustrated as a result of France's membership in the European Community. By giving General Motors grief, de Gaulle simply prompted the American automobile giant to shift operations to Belgium. The European Community agreement permitted General Motors to retain free access to the French market, but France lost the employment and tax advantages of having the plant on French soil. Facing reality, the French government eventually removed many of the foreign investment restrictions implemented by de Gaulle.

Just about every nation currently has several laws on the books which restrict foreign direct investment and trade activity. These specific restrictions will be discussed in Chapter 7. Furthermore, even when laws are not officially promulgated, methods are often employed to thwart foreign businesses from engaging in investment or trade activity. The Japanese, for example, have often stymied would-be foreign firms through excessive inspection systems and complex regulations. In an attempt to pressure Tokyo to make further cutbacks in the export of automobiles, French customs agents have from time to time stopped delivery on thousands of Japanese cars by withholding certificates of conformity to local technical standards. This action was taken by French officials even at a time when Japan was faithfully honoring a written quota agreement with the French government. Because of the lackluster sales record of French car manufacturers and the impending threat of layoffs in the local automobile industry, the French government opted to reduce even further the inflow of Japanese-made cars into the country, while at the same time paying lip service to the virtues of free trade and the free movement of capital.

As a state policy, economic nationalism is here to stay. Even international law supported by the United States and other major industrialized nations recognizes the right of states to expropriate foreign-owned property and businesses, as long as fair and prompt compensation is paid. Moreover, tariff and nontariff barriers and investment restrictions will continue to hamper international trade and capital flows. The director-general of the General Agreement on Tariffs and Trade has warned that "international trade is threatened to an extent not experienced since the Depression years of the 1930s," with one-fifth of all world trade already restricted by protectionist measures.[36] The pressure to import less, to export more, and to limit profit remittances in order to pay for onerous oil bills may well intensify pressure for economic-nationalist measures. Labor unions in the United States, the United Kingdom, and Sweden would also like to place limits on the outflow of foreign direct investment, claiming that such investment transfers much-needed jobs abroad. They also add that jobs are lost because subsidiaries in foreign countries now service overseas markets which used to be supplied by exports and that such investment drains the nation of capital which could be used for domestic economic development. Other critics complain that the technology transfer that accompanies outward investment is at times counter to the best interests of the nation. Almost 90 percent of the world technology transfer takes place among the industrialized countries, and there have been some concerns voiced about the implications of technology transfer on East-West and intra-West relations. Some observers in the Western democracies complain that the flow of technology to the Communist bloc of nations may provide a potential enemy with economic and even military advantages. In terms of linkages with the other Western nations, some American commentators have contended that the United States has exported too much technology which is now being used by Japanese and Western European businesses to beat out U.S. products in markets around the world. Moreover, some insist that the recent upsurge in foreign direct investment activity in the United States is partially attributable to the desire of overseas firms to acquire American technological innovations and then to export this technology back to their home countries.

Proponents of economic nationalism also remain very wary of the intentions of multinational corporations. Because these global firms operate largely beyond the control of the parent nation, the state faces greater difficulty in managing the domestic economy, international trade, and monetary policy. Multinationals have even been blamed for precipitating the crisis of the U.S. dollar from 1971 through 1973 by engaging in currency speculation, by shifting from the weakened dollar to stronger currencies, and by diverting funds from the United States to offshore tax havens.[37]

Mercantilist tendencies are also showing up in both regional and subnational government bodies. The European Community and the Andean Pact group are among the regional organizations which have official policies concerning trade and foreign direct investment activities. Powerful subnational governments, such as the provinces in Canada, have also formulated investment restrictions which are at times at odds with the policy preferences of the national government or other subnational governments. For example, the government of Ontario has supported major restrictions on certain types of foreign direct investment both within the province and in Canada as a whole, whereas several other industry-poor provinces have bitterly opposed Ontario's policy stance.

Because of the growing interdependency of the global community of nations and the increasing vulnerability of national societies, many citizens are going to support economic-nationalist policy options as a panacea for protecting or enhancing their lifestyles. Furthermore, this policy preference will not simply be limited to developing nations seeking to strengthen their economic infrastructures. Indeed, a major test of economic-nationalist versus liberal principles in the 1980s and 1990s will be how well the advanced industrial societies react to the deluge of product lines from the nearly industrialized nations such as Taiwan, South Korea, Hong Kong, Singapore, Mexico, and Brazil. Although mercantilist policies may provide some short-term relief for both advanced industrial and developing nations, the long range implications of intense economic nationalist competition are ominous, as the 1930's beggar-thy-neighbor episode conclusively illustrates.

THE IDEOLOGICAL DILEMMA

Multinational corporations and international investors must be prepared through the remaining two decades of the twentieth century to cope with governments and political movements which reflect to a greater or lesser degree Marxist, dependency, or economic-nationalist sympathies. Indeed, international investment will be in the forefront of skirmishes between East-West and North-South coalitions of nations. As one observer notes, "in an age of economic interdependence and of mutual military restraint, international economic relations—to paraphrase Clausewitz—could well become the pursuit of policy by other means."[38]

The "world vision" associated with the liberal perspective of international economic linkages will be diluted by the loyalties of people not only to national units but also to fragmented ethnic groups and even at times to separatist movements. Moreover, as international linkages among businesses, subnational governments, and other societal groups multiply, national states will become more impotent in the economic sphere. The frustration associated with this impotence may cause state leaders to overreact and to clamp down unnecessarily on economic exchanges in an attempt to restore the illusion that the state remains fully in control even in an age of global interdependency. The liberal perspective is also threatened within the domestic national setting by groups which are hostile to the notion that the market should be the final arbiter in the allocation of economic goods and services. This hostility naturally increases when unemployment mounts and young people are unable to secure jobs, a situation which has recently been repeated far too often in countries on both sides of the equator.

In spite of these major differences of opinion concerning international economic relations, there is still room for optimism. Almost every nation in the world continues to seek foreign direct investment, regardless of ideological persuasion. The entry of China and the Soviet Union into the investment system is also very encouraging, although potential investors will face major problems in these countries for quite some time to come. Even the willingness of state-owned enterprises to invest overseas and to compete head-on with private companies is in certain respects a healthy sign.

It is entirely possible that an acceptable *modus vivendi* can be worked out by liberal and economic-nationalist representatives. This agreement, whether formalized or informalized, would recognize some of the realities of this new age of interdependency while safeguarding a degree of economic self-determination for the nation-state itself. North-South differences are more imposing, but even in this context limited intergovernmental guidelines governing multinational corporation activities, income and technology transfer, pricing, and taxation policies are feasible. The so-called North-South dialogue has been underway for several years now, and at least a small part of the rhetoric will be translated into workable agreements. Although the so-called Group of 77, representing the 120 or so developing nations, will not be satisfied with the limited concessions made by the advanced industrial nations, what little progress is made will help keep open the investment and trade links to most Third World countries.

Thus it is still quite conceivable that international investment will become much more extensive and pervasive in the years to come, regardless of ideologies and philosophical preferences which perceive such investment with suspicion and repugnance. However, investors will have to carefully pick and choose their overseas projects or face the risk of incurring major financial losses. What occurred in Iran after the fall of the Shah is bound to be repeated in other nations in the foreseeable future. Consequently, political risk forecasting is emerging as a popular tool to assist would-be investors to evaluate their investment options. The next chapter will discuss political risk forecasting and assess how useful it may be to the investment community in deciphering investment opportunities and pitfalls.

REFERENCES

[1] Kurt F. Reinhardt, *Germany: 2000 Years* (New York: Ungar, 1961, p. 119).

[2] Philippe Dollinger, *The German Hansa* (Stanford, Calif.: Stanford University Press, 1970, p. 174).

[3] David H. Blake and Robert S. Walters, *The Politics of Global Economic Relations* (Englewood Cliffs, N.J.: Prentice-Hall, 1976, p. 77).

[4] Dollinger, p. 188.

[5] Sidney Ratner, James H. Soltow, and Richard Sylla, *The Evolution of the American Economy* (New York: Basic Books, 1979, p. 37).

[6] Gary M. Walton and James F. Shepherd, *The Economic Rise of Early America* (New York: Cambridge University Press, 1979, p. 40).

[7] A. G. Kenwood and A. L. Lougheed, *The Growth of the International Economy, 1820– 1960* (London: Allen and Unwin, 1971, p. 40).

[8] Ratner et al., p. 219; and William Woodruff, *Impact of Western Man* (New York: St. Martin's, 1966, p. 119).

[9] Woodruff, p. 121.

[10] Ibid., p. 119.

[11] Ibid.

[12] W. Elliot Brownlee, *Dynamics of Ascent: A History of the American Economy*, 2d ed. (New York: Knopf, 1979, p. 400).

[13] Ibid., pp. 401–402.

[14] Paul E. Sigmund, *Multinationals in Latin America: The Politics of Nationalization* (Madison: University of Wisconsin Press, 1980, p. 21).

[15] J. M. Stopford, "The German Multinationals and Foreign Direct Investment in the United States," *Management International Review*, No. 1, 1980, p. 12.

[16] A classic example of this perception of U.S. foreign direct investment as a tool to fight Communism is found in a speech given by former Secretary of State Dean Rusk to the National Business Advisory Council. See Dean Rusk, "Trade, Investment, and United States Foreign Policy," *Department of State Bulletin*, November 5, 1962, pp. 683–688.

[17] Robert Gilpin, "Economic Interdependence and National Security in Historical Perspective," in *Economic Issues and National Security*, Klaus Knorr and Frank N. Trager (eds.), (Lawrence: Regents Press of Kansas, 1977, p. 37).

[18] Leonard Tivey, *The Politics of the Firm* (Oxford: Martin Robinson, 1978, p. 154).

[19] Peter F. Drucker, *Managing in Turbulent Times* (New York: Harper & Row, 1980, p. 170).

[20] Leonard Gomes, *International Economic Problems* (London: Macmillan, 1978, p. 124).

[21] *The Wall Street Journal*, December 21, 1979, p. 20.

[22] Robert H. Frank and Richard T. Freeman, *Distributional Consequences of Direct Foreign Investment* (New York: Academic Press, 1978, p. 112).

[23] Raymond Vernon, "Storm Over the Multinationals: Problems and Prospects," *Foreign Affairs*, January 1977, p. 246.

[24] Another important advocate of the economic liberalism thesis is Harry Johnson. See his books, *Selected Essays in Monetary Economics* (Boston: Allen and Unwin, 1978), and *Technology and Economic Interdependence* (London: Macmillan, 1975).

Most business representatives and middle-of-the-road politicians in the Western democracies could be characterized as accepting the liberal perspective on international investment.

[25] A good example of a Marxist version of dependency is Immanuel M. Wallerstein's *The Capitalist World Economy: Essays* (New York: Cambridge University Press, 1979). In this book, Wallerstein discusses the inequalities between core and periphery states and asserts that through neocolonialism the capitalists in the major Western nations are able to appropriate the surplus value of the proletariat in the developing nations.

[26] Raul Prebisch, *Change and Development—Latin America's Great Task* (New York: Praeger, 1971).

[27] This report is discussed in José J. Villamil, "Introduction," in *Transnational Capitalism and National Development*, José J. Villamil (ed.) (Sussex: Harvester Press, 1979, p. 13).

[28] In his oligopoly model, Stephen Hymer contends that firms undertake foreign direct investment in order to exploit certain monopolistic advantages. See his article, "The Multinational Corporation and the Law of Uneven Development," in *Economics and World Order*, Jagdish N. Bhagwati (ed.) (New York: Macmillan, 1972, pp. 113–135).

[29] Villamil, p. 5.

[30] Gomes, pp. 134–135.

[31] R. S. Olson, "Economic Coercion: North-South," *World Politics*, July 1979, p. 485.

[32] Osvaldo Sunkel, "Big Business and 'Dependencia,'" *Foreign Affairs*, April 1972, p. 530.

[33] Prebisch, pp. 239–242.

[34] A good book of readings on the dependency perspective is Luis E. DiMarco, (ed.), *International Economics and Development* (New York: Academic Press, 1972). Assessments of the dependency approach may be found in Robert Gilpin, "Three Models of the Future," in *Transnational Corporations and World Order*, George Modelski (ed.) (San Francisco: Freeman, 1979, pp. 353–372); Yale H. Ferguson, "Through Glass Darkly: An Assessment of Various Theoretical Approaches to InterAmerican Relations," *Journal of InterAmerican Studies and World Affairs*, February 1977, pp. 21–24; R. D. Walleri, "Political Economy Literature," *International Studies Quarterly*, December 1978, pp. 607–613; Jeanne G. Gobalet and Larry J. Diamond, "Effects of Investment Dependence on Economic Growth," *International Studies Quarterly*, September 1979, pp. 412–444; and Philip J. O'Brien, "A Critique of Latin American Theories of Dependency," in *Beyond the Sociology of Development*, Ivan Oxaal (ed.) (London: Routledge and Kegan Paul, 1975, pp. 7–27).

[35] John D. Daniels, Ernest W. Ogram, Jr., and Lee H. Radebaugh, *International Business: Environments and Operations*, 2d ed. (Reading, Mass.: Addison-Wesley, 1979, p. 11).

[36] *The Wall Street Journal*, December 21, 1979, p. 20.

[37] Blake and Walters, pp. 101–104.

[38] Gilpin, "Economic Interdependence," p. 63.

FORECASTING POLITICAL RISK IN THE INTERNATIONAL INVESTMENT ARENA

4

INVESTMENT RISKS IN THE CONTEMPORARY WORLD

As manifested in the previous chapter, quite a few people scattered around the globe are not buying the notion that unimpaired international trade and investment will necessarily benefit all of humanity. Most people wish their counterparts in other nations well, but security and pocketbook issues within their own respective countries take clear precedence over economic concerns occurring beyond their national borders. Above all, improvements in the economic health and standard of living of the home country plus the preservation of jobs rank extremely high on the priority list of a nation's populace. Furthermore, citizens and governments alike desire ultimate control over the economic destiny of their own nations, regardless of the trend toward global interdependence.

The fragmentation of the international political system, the entrenched parochial sentiments of national and subnational groups, divergent ideological allegiances, and a community of nations in which one-third of the national governments change every year, have all combined to make life rather hectic at times for international investors. At one time or another over the past few decades, multinational enterprises and individual investors have been negatively impacted by events which have transpired in Afghanistan, Algeria, Angola, Argentina, Bolivia, Brazil, Burma, Canada, Chile, China, Cuba, Eastern

Europe, Egypt, El Salvador, Ethiopia, France, Ghana, Guatemala, India, Indonesia, Iran, Iraq, Lebanon, Libya, Mozambique, Nicaragua, Nigeria, Peru, Somalia, South Yemen, Sri Lanka, Sudan, Tanzania, Uganda, Zaire, Zimbabwe, and a host of other countries.

American companies alone may have lost a billion dollars or more as a result of the downfall of the Shah of Iran. Prior to the Shah's ouster, one U.S. firm had signed a contract with the Iranian government to supply more than 500 million dollars in communications equipment. The company had agreed to advance the Iranians almost 100 million dollars in open letters of credit with no specifications concerning when and under what conditions the government of Iran could utilize the credit letters. A U.S. housing-construction corporation also fell into the Iranian quagmire when it agreed to build two major housing projects in the Middle Eastern nation. The potential losses suffered by the housing firm were far greater than its total net worth. In both cases, neither company had any insurance to mitigate the investment disasters.[1]

U.S. companies were not the only victims of the Iranian investment debacle. Japan's largest foreign direct investment in the postwar period has been seriously jeopardized by the revolution in Iran. Mitsui and the Japanese government agreed in 1971 to a fifty-fifty joint venture with the National Iranian Oil Company to build a huge petrochemical complex on the Persian Gulf. The project suffered through many years of delays, serious labor disruptions after Ayatollah Khomeini came to power, and several bombing strafes during the Iran-Iraq war. Mitsui still hopes to salvage parts of the investment agreement but stands to lose hundreds of millions of dollars in the process.[2]

Stephen Kobrin has documented 511 "acts" of forced divestment involving over 1500 firms in seventy-six developing nations from 1960 to 1976.[3] Moreover, according to one executive recruiting firm based in New York City, more than 60 percent of U.S. companies doing business abroad suffered politically inflicted damage from 1976 to 1981.[4]

The political risks for international investors may be quite substantial, especially in the 100 or so nations which have gained independence in the postwar era and are strenuously engaged in the modernization and development of their political and economic systems. The quest for control over the nation's economic destiny and the collective push for a new international economic order also present special challenges for the investment community. The polarization of the Western alliance and the gradual erosion in the U.S. economic hegemony cloud the investment picture even further. One bank executive has succinctly summed up the risky nature of some investments, "one bad call wipes out 15 years of profits."[5] Such a bad call was made by a U.S. oil company in 1968 when it decided to invest tens of millions of dollars in offshore oil developments in Vietnam. Aris Gloves, a division of Consolidated Foods, went ahead in 1976 with the establishment of a facility in El Salvador after receiving assurances from the U.S. Embassy that this Central American nation was a "happy, sleepy country." Within twenty-four months, leftist groups were holding the subsidiary's president and 120 local employees hostage, demanding higher wages and a better working environment, along with a host of other conditions. The company finally acceded to some parts of the ultimatum but in doing so rendered the business venture unprofitable. It subsequently ceased operations completely in El Salvador six months later.[6]

In addition, the source of political risk is not always found in the host country. As an illustration, Sweden's giant electrical firm, ASEA, faced intense criticism at home for proposing to take part in a power-plant project in what was then the Portuguese colony of Mozambique. The widespread rebuke of ASEA was linked to the Swedish company's alleged support for colonialism. Many U.S. firms have also faced vehement criticism and even boycotts of their products and stock because of their investments in South Africa. In 1965, Firestone Tire and Rubber Company decided to cut off negotiations to design and equip a synthetic rubber company in Rumania because of political pressure from conservative youth organizations in the United States.[7] Many other firms have desisted from engaging in what may have been sound overseas investments because of organized interest-group opposition at home.

In spite of the wholesale confiscations in Cuba in 1959 and 1960, as well as in certain other countries, most government interference in the foreign direct investment sector tends to be very selective and limited. One should keep in mind that an "expropriation" is aimed at a particular enterprise or property, such as the Quebec government's expropriation of Asbestos Corporation, a subsidiary of General Dynamics of St. Louis. A "nationalization" is directed at a general type of industry, property, or economic sector, such as the nationalization by several Middle Eastern governments of their entire petroleum industries, which had been predominantly foreign-owned. Both expropriations and nationalizations provide compensation to the former owners, whereas "confiscations" à la Cuba or China under Mao are carried out without providing compensation to the foreign owners.

Stephen Kobrin has shown that even in the case of forced divestments in Third World nations, almost 90 percent of the incidents had been very selective and did not represent wholesale nationalizations.[8] Much more widespread but lower-profile political risks to be faced by international investors in the future will probably emanate from governments limiting the multinational enterprises' strategic flexibility.

Because of government regulations, firms will find it much more difficult to protect product lines and technological innovations, marketing and transfer strategies, and profit margins. IBM, for example, withdrew completely from India because it refused to comply with the New Delhi government's insistence on a greater role in product development and equipment allocation.[9] The Australian national telecommunication administration has also adopted a tactic which foreign-based enterprises will repeatedly face all over the world. This Australian government agency now mandates that those subsidiaries of multinational firms desiring to secure contracts from the government must supply equipment which conforms to tailor-made standards. These standards generally mean that the subsidiaries must farm out some of the key work to indigenous Australian companies, thus making it very difficult for the multinational enterprise to protect its proprietary hold over newly developed technology.[10] Local content and ownership standards, foreign exchange and export stipulations, and government export promotion and subsidy programs which openly support home-grown firms are among the other tactical measures available to host governments which may adversely affect foreign direct investment. For example, in order to gain a foothold in the Spanish market, Ford Motor Company had to agree in 1973 to limit sales to 10 percent of the previous year's total domestic automobile purchases in Spain. Moreover, Ford acceded to a government edict to export at least two-thirds of its entire production from its new Spanish plant and to refrain from introducing a broader range of models in the Spanish market without the prior approval of the Madrid authorities.[11]

With the recent history of some major overseas investment setbacks, the uncertainty associated with complex interdependence, the push for a new international economic order more favorable to the developing nations, and much more extensive government intervention in the economic sector, many global companies have begun to establish their own political risk-assessment units. Heeding the old adage that an ounce of prevention is worth a pound of cure, these firms have begun to recognize that it is far more preferable to predict risks beforehand than to minimize losses once an investment setback has occurred. According to a Conference Board survey, approximately 55 percent of 193 major U.S.-based multinationals have institutionalized to one degree or another their political analysis activities. Because of a bitter experience in Chile, Dow Chemical was prompted several years ago to establish an ad hoc Economic, Social, and Political (ESP) Committee, composed of a half dozen executives, to keep management aware of political shifts which might adversely affect Dow's overseas investments. Shell Oil uses panels of experts which assess political and economic factors that may impact upon the company's operations. Their responses are then weighted according to a predetermined formula, and both the individual assessments and the aggregated results are forwarded to Shell's top management for analysis. In 1977, American Can introduced its computer program nicknamed PRISM (Primary Risk Investment Screening Matrix), which is specifically intended to provide guidance for business expansion in Third World regions.

Banks were actually among the first business enterprises to establish such units, largely because upwards of 50 percent of their profits come from overseas operations and several have been stung by a series of setbacks in Peru, Sudan, Jamaica, Iran, Zaire, and selected other countries. Citibank set up a special country-risk management team in 1974, and Chase Manhattan followed in 1979. The Bank of America is experimenting with an advisory team chaired by the executive vice-president, the senior credit officer, and the chief economists from the four regional divisions in Los Angeles, Caracas, London, and Hong Kong.[12] Petroleum companies, which suffered through many nationalization campaigns, were also among the first business organizations to establish in-house political assessment groups. Recently many large manufacturing concerns have jumped on the bandwagon, with General Motors, Eaton, TRW, and General Electric among the manufacturing and high-technology companies setting up in-house units.

Independent consulting firms specializing in political risk forecasting have also multiplied rapidly over just the past few years. Some of the better known companies include Frost and Sullivan, Business International, BERI, Multinational Strategies, Risks Insights, and Probe International. Some of these firms engage in country-by-country surveys, and their conclusions are scrutinized very closely not only by subscribing business organizations but by host countries as well. As an illustration, one report ranked Thailand as a very risky nation and predicted that within eighteen months rising oil and other energy costs would tempt the Thai government to strengthen popular support by adopting nationalistic policies toward foreign direct investment. This appraisal prompted the Prime Minister of Thailand to respond immediately and to deny the firm's conclusions. As part of his rebuttal, the Prime Minister stressed that other political risk-forecasting groups had assigned Thailand much more positive ratings and that foreign investment would continue to be welcomed in his country.[13] Of course, the discrepancies among forecasting firms in predicting the most volatile national settings may be partially explained by the fact that the latitude for change is so much greater in these countries than in the most stable advanced industrial societies. Thus, it should be much easier to predict the 10 most stable nations than the 10 that are the least stable among the more than 150 sovereign countries in the world.

Businesses with extensive investments abroad have also rushed to acquire the part-time services of retired foreign service and intelligence officers or academicians with overseas expertise who are able to provide some guidance as to the linkage between political phenomena and investment potential and risk. Henry Kissinger, for one, has formed his own risk assessment firm and in the past has provided occasional advice to Chase Manhattan, Goldman, Sachs, and Merck.[14] The Association of Political Risk Analysts (APRA) has also recently been established in New York City. This association has already attracted hundreds of members, holds a yearly convention, and publishes a quarterly newsletter.

In light of this rapid expansion in political risk-forecasting activities, the next two sections of this chapter will zero in on some of the techniques used in forecasting and assess their strengths and weaknesses. One must recognize that the effort to systematize and integrate political science and business research endeavors is still in the early stages. On the whole, business people underestimate the impact which political phenomena may have on their investment activities and perceive the political arena in a simplistic, stereotypical fashion. The perceptions of political scientists toward the intricacies of international business operations generally fall within the same stereotypical abyss.

Companies which rely on intuitive, seat-of-the-pants methods to assess investment opportunities are inviting major disasters in the years ahead. Some organizations are writing off not only individual countries for investment purposes but entire regions as well, an outlook which will be extremely costly in this highly competitive interdependent age. American businesses in particular must realize that they face formidable competition from foreign multinationals in both developing and advanced industrial countries. Not only must these U.S. businesses provide highly respected products and services at a reasonable price, but they must also accurately gauge the investment climate in a myriad of nations and regions if they are to remain internationally competitive. Indeed, in some cases U.S. firms will have to work harder than their overseas counterparts because of certain prejudices which linger within the international community of nations. In essence, the U.S. economic hegemony in the world is definitely decreasing, but many national governments persist in using the United States as the scapegoat for their societal ills. Consequently, some American firms suffer from the spillover consequences of this scapegoat phenomenon, whereas foreign competitors often emerge unscathed or even benefit from the anti-American policies. Incidents in Iran, Mexico, India, and several other nations have conclusively shown the disadvantages which American firms often face abroad vis-à-vis their competitors from other advanced industrial or developing countries.[15]

International investors will also have to go beyond the superficiality of country and region surveys and recognize that risk assessment must be company or even project specific. In effect, what may be a major risk for one economic sector may represent only a minor gamble for another industry or sector. Furthermore, risk assessment will have to become much more sophisticated in order to take into account investment climates within the jurisdictions of subnational governments. In addition, the assessments must go beyond simply ideological parameters and identify good investment opportunities in nations which are seemingly hostile to capitalism. For example, Gulf Oil has been hurt more than most petroleum companies by nationalization policies, but was successful in ascertaining that it could continue to carry on a profitable operation in Angola even though that nation swung over to a Marxist government in 1975. And lastly, the investors with extensive overseas operations will have to learn to mitigate their risks through insurance, pricing transfer, profit repatriation, joint venture, lobbying, and assorted other defensive strategies.

THE STATE OF THE ART

Political risk forecasting is a relatively recent phenomenon. This is clearly illustrated in a survey completed in mid-1981 by the Association of Political Risk Analysts. This survey of that organization's membership found that the vast majority had been involved in full-time risk analysis for less than three years.

These analysts use a variety of approaches in their efforts to forecast political risks for businesses. Some even distinguish political risk from political uncertainty, with the latter described as "an unmeasured, subjective doubt about a political environment," and the former as "a relatively objective measurement, usually resulting in a probability estimate of that doubt."[16] Thus, by converting political uncertainties into probability terms, "political risk provides a mechanism for the objective evaluation of foreign investment climates."[17] Rummel and Heenan identify at least five major approaches which are employed to ascertain political risk. The first is the grand-tours approach, wherein a company engages in some preliminary market research toward a country where it is considering investing and then dispatches an executive or a team of people on an in-country inspection tour, usually lasting several days. Once the tour has been completed, the team meets with top management and discusses the potential strengths and pitfalls of the proposed investment. The second is termed the old-hands approach, with a company placing great stock in the recommendations made by academicians, diplomats, business representatives, and other outsiders who have great knowledge about the target country. The third approach utilizes Delphi techniques. The potential investing firm initially lists selective elements which might influence a nation's political future, such as the size and composition of the armed forces or the history of leadership succession. The firm then asks a number of outside experts to weigh or rank the importance of these factors for the country under consideration. The data may then be aggregated and the country ranked on a high-, moderate-, or low-risk basis. The fourth major approach stresses quantitative methods, somewhat akin to econometric forecasting of economic events. Multivariate analysis is used to predict political trends based on contemporary and historical information and to provide underlying political, economic, sociological, and cultural relationships which may affect the future of the nation-state under consideration. The fifth approach, which is strongly favored by Rummel and Heenan, utilizes integrated analysis. This type of analysis combines both subjective and objective approaches and provides a systematic framework for both the qualitative and quantitative interpretation of data. The authors add that this fifth approach combines both insight and wisdom with the best features of management science and permits an analyst to zero in on the most salient aspects of domestic instability, foreign conflict, and political and economic "climates."[18]

Rummel and Heenan proceed to provide a concrete test case of the fifth approach, applying their version of political risk forecasting to Indonesia. They concluded back in 1978 that Indonesia would face in the future minimal foreign conflict and few shifts in political ideology but major problems in terms of domestic turmoil, increased expropriations, and high external debt. The authors assigned Indonesia a "moderately high risk" rating and investors were warned to proceed with considerable caution.[19] With the passage of time and the benefit of hindsight, members of the investment community should now be able to gauge the accuracy of this specific political risk forecast.

Almost all of the professional forecasting services incorporate the major features of integrated analysis. The Frost and Sullivan World Political Risk Forecasts cover more than sixty countries and utilize the qualitative and quantitative analyses of 150 political scientists, business representatives, government officials, and other country specialists. At least three experts evaluate a country every few months and the Frost and Sullivan permanent staff may also add its own input. An eighteen-month forecast is provided for each country, with emphasis placed on the probability of regime change, political turmoil, expropriation, and equity and repatriation restrictions. A five-year forecast is also included, with each expert analyzing the likelihood that political change will result in major losses to multinational enterprises as a result of socioeconomic conditions, factional or political activities, or government decisions. Major domestic actors are identified, their positions on issues crucial to businesses scrutinized, and their potential for influencing change estimated. The Frost and Sullivan country-reports average thirty pages and each client is provided with a concise political risk forecast similar to the following: "There is a 25 percent chance of a major business loss because of political developments in the next 18 months, a 45 percent chance of a loss within five years."[20]

Business International Corporation also employs a panel of outside experts who rank more than seventy countries twice a year according to risk, opportunity, and operating conditions. These specialists provide ratings for fifty-five topics ranging from government attitudes toward the private sector to the composition, size, and influence of the middle class.[21] Business International's reference service on investing, licensing, and trading conditions abroad also covers the laws and regulations of most "free world" countries and highlights the actual experiences of companies as they pertain to (a) the establishment of new operations, (b) limitations on foreign ownership and management, (c) financial transfers, (d) antitrust, licensing, patent, labor, tax, and incentive practices, and (e) other regulations and controls that will or may in the future affect business operations.

The Business Environment Risk Index (BERI) was conceived by Professor F. Theodore Haner. BERI reviews more than forty-five countries three times a year. A panel of outside experts ranks the countries according to fifteen factors that affect the business climate, with ratings ranging from zero (unacceptable) to four (superior). The ratings are then weighted, and countries are classified as low-risk, moderate-risk, high-risk, or excessive-risk. Political risks are isolated into various categories, including splits among different language, ethnic, and religious groups which might undermine stability; unfavorable social conditions such as extremes in population density and distribution of wealth; conflicts in society such as the frequency of demonstrations, violence, and general strikes; and dependence of a country on a major power unfriendly to a company's parent nation.[22]

Dan Haendel has also introduced a Political System Stability Index (PSSI) which is geared exclusively toward developing nations. Fifteen indicators of political stability are distributed among three equally weighted indexes—socioeconomic, governmental processes, and societal conflict. The indicators for the societal-conflict component, for example, are public unrest, internal violence, and the coercion potential of the society.[23] Each country is then ranked according to the stability of its political system, and the reader is also provided with a rating of the reliability of the estimate. Using data gathered for the period 1961 through 1966, Haendel ranked Israel as the most politically stable nation and the Dominican Republic as the least stable. Unfortunately, Haendel was not able at the time to ascertain the predictive value of the PSSI by comparing his ratings with more recent empirical data, but he does assert that his index can be used as a forecasting tool.[24]

Almost without exception, each of these organizations and scholars is convinced that politics will play a progressively greater role in affecting the global strategies of multinational enterprises. Stephen Kobrin also endorses this notion, claiming that the increased politicization of economic activity, changes in the nature of nationalism in the postcolonial era, an upsurge in political instability and conflict, the growing importance of nongovernmental actors, the decline of American economic hegemony, and the partial disassembly of relationships between political, economic, and military power will all contribute to the political sector, having a much greater impact on international business activities.[25]

In one of the first studies devoted to political risk, Stefan Robock and Kenneth Simmonds identify the sources of political risk as (a) latent philosophies (socialism, economic nationalism, etc.), (b) social unrest and disorder, (c) ineffective law enforcement, (d) extreme economic hardships, (e) racial disorders, (f) political influence of local business interests, (g) political uncertainty, particularly in newly independent nations, (h) armed conflict between nations, and (i) new international alliances.[26] The authors also provide four basic steps in the political risk-forecasting process. The first involves understanding the type of government presently in power. The second step calls for an analysis of the multinational corporation's own product or operations in order to isolate the specific kind of political risk likely to be encountered. For example, macropolitical risk would involve politically motivated environmental changes broadly directed at many if not all foreign enterprises, whereas micropolitical risk would deal with selected economic sectors or specific foreign-owned operations. The third step would provide a determination of the source of political risk. As an illustration, if the risk is an operational restriction, an analyst might be able to trace the source of that restriction to local businesspeople, thereby pinpointing the target group which must be lobbied by the foreign-based firm. The last step entails projecting into the future both time parameters and probability of political risk.[27]

THE UTILITY OF POLITICAL RISK ASSESSMENT

Because of the paradox of complex economic and resource interdependence and continuing political fragmentation, political risk assessment must become an essential task of prudent international investors. Interdependence is, of course, a fact of life, as evidenced by the United States being more than 50-percent dependent on twenty-four strategic metals, including a 90-percent or more dependence on bauxite, chrome, cobalt, manganese, and the platinum-group metals, and a 75-percent or greater dependence on antimony, fluorspar, gold, and nickel.

Yet in spite of this interdependence, the world continues to be organized politically on the basis of sovereign national states. This is clearly illustrated by the growing membership in the United Nations. When the first meeting of the General Assembly of the United Nations was held in London in January, 1946, 51 states were represented. By 1952 the membership had increased to 60, in 1960 it was up to 100, in 1970 it stood at 125, and in 1980 at 153. Moreover, many of these states are in the difficult transition period between traditional and industrialized economies, a period often characterized by rampant political instability and intense political violence.[28]

Investment risks may therefore be quite high, but the tremendous competition faced by U.S. firms abroad, especially from enterprises based in other advanced industrial societies, necessitates that U.S. companies be very active overseas investors. For the moment, these U.S. businesses have an advantage in the political risk-assessment field because so few foreign firms have adopted sophisticated assessment techniques. On the other hand, as explained earlier, some of this current advantage is mitigated by the fact that in more than a few Third World nations there is seemingly greater resistance to accepting direct investment from U.S.-based enterprises than from businesses situated in other countries. As a superpower and the military leader of the Western alliance, the U.S. government is sometimes forced to take strong stances against political developments in other nations or blocs of nations, stances which may prove to be injurious to U.S. business interests in those countries or regions. Other members of the Western alliance may well be in full agreement with the U.S. policy stance, but are able to maintain a lower profile and thereby minimize the criticism which may be lodged against their own multinational enterprises in the impacted nations. Furthermore, U.S. domestic laws, such as foreign corrupt-practices regulations, make it much more difficult for U.S. firms than their foreign counterparts to cope with the special investment challenges which may be faced abroad.

Even though political risk assessment is more in vogue in the United States than abroad, its utilization by U.S. firms is still relatively sporadic and leaves much to be desired. Business men and women are frankly ill-equipped to understand the subtleties of a foreign political environment. Generally, they tend to oversimplify, to rely on ethnocentric stereotypes and misperceptions, and to believe steadfastly that business practices can generally remain aloof of the political arena. Some firms insist that by hiring business managers who are born and raised in the foreign country, they will be able to ascertain the political "pulse" of that nation. Certainly, this action will help to mitigate the ethnocentric bias, but there is no guarantee that a manager who has graduated from a business school and who is generally from an upper- or upper-middle-class background will have a good grasp of political realities. This was very clearly and painfully illustrated in Vietnam when both the U.S. government and U.S.-based multinationals relied on the political advice of upper-class, European-trained, French-speaking Vietnamese. In effect, a business representative easily recognizes that a political scientist is not adequately prepared to accept a senior management position in a firm simply by reading a couple of management books and *The Wall Street Journal* and *Business Week* on a regular basis. Unfortunately, too many business people do not recognize that they cannot become sophisticated political analysts simply by reading a few political science texts and by perusing *The New York Times* and *Time* magazine.

Even when astute political analysts are retained by firms considering major investments abroad, there is only a marginal chance that their recommendations will be given proper consideration at the highest corporate levels. A Conference Board study completed in the mid-1970s has indicated that multinational enterprises generally (a) pay very little attention to political assessments, (b) do most of their political analyses only during entry or exit from a host country, (c) do not attach sufficient importance to political intelligence at corporate headquarters, and (d) do not sufficiently integrate political assessments into the overall corporate decision-making process.[29]

International investors must begin to take political risk forecasting very seriously, while at the same time recognizing the limitations of the approach. Political analysis is inextricably linked to the activities of people, a complicated species replete with irrationalities and uncertainties. Moreover, a person involved in the political sphere may exhibit extreme narcissistic drives which make it very difficult to ascertain whether his goals are linked primarily to self-gratification and glory or to the welfare of his constituency. It is precisely these imponderables of human behavior which call into question the validity of the current theory of nuclear deterrence. According to this theory, nations should strive to achieve a second-strike nuclear capability, which means even if attacked first by an aggressor nation, the besieged country could still retaliate and inflict unacceptable damage on the aggressor. Under such circumstances, a nuclear balance of terror would theoretically exist and no rational leader would launch a nuclear attack because that action would be tantamount to committing suicide. Unfortunately, "rationality" seems to be based on Western Judeo-Christian principles and does not take into account the value systems of other cultures, nor the extremist motivations and goals of selected political leaders. Thus in an era of nuclear proliferation, one shudders to think what damage certain contemporary national and ethnic leaders could inflict on the world if given access to devastating weaponry and sophisticated delivery systems.

It is quite clear that political risk analysts are not working with closed systems where one can control all of the variables and predict with great certainty the pertinent inputs and outputs. Therefore, one must always keep things in perspective and remember Edgar R. Fiedler's six forecasting rules:[30]

1. Forecasting is very difficult especially if it is about the future.

2. The moment you forecast you know you are going to be wrong, you just don't know when and in which direction.

3. The herd instinct among forecasters makes sheep look like independent thinkers.

4. When asked to explain a forecast, never underestimate the power of a platitude.

5. On the use of survey techniques in forecasting: When you know absolutely nothing about a topic, make your forecast by asking 300 others who don't know the answer either.

6. Forecasters tend to learn less and less about more and more until they know nothing about everything.

Nonetheless, these very apparent weaknesses should not serve as an excuse for simply writing off overseas investments or for falling back to intuitive, seat-of-the-pants approaches to risk forecasting. Investors must begin to utilize a systematic risk-assessment approach which is tailor-made to a specific business operation or project in a single country or even subregion of a country. The general services provided by Frost and Sullivan, Business International, BERI, and other such organizations or individual analysts may be a good starting point for the assessment process, but eventually the analysis must be customized to take into account the specific requirements of the individual company.

It should also be remembered that what might be risky for one industry might offer little risk or even special advantages for another. For example, extractive industries tend to be quite vulnerable because foreign control of a nation's natural resource base evokes strong emotions on the part of the nation's citizenry. This is particularly true in Third World countries where extractive enterprises account for the great bulk of a nation's export activity and gross domestic product. However, even most of the advanced industrial nations place strict controls on foreign access to their natural resources, as exemplified by the fact that most do not permit nonresident aliens or corporations to acquire farmland and severely restrict their activities in the energy and precious-metal sectors. Businesses engaged in infrastructure activities considered crucial to national security, such as public utilities and mass communications, or sectors affecting the control of the economy, such as banking and insurance, also tend to be very vulnerable to government-mandated takeovers or major restrictions.[31] Companies with heavy capital investments must also be very wary of political events because it is virtually impossible to transport a large plant, lock, stock, and barrel, out of a country. On the other hand, even in countries with strict controls, lucrative incentives may be available for foreign firms willing to invest in the high-technology sphere, and these firms also tend to be the least vulnerable to takeovers after entry into the country. Furthermore, companies involved in complicated international production procedures and which assign only one phase of production to a subsidiary in any single country are relatively immune from expropriation and nationalization. In effect, the national government always desires to maintain the jobs created by the subsidiary. Consequently, an unfriendly takeover of the subsidiary might jeopardize that country's place in the international production network and thereby cost many jobs as well as much-needed tax revenues. In the same vein, a company may decrease the chances of government interference by retaining control over the distribution and marketing network for the subsidiary's products.

Instead of being mesmerized by the rather infrequent episodes of mass nationalization, companies must pay much more attention to the potential risks of micropolitical changes and must monitor in-country developments continuously *after* entry into a country. For example, central bank and government economic policies may dramatically impact on interest rates and currency-exchange rates, and this may work either to the advantage or disadvantage of the foreign investor. In the early 1980s, the tight-money emphasis of the U.S. Federal Reserve

Board, when combined with the budgetary and tax policies of the Reagan administration, drove the value of the dollar way up against most other major currencies. For foreign-based firms situated in the United States which were doing well financially and could repatriate a fair share of their profits, the Federal Reserve and government policies were a windfall. However, for those companies making an initial investment, having to pump large sums of money into their U.S. subsidiaries, or needing to export a large percentage of their U.S. production, these policies could be very costly. As an illustration, Thyssen AG, the number one steel producer in West Germany, offered to pay 275 million dollars in January 1978 for the Budd Company, a U.S. automobile and railroad-car supplier. This purchase cost Thyssen approximately 577 million marks, whereas the same deal, consummated in August 1981, would have cost 674 million marks because of the dramatic increase in the value of the American dollar versus the German mark. The Trudeau government's "Canadianization" strategy of the early 1980s was also a major factor in the precipitous drop of the Canadian dollar to a fifty-year low vis-à-vis the U.S. dollar. Thus it is very important that companies engage in currency risk analysis and understand the impact which specific government actions may have on a company's foreign-exchange dealings, both in the investment and exporting spheres.[32]

Foreign firms must also keep abreast of host government decisions which might favor indigenous or state-owned competitors. Because the maintenance and creation of jobs are so vital to the electoral fortunes of government leaders, labor policies must also be watched very closely. Indeed, investors must recognize that the time horizons of politicians only extend to the next election and that short-term remedies to economic problems will almost invariably take precedence over long-run solutions. Therefore, emphasis will often be placed by incumbents on holding down inflation and interest rates just prior to an election, even though this strategy may have negative long-term economic implications. In order to whittle down a growing federal government deficit, the Trudeau administration announced plans to place a special tax on natural gas but not on hydroelectric production. This tax, which would prove costly to several major multinational oil and gas companies operating in Canada, had clear political overtones. The Trudeau government was unhappy with the degree of foreign ownership in this resource sector and also resented the policies of provincial governments which controlled most of the nation's gas and oil reserves. Because his party had little electoral support in these regions, Trudeau proceeded with the tax. However, hydroelectricity is generated mainly by the provinces in Central Canada which provide the bulk of electoral support for Trudeau's Liberal Party. Thus hydroelectric production was not subjected to the new tax, even though additional revenues were desperately needed to decrease the government's budget deficit. With few exceptions, the electorate is also guided in its selection of candidates by pocketbook issues, and although certainly not an absolute truth, the following maxim rings true in many electoral situations: "As goes politics, so goes economic policy and performance. This is the case because as goes economic performance, so goes the election."[33]

Local content standards, tax laws, exporting provisions, protectionism, repatriation and currency limitations, antitrust stipulations, ownership formulas, boycott provisos, and wage and price controls are among the day-to-day regulatory activities of host governments which must be monitored on an ongoing basis. Firms must also be in tune with how government bureaucracies and individual bureaucrats operate within a specific national setting and be able to ascertain the complexities of the policy formulation and implementation processes. In addition, international companies must become familiar with the interaction of interest groups, such as environmental and consumer organizations, and recognize that small single-minded groups may have more influence at times on governments than a complacent, consensus-minded majority.[34] Moreover, the impact which the host country's media may have on government policy and business practices should not be underestimated. Special emphasis must also be given to the "politics" of unfriendly takeover bids pursued by a foreign firm against a local business. For example, several major foreign multinationals have been surprised recently by how local U.S. companies have been able to frustrate unsolicited takeover bids through state and federal court actions, media blitzes, and appeals to congressional committees and federal agencies.

Multinational enterprises must not overreact to episodes of terrorism, political kidnappings, student demonstrations, palace coups, or other similar events. The media survive on such spectacular occurrences and almost always depict such episodes as having an awesome and overbearing effect on the nation's populace as a whole. In actuality, this rarely occurs; life goes on as usual for most people, and everyday business activities suffer hardly at all. However, because of the stigma of major unrest, dissatisfaction, and instability, investors may shy away from the impacted nation, even though the investments might be very secure and return respectable profits. In such cases, political risk forecasting, when properly utilized, will be able to show an international business that excessive caution may be just as debilitating as too little caution.

Other superficial signs of instability or ideological commitments can be placed in proper perspective by a thorough study of a nation's historical development and its political, economic, social, and cultural tendencies. Third and Fourth Republic France rarely had governments which could count on continuous majority support in the National Assembly. As a result, Prime Ministers and their Cabinets averaged less than two years in office and chaos often typified parliamentary and Cabinet proceedings. Nonetheless, an effective civil service remained in place, and continuity was maintained in spite of France's reputation for unstable governments. Brazil also went through eleven Presidents from 1947 to 1970, but generally enjoyed consistent economic growth. The Parti Québécois government in the province of Quebec is dedicated to social-democratic principles and, as a result, has frightened many businesses in the United States. With few exceptions, however, the Parti Québécois continues to seek foreign investment and will even assist potential investors to overcome the hurdles erected by Canada's Foreign Investment Review Agency (FIRA).

The Parti Québécois example also illustrates that international businesses must not be content to concentrate solely on national-level policies. As will be discussed in a later chapter, subnational governments and groups may be very powerful actors within a national setting and may be in the process of expanding their own international linkages. In the United States and Canada, state and provincial governments compete against one another in an effort to entice international investors to their respective locales, thus allowing overseas firms to shop around for the most lucrative incentive package. Even municipalities have begun to sponsor overseas missions in an effort to bring new direct investment and jobs to their communities. For example, more than seventy American cities joined together in the autumn of 1981 to sponsor an "investment fair" in Zurich, hoping to attract European investment to their respective localities.

On the other hand, a nation may generally offer good investment opportunities for overseas firms, but special problems may face such investors on a regional basis. For example, one American firm which was enticed by French-government regional-development subsidies opened a manufacturing facility in a part of Normandy which had traditionally experienced militant labor unrest. This militancy plagued the operations of the new firm and made the business much less profitable than if it had been set up in another region of France. The government of Great Britain also offers investment incentives to firms willing to establish facilities in Northern Ireland, and such incentives may be either very worthwhile or worthless depending on the area of Northern Ireland selected for the new facility. Several "free-enterprise zones" have also been established in major urban centers in the United States and may prove to be a boom or bust for international businesses, depending on labor conditions, quality-of-life considerations, and the specific policy supports and constraints available from local municipal and state governments. Consequently, risk-assessment studies must begin to pay close attention to developments and trends at the subnational levels.

Political conditions in the home country may also impact upon the international investor, and therefore they deserve close scrutiny. Government policies toward the tax treatment of nationals assigned abroad, boycotts, antitrust matters, extraterritoriality, investment-risk insurance, overseas business conduct (linked to such laws as the Foreign Corrupt Business Practices Act), interest-rate and balance-of-payments considerations, and alliance politics may either hinder or enhance investment opportunities abroad. In addition, government policy and the positions of powerful interest groups may make the pursuit of profits in particular nations pale in comparison to the grief which a company may face at home. This has certainly deterred several businesses from investing in South Africa. Labor criticism that investment abroad exports jobs has also occasionally made life uncomfortable for multinational enterprises, especially in countries suffering from endemically high unemployment. Because interdependence has helped to blur the distinction between domestic and foreign policy and because nationalism remains strong, multinational enterprises must anticipate that political developments at home will impact upon their investment strategies. This dimension of political risk analysis has thus far received scant attention.

The influence on overseas investment wielded by international relations and alliance policies must also become an integral part of the risk-assessment process. As an example, businesses seeking to service the Argentine market from Chile, or vice versa, found during the 1970s that borders were closed twice for long periods of time because of lingering disputes between the two Latin America neighbors. For U.S.-based firms, investment in nations which are opposed to the United States militarily and politically may present special difficulties. Although empirical data are unavailable, it is conceivable that nations not receiving substantial U.S. military and economic assistance may find it much easier to clamp down on the subsidiaries of U.S. firms than countries tied into the U.S. foreign and military aid network. On the other hand, the "presence" of other nations on a regional basis may also influence a host nation's investment policies. For example, most Canadians perceive the United States very favorably and consider that Canada must remain faithful to its commitments to the North Atlantic Treaty Organization (NATO) and the North American Air Defense Command (NORAD). However, they also perceive that there is too much American direct investment in most of Canada's key economic sectors and that American cultural values have stifled the development of an indigenous Canadian culture. These perceptions provided the popular support which Prime Minister Trudeau needed to introduce his Canadianization strategy in the oil and gas sectors. Moreover, the resurgence in Canadian economic nationalism prompted the Trudeau administration to think about permitting the Foreign Investment Review Agency to begin to review the records of existing foreign subsidiaries in terms of research-and-development allocations, export activity, subcontracting practices, and profit-repatriation practices, and then to mandate performance standards for those firms found to be deficient. If the FIRA retroactive review process is fully implemented, the failure of foreign firms to comply with these standards could lead to a loss of government contracts, financial penalties, or even the forced divestiture of assets. The Canadian experience will certainly be replicated in other countries and definitely indicates that businesses must be prepared to renegotiate arrangements with host governments after an investment has been made.

MITIGATING POLITICAL RISK

Political risk assessment will be of little use to multinational firms and individual investors unless mechanisms are developed to offer protection against anti-investment government policies or political forces. Government-sponsored insurance offering coverage against such contingencies represents one such protective mechanism. The U.S. government began to offer such insurance back in 1948 through the U.S. Agency for International Development (AID). This function has now been transferred to the Overseas Private Investment Corporation (OPIC), which can offer up to 90 percent coverage for three types of risk: (1) inconvertibility of assets; (2) war, revolution, or insurrection; and (3) expropriation. It has been estimated by the Congressional Research Service that up to 20 percent of U.S. private investment in the oil industry would not have been made without the availability of OPIC insurance.[35] However, as is the case in several other countries, this government-backed insurance program is limited in terms of the amount of coverage it will provide, the types of risk involved, and the nations eligible for coverage. Firms do have the option of supplementing government-backed insurance or seeking alternative coverage from private underwriters such as Lloyd's of London or a growing number of American companies.[36] The premiums may be more expensive, but it is much easier to tailor-make a policy with a private underwriter, and the types of risk can be expanded to include hijackings, riots, political kidnappings, boycotts, etc. In addition, rates may differ rather substantially from firm to firm, with British companies generally charging less for coverage in Africa, and American firms less for policies in South America.[37]

Particularly in Third World areas and in extractive industries, joint ventures will become an increasingly prominent vehicle for making a direct investment while at the same time hedging against the contingencies of political risk. Such ventures may provide the foreign firm with a minority position (most likely a 49-percent interest) in a new enterprise. Reliable local partners who have a good feel for the turf will be selected, and local borrowing, preferably spread out among several banks, will account for a significant portion of the overall debt structure. By having prominent local citizens and lending institutions integrally involved in the new venture, the chances of expropriation or other negative government actions are diminished and the foreign enterprise's initial capital commitment to the project is minimized. In high-risk areas, the foreign investor may also push for a fairly rapid repatriation of profits and engage in transfer-pricing practices which will help to recoup the initial capital outlay in a relatively short period of time. Efforts should also be made to cultivate international support against expropriation or other drastic measures, with specific appeals made to the World Bank and the International Monetary Fund (IMF) in particular.

Above all, the foreign enterprise must understand that assistance from the parent government, aside from insurance protection or influence in money-lending institutions such as the World Bank and IMF, will generally be very minimal and may well be counterproductive in the long run. In the case of the United States, the era of gunboat diplomacy has fortunately ended and the retaliatory provisions contained in the Hickenlooper and Gonzalez Amendments and other relevant legislation pack very little wallop. Kennecott, of course, was able several years ago to help protect its mining operations in Chile by making sure that an Ex-Im Bank loan to Chile was unconditionally guaranteed by the Chilean government and that the provisions of the loan would be governed by the laws of New York State, and not Chile.[38] However, this type of tactical move has had only limited success.

The foreign subsidiary must above all take very seriously its role as a good corporate citizen. It must also be an adroit lobbyist vis-à-vis the government apparatus and the attentive public, but this lobbying effort must be reinforced by genuine support for the nation's societal and economic advancement. Multinational corporations generally have a very poor reputation among Third World nations, and in the case of U.S. firms, students in both developing and advanced industrial nations often accept as an act of blind faith that U.S. enterprises and the CIA work hand-in-hand to spread American domination abroad and therefore should be blamed for most of the unrest in the world.[39] This built-in bias can only be overcome by showing a strong and sincere commitment to the progress of the host nation's society and by a generous and appropriate transfer of technology, management, and marketing expertise.

THE FUTURE OF RISK FORECASTING

In summary, great progress has been made in recent years in the field of political risk assessment, and dividends are already accruing to those companies which take this function seriously. Methodologies will become somewhat more sophisticated in the future as systemic and quantitative techniques are refined, but real headway will still have to be made in the area of conceptualization. Too often, current risk analysis is based on the model of advanced industrial, democratic, pluralist societies and is of limited utility when analyzing developing nations. Much greater concern must also be given to a nation's particular cultural-historical context, and analysts must be very familiar with the literature of modernization and the special tensions present in a nation making the transition from a traditional to an industrial society. Staffs assigned to political analysis functions must have a wide variety of talents, including extensive in-country experience, language abilities, and opinion research, political science, social psychology, communication, and cultural skills. Companies must also be committed to giving the political analysis a priority status at the top corporate levels, otherwise the effort may be an exercise in futility. Already, large corporations such as Eaton and United Technologies have disbanded political risk groups which were formed only a short time before. Thus, whether a company utilizes individuals in existing staff positions for part-time risk forecasting, or a coordinator who brings together both in-house and outside expertise, or goes the full way and establishes a sophisticated and comprehensive political intelligence group, access to the very top strategic decision-making circles must be guaranteed for the project to be cost-effective.[40]

Business leaders should learn to mesh the political risk-assessment recommendations into the overall corporate decision-making process and be able to reconcile the recommendations of line managers with those of the assessment team. Furthermore, top decision makers must be able to "translate" analyses and recommendations of political scientists and other country experts and place them within a business and management framework, recognizing that government regulation can substantially influence the strategic choices available to the multinational enterprise. In terms of this much-needed expertise, one analyst has succinctly remarked: "It is self-delusion to think that by following a certain checklist or by plugging in some numbers to a model, someone who is not familiar with a given country can come up with something worthwhile."[41] The same can be said about the inutility of having a country expert gather sophisticated data at the national or subnational levels unless that information is directly applicable to the specific project being considered back at corporate headquarters.

Chief concerns of the corporate leadership will be to isolate subjective and ethnocentric biases and to base decisions on objective knowledge about the nation and society under consideration. For example, line managers native to the country under scrutiny may have difficulty openly criticizing their homeland. In addition, it is difficult for managers to support a cutback in projects which are so important to their own career advancement and to the welfare of their workers. As for advice from parent nation governments, one should remember that during the last days of the Shah's reign in Iran, many American officials were unwilling to provide frank advice for fear that an American business exodus would be viewed as an abandonment by the United States of the Iranian regime. On the other hand, overcaution in investment decisions must also be recognized as just as dangerous as lack of caution, because in an increasingly interdependent world, remaining competitive abroad will be an essential fact of life for healthy business enterprises.

Undue importance must not be attributed to dramatic events which receive so much publicity in the media age. Such events may have minimal short-term or long-term implications for the daily activities of the citizenry as a whole or the business community in particular. Moreover, political forecasting must be specialized to the point that only the specific business or even a single project is considered, for what may be a major risk for one business may be a minimal risk or even an advantage for another enterprise or project.

International investors must also learn to go beyond the national setting to consider the impact of international and regional tendencies on the one hand and subnational trends on the other. In this era of complex interdependence, more and more subnational actors are establishing links beyond international borders, and their activities must be given proper scrutiny. In Chapter 6, this subnational dimension will be discussed in greater detail and several examples will be given of choice investment opportunities at the subnational level within more hostile or ambivalent national settings. This upcoming chapter will also pinpoint the distortions which might result in giving too much attention to what transpires at the national governmental level.

Corporations must also explore very carefully the risk-reduction options available to them and decide what level of return is required in order to invest in any given country. The corporation must carefully delineate its business goals and determine how well or poorly these goals correspond with the prevailing political and economic goals of the society in question. Furthermore, much greater attention should be assigned to postinvestment political risk analysis, and strategies for on-going negotiations with government agencies and important interest groups should be developed. International investors will also recognize that potential pitfalls are not limited simply to developing nations, as Trudeau's Canada and Mitterand's France illustrate. But whether within an advanced-industrial or developing-nation framework, complex interdependence and political fragmentation dictate that "the political acumen of the management of the parent company will be as important as their financial skills in making any foreign investment decision."[42]

REFERENCES

[1] The two companies were G. T. & E. and the Starrett Housing Corporation. See Louis Kraar, "The Multinationals Get Smarter About Political Risks," *Fortune*, March 24, 1980, pp. 95–96.

[2] *The New York Times*, November 30, 1980, pp. F4–5.

[3] Stephen Kobrin, "Foreign Enterprise and Forced Divestment in LDCs," *International Organization*, Winter 1980, pp. 73–74.

[4] *The Wall Street Journal*, March 30, 1981, pp. 1 and 16.

[5] "Meet the New Breed of Banker: The Political Risk Expert," *Euromoney*, July 1980, p. 10.

[6] Kraar, p. 87.

[7] Stefan H. Robock, "Political Risk: Identification and Assessment," *Columbia Journal of World Business*, July–August 1971, p. 7.

[8] Kobrin, p. 86.

[9] Yves L. Doz and C. K. Prahalad, "How MNCs Cope with Host Government Intervention," *Harvard Business Review*, March–April 1980, p. 152.

[10] Ibid., p. 150.

[11] Ibid.

[12] "New Breed of Banker," pp. 17–18.

[13] *Christian Science Monitor*, April 24, 1981, p. 11.

[14] "New Breed of Banker," pp. 17–18.

[15] In the case of Mexico, the enmity which existed between the Lopez Portillo and Jimmy Carter administrations definitely prompted the Mexican government to discriminate against U.S. firms in the awarding of government contracts.

[16] R. J. Rummel and David H. Heenan, "How Multinationals Analyze Political Risk," *Harvard Business Review*, January–February 1978, p. 68.

[17] Ibid.

[18] Ibid., pp. 68–72.

[19] Ibid., pp. 72–76.

[20] "New Breed of Banker," p. 19.

[21] *Business Week*, December 1, 1980, p. 69.

[22] Ibid., and "How Safe Is It to Invest Abroad," *International Management*, October 1979, pp. 68–70.

[23] Dan Haendel, *Foreign Investments and the Management of Political Risk* (Boulder, Colo.: Westview Press, 1979, pp. 161–169).

[24] Ibid., pp. 112–113.

[25] Stephen J. Kobrin, *Political Assessment by International Firms: Models or Methodologies* (New York: New York University Faculty of Business Administration Working Paper Series, February 1981, pp. 1–2).

[26] Stefan H. Robock and Kenneth Simmonds, *International Business and Multinational Enterprises* (Homewood, Ill.: Irwin, 1973, pp. 362–364).

[27] Ibid., pp. 370–371.

[28] See, for example, two books by Ted Gurr, *Why Men Rebel* (Princeton: Princeton University Press, 1971) and *Handbook of Political Conflict* (New York: Free Press, 1980); and Samuel P. Huntington's *Political Order in Changing Societies* (New Haven: Yale University Press, 1971).

[29] See Haendel, p. 153, and two publications by Joseph LaPalombara and Stephen Blank, *Multinational Corporations and National Elites: A Study in Tensions* (New York: Conference Board, 1976), and *Multinational Corporations in Comparative Perspective* (New York: Conference Board, 1977).

[30] Quoted in Diane Marie Eckland and Thomas Schneeweis, "Environmental Scanning for Multinational Enterprises," paper presented at annual conference of Academy of International Business, Montreal, October 1981.

[31] Kobrin, "Foreign Enterprise," p. 86.

[32] See S. L. Srinivasulu, "Strategic Response to Foreign Exchange Risk," *Columbia Journal of World Business*, Spring 1981, pp. 13–23.

[33] Edward R. Tufte, *Political Control of the Economy* (Princeton: Princeton University Press, 1978, p. 137).

[34] Drucker, p. 220.

[35] Haendel, p. 44.

[36] American companies include the American International Group, INA, Continental, and Chubb. See Lynn Brenner, "How to Insure Against Political Risk," *Institutional Investor,* April 1981, pp. 211–220.

[37] Ibid., p. 220.

[38] Ibid., p. 16.

[39] The author has lectured extensively in several countries, including a year's stint as a Fulbright Lecturer at the Sorbonne in Paris. It is quite amazing how many university students wholeheartedly accept the premises that the CIA is responsible for most societal ills in the world and that the U.S. government's ultimate task is to make sure that as much of the world as possible is open to exploitation by American corporations. Major texts devoted to U.S. foreign policy which are used extensively in overseas classrooms are often very polemical and occasionally plagiarize from radical-left publications in the United States. Certainly both the CIA and U.S.-based multinationals have engaged at times in reprehensible activities, but the one-sided, unscholarly treatment of U.S. foreign policy and the reliance on "scapegoat" explanations are very alarming. One should also remember that these students will become leaders in their own societies and that most will become part of the influential attentive public in their respective countries.

[40] Stephen Kobrin discusses the strengths and weaknesses of the organization of political assessment units in his article, "Assessing Political Risk Overseas," *The Wharton Magazine,* Winter 1981–82, pp. 25–31.

[41] Roman I. Senkiw, "Using Country Risk Assessments in Decision-Making," *Journal of Commercial Bank Lending,* August 1980, p. 32.

[42] Ranjan Das, "Impact of Host Government Regulations on MNC Operations: Learning from Third World Countries," *Columbia Journal of World Business,* Spring 1981, p. 90.

5 | PROFILE OF A HOST NATION— CANADA

INTRODUCTION

With a population base not much greater than the state of California, Canada ranks as the world's seventh major industrial power and trails only the Soviet Union in terms of territorial size. Canadians are among the most prosperous people on earth and enjoy virtual cradle-to-grave economic security. Canada is also one of the world's major breadbaskets and is richly endowed with an enviable variety of vital natural resources.

Canadians on the whole are also a highly governable people who have a very stable political system and enjoy free elections and a peaceful, orderly transition of power at all governmental levels. They generally appreciate their way of life and accept Canada's role in the world as a "middle power." Yet as is the case with many populaces throughout the world, Canadians are having a tough time reconciling the demands of economic and resource interdependency with nationalist and subnationalist loyalties. In effect, many Canadians desire a clear-cut answer to the following question: How can Canada retain sovereign control over its political and economic destinies when it is so dependent on outside forces for its economic prosperity?

Until recently being overtaken by the United States, Canada long held the distinction of being the number one host nation in the world for foreign direct investment, and much of the prosperity of its people was attributable to the pivotal role which foreign capital played in the development of the Canadian economy. Entering the 1980s, Canada had attracted 52 billion dollars in foreign direct investment, not including retained earnings reinvested by foreign-controlled enterprises already established in Canada. Almost 70 percent of Canada's oil and gas industry was foreign-controlled in 1980, as were 51 percent of the mining sector and 54 percent of the manufacturing sphere.

Frustration attributable to lack of control over Canada's economic destiny is also closely linked to the fact that Canada must share a continent with an economic superpower. In essence, whenever the United States has sneezed, Canada has traditionally caught cold or at least developed the shivers, regardless of the policies or rhetoric forthcoming from the government leaders in Ottawa.

No two sovereign nations in the world are so closely intertwined as Canada and the United States in terms of trade, investment, resource, and tourist linkages. In the trade sphere, a far greater percentage of imports and exports are shipped between Canada and the United States than any other dyad of nations in the world. Sixty-seven percent of Canada's total imports come from the United States and almost 67 percent of its total exports are destined for U.S. markets. More than one-fifth of U.S. exports go to Canada, nearly twice the amount which end up in Japan, America's second largest customer. Moreover, U.S. shipments to Canada are greater than American exports to all of the European Community countries combined. Once the Tokyo Round provisions are fully implemented, 85 percent of Canadian exports to the United States and 65 percent of U.S. exports to Canada will be duty-free, as will almost all service-related transfers.

American-based investors and corporations also account for four-fifths of all foreign direct investment in Canada. Consequently, important corporate decisions linked to economic development are often made in New York City rather than Toronto. Canadian governments at all levels and major corporations must also travel south of the border to raise capital for both new and continuing projects. Bond ratings assigned by Standard and Poor's and Moody's may thus have a greater impact on economic life in Canada than in the United States. Approximately 40 major Canadian companies are also among the 1000 firms listed on the American Stock Exchange, but the Canadian businesses have oftentimes accounted for at least one-third of the total value of the list and one-fifth of the trading volume. Because of the high degree of economic interdependence which exists between Canada and its southern neighbor, which has a population and gross-national-product base ten times larger, inflation, unemployment, and interest rates in Canada are determined to a much greater extent by decisions rendered in Washington, D.C., than in Ottawa. The roller-coaster performance record of the Canadian dollar, which stood at 1.03 U.S. dollars in October 1976 and at close to 80 U.S. cents in the autumn of 1982, has also been influenced almost as much by American policies as Canadian actions.[1]

Consistently in recent public-opinion polls, Canadians have expressed resentment that so much of their economic destiny is determined by forces outside of Canada. Moreover, strong support has been expressed by the Canadian public for greater Canadian investor control of key sectors of the economy. Economic nationalist groups demanding drastic restrictions on foreign investment are also highly visible and have found strong support in one national party organization and moderate support in another. In response to this public sentiment, Canadianization has become a top priority of the federal government. The task facing public officials in Ottawa is to minimize the impact which foreign corporations and investors have on Canadian economic decision making, while at the same time providing enough investment opportunities to attract the tens of billions of dollars of outside capital desperately needed to expand Canada's economic base.

Governments in many national capitals are following Canadian developments with great interest. Indeed, how well or how poorly the Canadian government is able to reconcile the divergent forces of economic interdependence and political nationalism and subnationalism may have a great influence on the future policies which many governments enact toward foreign direct investment. Keeping this in mind, this study of Canada as a host nation for direct investment may provide some useful insights for the political maneuverings and stratagems which will eventually be commonplace in both advanced industrial and Third World host countries.

THE EVOLUTION OF CANADIAN INVESTMENT POLICY

Concern about the influence of foreign investment on the Canadian economy surfaced in the 1960s with various economic-nationalist groups claiming that Canada was little more than a branch plant and resource colony of the United States. The Watkins Report of 1968 warned that the most serious cost for Canada resulting from foreign ownership was the intrusion of American law and policy on Canadian society. Indeed, the issue of extraterritoriality irked many Canadians. As an illustration, the U.S. Justice and Commerce Departments and other federal agencies attempted to force subsidiaries of U.S. firms to cease and desist from trading with China and Cuba at a time when Ottawa had normalized relations with both countries. In addition, zealous government lawyers in Washington seemed to neglect time and again the fact that a sovereign border separated Canada and the United States and that U.S. antitrust regulations were not applicable to Canadian businesses.

Already saddled with regionalism and a small domestic market, some Canadians began to complain that Canada's branch-plant economy would not be able to sustain sufficient growth in the manufacturing and high-technology sectors. Indeed, studies indicated that subsidiaries of foreign-controlled firms were spending very little on research and development activity and that Canada ranked far behind other major OECD nations in expenditures on research and development as a percentage of the gross domestic product.[2] This was particularly the case in the foreign-dominated manufacturing sector. In Canada, the manufacturing sphere accounted for only one-third of overall research-and-development activity up to 1980, whereas in other major industrialized nations this figure was one-half or even greater.[3] Moreover, even though Canadian-controlled firms have tended to maintain a higher research intensity than their foreign counterparts, over 90 percent of Canadian patents are granted to foreign residents or foreign-controlled corporations.[4]

In 1965, Canada concluded an Auto Pact with the United States which provided for duty-free trade in finished vehicles and original equipment and parts. Over the past few years, Canada has experienced an annual deficit of 2 billion dollars or more in automobile trade between the two nations, and of the 326 million dollars spent for research and development in the North American automobile industry in 1979, only 4 million dollars was expended in Canada (1.2 percent). With this dearth of research-and-development projects and the U.S. domination of the automobile industry, some Canadian economic nationalists have vehemently claimed that Canada will eventually be stuck with plants that produce only gas-guzzling cars.

Canadian malaise over perceived foreign domination spills over to the cultural domain as well. In recent years, foreign films have accounted for more than 90 percent of all box-office receipts, foreign magazines for 85 percent of the total magazine circulation, and foreign books for more than 80 percent of total domestic book sales. More than two-thirds of all Canadians live within 100 miles of the American border, and they are inundated with U.S. television programs. As an exasperated director of the Canadian Broadcasting Corporation (CBC) has asserted, through the medium of television Canadians have invited in "the American value system, American heroes, American institutions and American touchstones." He further contends that no other country in the world allows such a massive intrusion of foreign culture and laments that this has led to "the importation of massive doses of U.S. programming with its frequent emphasis on violence and materialism through the scheduling of fast-paced, action-oriented, maximum 'jolts per minute' American entertainment programming."[5]

Recognizing that this issue was of significant importance to a large number of Canadians, Prime Minister Trudeau and his government began in the late 1960s to push for a "third option" in Canada's external political and economic relations. Trudeau explained that the first option was to maintain the status quo and the second was to move toward even closer economic ties with the United States. His preferred option, however, would be to decrease Canada's economic dependency on the United States by strengthening links with other nations, especially Japan and the European Economic Community. After years of negotiations, Canada and the EEC finally signed a commercial and economic cooperation agreement in July 1976. Three months later, a similar accord was signed with Japan.

Both Canadian and U.S. leaders also began to speak of an end to the "special relationship" between the two countries and a willingness to agree to disagree on certain major substantive issues.[6] The Canadian Radio-Television and Telecommunications Commission (CRTC) also embarked upon its own domestic version of the third option by mandating Canadian content requirements for radio and television programs. In addition, tax write-offs were eliminated for Canadian companies placing advertisements on American television stations situated along the border. Furthermore, the Canadian government demanded that popular foreign magazines which produced special editions in Canada sell more stock to Canadian investors and significantly increase the Canadian content in their publications. Because of this government pressure, *Time Canada* ceased operations in 1976.

Ardent Canadian nationalists have claimed that Canada (or at least English-speaking Canada) has been unable to develop a sense of national identity because of the stifling cultural and economic influence of the United States. They insist that the pursuit of the third option is necessary in order to combat the Americanization of Canada. However, an analysis of the third option strategy through its first decade reveals that it has been far from successful. Canada remains as dependent as ever on the economic benefits derived from trade, investment, and tourist linkages with the United States. Whereas economic integration has continued to march forward in North America, Canada's trade and investment ties to Japan, Western Europe, and other regions of the world have been very slow in developing. Canadians also continue to favor American television programs because they are generally better produced and more entertaining than the slim array of Canadian productions. *Time* now distributes its regular U.S. edition in Canada and ranks near the top in total Canadian magazine sales.

Disappointed with the results thus far achieved and bolstered by continued public concern with the foreign-domination issue, the Trudeau government moved in 1980 to a new variant of the third option called Canadianization. After more than a decade in power, Trudeau and his Liberal Party had been dumped from the national leadership position in 1979 but managed to provoke new elections when the Clark government's budget was defeated in the House of Commons. During the 1980 election campaign, Trudeau and his cohorts promised to provide greater Canadian control of the economy if voted back into power. Although survey data showed that during the election campaign, and indeed up to the present, foreign investment ranked far behind inflation, unemployment, and environmental issues in order of importance for the electorate, the new Trudeau government decided to introduce in October 1980 a very significant Canadianization bill.

Canadianization was first enshrined in the National Energy Program (NEP), but federal officials have promised that nonresource sectors of the economy would also eventually be Canadianized through the stiffening of the Foreign Investment Review Agency's (FIRA) standards and through incentives to promote Canadian takeovers of foreign-controlled firms.

Acting on protests from American corporations, officials in the Reagan administration openly criticized Ottawa for its alleged abandonment of free-market principles. The Secretary of Commerce and the Special Trade Representative also dispatched letters to Ottawa complaining about FIRA's tough standards. In particular, the U.S. officials complained about FIRA's "extraterritorial" application of Canadian law to the takeover of U.S. firms by other U.S. corporations. This allegation was linked to FIRA's efforts either to impose performance standards for the takeover of the Canadian subsidiaries of these U.S. companies or even to force the divestiture of part or all of the Canadian holdings. This war of words and nerves between governments and transnational enterprises promises to continue for many years to come and will certainly expand beyond the parameters of North America.

THE POLITICS OF INVESTMENT RESTRICTIONS

The Canadianization Strategy

With the broad electoral mandate provided the Liberal Party in 1980, the stage was set for a new wave of economic nationalism in Canada. Prime Minister Trudeau early on underscored his commitment to investment-restriction policies by naming Herb Gray, an ardent economic nationalist from southern Ontario, to the pivotal post of Minister of Industry, Trade, and Commerce.

The newly rekindled enthusiasm for dampening the impact of foreign direct investment was, of course, tempered somewhat by Trudeau's pragmatic reading of the political and economic situation. For one thing, the enviable economic prosperity and standard of living achieved by Canada's sparse population was largely attributable to the massive infusion of foreign capital and the technology transfer and management know-how which are such an integral part of the direct investment package. Consequently, a concerted campaign to make drastic cutbacks in foreign direct investment would necessitate at least short-run economic sacrifices on the part of the Canadian people. The same polls which showed public support for a diminution in foreign control of the oil and gas industry also revealed that most Canadians were not prepared to go along with tough government measures to attain this goal if it meant a precipitous rise in the price of gasoline and home-heating fuels. In addition, public support had soured toward the previous Clark administration, and thereby provided the Liberal and New Democratic Parties with the impetus to vote down the government in Parliament, because of Clark's resolve to bring Canada closer to world oil prices. In many respects, the budget introduced in the House of Commons by Clark's Minister of Finance was a bold and realistic document which would have eventually brought Canada into line with world energy prices and thus ended the nation's reliance on an artificial pricing structure buttressed by indirect taxation and low domestic oil-production payments. Indeed, in October 1980 the wellhead price of a barrel of Canadian-produced oil was 17 dollars, less than one-half of the world price. Because of this artificially low price, oil rigs were leaving Canada en masse to go to the much more lucrative fields in the United States, and the governments in the oil-producing provinces, disgruntled by the pricing arrangement, stood ready to cut back on production at the wellhead. Nonetheless, Canadians living in the non-producing areas, who represented a solid majority of the entire national population and who provided the backbone of electoral support for Trudeau's Liberal Party, seemed quite content to sacrifice Canada's long-range energy future for the short-run benefits of lower domestic oil and gas prices.

The Trudeau administration also had to take into account what impact new restriction policies would have on Canadian unity and on Canada's relations with the United States. A much more important priority to Trudeau than investment policies was the formulation of a new Canadian constitutional arrangement which would enshrine and foster national unity. Canada has the most decentralized federal system in the Western world, with the provincial governments exercising a broad range of policymaking powers, including control over natural resources. Canadians were visibly shaken in November 1976 when the Parti Québécois, an ardent independence group, was chosen by the Quebec electorate to form a new provincial government. In May 1980 the nation as a whole had to sweat out a referendum in Quebec which was designed to give the Parti Québécois government a mandate to negotiate political sovereignty and economic association with the rest of Canada. This issue failed to pass, 59 percent to 41 percent, but defeat was largely predicated on favorite son Pierre Trudeau's pledge to bring about renewed federalism which would be much more beneficial for Quebec's French-speaking people, representing 80 percent of the province's entire population. Consequently, the Quebec electorate adopted a wait-and-see attitude toward Canadian federalism but later on expressed their impatience with the lack of progress on reforms by reelecting the Parti Québécois government in April 1981.

Trudeau also had to contend with governments in the Western producing provinces, particularly Alberta, which felt that they had always been treated as second-class provinces and that their economic interests had invariably been subordinated to the needs and demands of the much more populous and industrialized region of Central Canada. The lack of progress on the formulation of a new oil and gas pricing agreement which would realistically reflect world prices became the issue of prime concern for Alberta and its neighbors. Although representing a very small percentage of the population of the West, very vocal separatist groups began to spring up and boldly claimed that the West could be much more prosperous as a national entity divorced from the rest of Canada. In many parts of the West, Pierre Trudeau was considered as persona non grata because of his policies which seemed to favor disproportionately the Central Canadian region which had swept him back into power. Indeed, the deep-seated regional cleavages which have long plagued Canada were strongly in evidence during the 1980 elections to choose the 282 members of the House of Commons. The majority achieved by Trudeau's Liberal Party was attributable almost totally to support in just two provinces, Ontario and Quebec, whereas his party managed to elect only two representatives from the four Western provinces and none whatsoever west of Winnipeg. Consequently, in spite of solid majority support in the Parliament in Ottawa, Trudeau could hardly claim that he had a nationwide mandate to push forward boldly with the imposition of investment restrictions, particularly if such restrictions would prove to be much more injurious to certain regions than others. Of course, because Canada's population is largely concentrated in the provinces of Ontario and Quebec and the Liberal Party could gain a majority in Parliament simply by sweeping those two provinces, Trudeau could have conceivably ridden roughshod over the rest of Canada and implemented an investment strategy tailor-made to the interests of Central Canadians. However, Trudeau's top priority was the bolstering of national unity, and he keenly desired to leave behind a legacy of being the statesman who finally brought Canadians a constitutional arrangement dissipating regionalism and fostering a strong sense of Canadian national pride and identity. He knew that he could never achieve this lofty goal by casting aside the special interests and concerns of the regions in Western and Atlantic Canada.

Taking into account the realities of economic interdependence, the Trudeau government also had to be extremely careful in putting together an investment-restriction package which would not drastically impair relations with the United States. In the past, Trudeau consistently spoke of the United States as Canada's closest ally, but he would occasionally appeal for greater national unity based on the premise that Canadians must stick together in order to mitigate the dominant American economic presence in Canada. Therefore, the new economic-nationalist stance of the 1980s would be couched within the framework of Canadianization with the implicit assumption that this would mean less Americanization in Canada. Moreover, strong overtones of disenchantment with American investment would be easily discernible in the rhetoric accompanying the new Canadianization quest, but actual policies would fall well short of what the rhetoric insisted should be done. Although he had chosen a very difficult strategy to implement successfully, Trudeau was nonetheless ready to walk an investment-restriction tightrope which would incite a great deal of vindictive jaw-boning on the part of the United States, but which would not go so far as to provoke Washington to impose retaliatory measures able to inflict significant damage on Canada's economic infrastructure. Trudeau pointed out many times during his long tenure as Prime Minister that when an elephant and a mouse share the same bed, the mouse must remain constantly on guard regardless of the sincere and honorable intentions of the elephant. Trudeau also recognizes that in many respects, Canada and the United States have achieved over the years an economic interdependence which is much more profound than the Common Market arrangement which currently exists in the European Economic Community, but which is dominated by the United States. If his new investment policies would do little more than provoke heated rhetoric south of the border, Trudeau would be able to cultivate an image among his own people of Canada's stalwart defender vis-à-vis a dominant economic power and thereby promote much-needed national unity. On the other hand, extremist policies, going against the grain of traditional Canadian pragmatism and generating a U.S. response injurious to Canada's economic well-being, would leave Trudeau exposed to charges of political and economic mismanagement and the exacerbation of regional tensions within Canada.

Investment in the Natural-Resource Sector

After careful consideration, the Trudeau government decided that the first target for the Canadianization campaign would be in the oil and gas sector. At the time the new National Energy Program (NEP) was presented to Parliament in October 1980, foreign investors controlled seventeen of the top twenty-five energy companies, 68.7 percent of total oil and gas production, and assets exceeding 25 billion dollars in value. Representatives of the federal government pointed out with great justification that no other advanced industrial nation permitted such overwhelming foreign investor control of such crucial nonrenewable energy sources. In addition, the NEP goal was simply to decrease the amount of foreign control over gas and oil production to 50 percent by 1990. At the same time, foreign companies would be encouraged to reinvest more of their profits in the Canadian economy. A 1979 audit by the Energy Department had indicated that the dividend payments of foreign companies (as a percentage of cash flow) were twice as great as those of Canadian-owned firms and that through dividends and equity reductions, subsidiaries of foreign corporations had shipped almost three-quarters of a billion dollars back to their head offices during that year.[7] The Canadian government expressed deep concern over this practice pursued by foreign-owned subsidiaries in the energy sector.

Theoretically, the NEP was not intended to discriminate directly against foreign-owned energy companies but rather to give special exploration and development incentives to Canadian-controlled companies. Under the provisions of the Petroleum Incentives Program (PIP), companies with Canadian control and at least 65-percent Canadian ownership in 1981 would be eligible for incentive grants covering up to 80 percent of exploration costs on federal land. The minimum ownership requirements for these maximum grants would rise by two percentage points annually to reach 75 percent by 1986. A rather complicated Canadian Ownership Rating (COR) is to be used to ascertain the degree of Canadian control in an oil or gas company.[8]

Because of the differential in incentives offered to Canadian-controlled versus foreign-controlled companies, the foreign corporations were to be placed at a distinct disadvantage in future exploration and development activities. Furthermore, the federal government added another major disadvantage by providing Petro-Canada, the state-owned petroleum company, with a retroactive 25-percent interest in all leases on federal land which were not already in production. Oil companies quickly claimed that this edict was tantamount to expropriation without compensation. Federal officials countered by saying that the land is owned by the federal government and was made available under exploration permits for which no payment was required, unlike the U.S. system of bidding for exploration leases. Moreover, these officials insisted that this 25-percent Crown share is not any more confiscatory nor retroactive than the U.S. windfall-profits tax.

Regardless of the rhetoric spewing forth from Canadian officialdom, foreign-controlled firms in the oil and gas industry have indeed been placed at a distinct disadvantage in relationship to their Canadian competitors, and several have already decided to sell their assets and leave the nation. Petro-Canada paved the way by acquiring Petrofina Canada, a subsidiary of the Belgian state-owned firm, for 1.2 billion dollars (Canadian). Dome Petroleum then raided the U.S. stock market and pulled off a major but controversial coup. Dome purchased 22 million shares of Conoco, a much larger American firm, and then agreed to swap those shares plus 245 million dollars (Canadian) for Conoco's 53-percent stake in the Calgary-based Hudson's Bay Oil and Gas Company. Later on, Seagrams made an unsuccessful bid to acquire a controlling interest over the rest of Conoco. Several other U.S.-based companies soon announced that they were willing to relinquish their Canadian energy interests because of the discriminatory provisions in the NEP and were thus looking for suitable buyers. On its part, Ottawa has established a Canadian ownership account, which is a special tax to be imposed on all consumption of oil and gas in Canada. This tax, which may go as high as 14 cents a gallon and could raise 3.5 billion dollars annually, is to be used to "repatriate" Canadian oil and gas industry assets.

Both business and government representatives in the United States bitterly protested against the NEP and the negative impact it was having on the U.S. market itself. In effect, allegations were made that the Canadian government was using anti-free-enterprise tactics in order to drive down the stock values of U.S. energy companies with substantial interests in Canada, thereby making it possible for Canadian firms to raid the U.S. market and buy stock at distressed price levels. The Special Trade Representative in the Reagan administration even went so far as to brand the NEP as a Canadian government tactic to "expropriate" American-controlled assets in Canada.

Ottawa has continued to insist that a goal of 50-percent Canadian ownership over its own oil and natural gas industry is very modest and that incentives available to foreign-owned companies in the Canadian resource sector are still far better than those available from Norway, the United Kingdom, and many other major oil- and gas-producing nations. Both assertions are quite accurate. In addition, Canadian control over this key resource and industrial sector is being steadily increased, and for the first time ever, Canadian firms are now investing more in this sector than their foreign-owned counterparts.

However, the federal government must still face up to the monumental question of whether or not the NEP will accelerate the quest for energy self-sufficiency in Canada. A thorough analysis of the NEP and the pricing agreements between Ottawa and the oil-producing provinces generally indicates that the investment climate for foreign-controlled energy firms is still better in Canada than in Western Europe or many other areas of the world. Nevertheless, Canada is still situated right next to the United States, and the American government has turned toward deregulation of the oil and gas industry. Consequently, many drilling rigs have left Canada and headed toward the United States, where the net return after taxes on conventional oil is at least four times as great and where the return on natural gas is even more lucrative.[9] Consequently, Ottawa has not as yet been able to attract the rate of investment which it had anticipated from Canadian-controlled firms. In addition, Canada's economic prosperity over the next two decades is largely predicated on resource development, and literally hundreds of billions of dollars in foreign capital will be needed to expand the economy. The combination of Canadianization, which will expend capital for takeovers of foreign firms at the expense of job creation and economic expansion, and deregulation in the United States will complicate the fulfillment of this goal. Furthermore, in order to achieve greater Canadian ownership and a lucrative revenue-sharing arrangement between Ottawa and the governments of the producing provinces, have not federal officials actually retarded the quest to attain energy self-sufficiency and economic prosperity based on resource development?

The Foreign Investment Review Agency

What the National Energy Program is supposed to accomplish for the Canadian oil and gas industry, the Foreign Investment Review Agency (FIRA) is supposed to achieve for Canada's other economic sectors. As mentioned previously, Canada's manufacturing sphere is 54-percent foreign-controlled, and pricing policies, production plans, and capital movements have quite often been determined by the foreign parent rather than the Canadian subsidiary.

Pressure was placed on Ottawa in the 1960s and early 1970s by Independent Canada associations to diminish the influence which multinational corporations were wielding over domestic economic development. The Trudeau government finally responded by establishing in 1970 a task force which would scrutinize the issue of foreign investment in Canada. The recommendations offered by the task force eventually led to the creation of the Foreign Investment Review Agency, which began operations in 1974.

FIRA has been given a mandate to screen all new foreign direct investment proposals, as well as the expansion into new economic sectors by foreign-owned firms already operating in Canada. A potential foreign investor or corporation is sent a bulky FIRA investment-information kit which includes booklets entitled *Businessman's Guide to the Foreign Investment Review Act, A Guide to Filing Notice with the Foreign Investment Review Agency,* and the *Foreign Investment Review Act.* A lengthy FIRA application form in either English or French is also included, and once the form is submitted to Ottawa, the foreign investor must usually wait 100 days or longer before receiving an official decision. Although FIRA is an appendage of the new Department of Regional Industrial Expansion, the entire federal Cabinet in Ottawa renders the final decision, based heavily on FIRA recommendations (see Figure 5-1).

The verdict is supposed to be based on whether or not the proposed investment is of significant benefit to the Canadian economy as a whole. Five specific criteria are used to ascertain the significant benefit stipulation: (1) the effect on employment; (2) the productivity, industrial efficiency, and degree of Canadian participation; (3) technological development and product diversification; (4) the impact on competition; and (5) the compatibility with national and provincial industrial and economic policies.[10] The FIRA review process is very secretive, and the Cabinet's determination of what is or is not of significant benefit to the Canadian economy cannot be appealed within the judicial system.

During its first seven years of existence, FIRA approved 91 percent of all U.S. investment proposals and 93 percent from other parts of the world.[11] Some Canadians consistently complained that FIRA was acting more like a lapdog than a watchdog and that Canada's "open door" policy toward foreign direct investment had not actually changed since 1974. Conversely, a few U.S. companies insisted that FIRA was arbitrary in rejecting their applications and pointed out that many foreign investors were deterred from submitting proposals to FIRA in the first place because of the complicated nature of the forms and the secretive, arbitrary nature of the review process.[12]

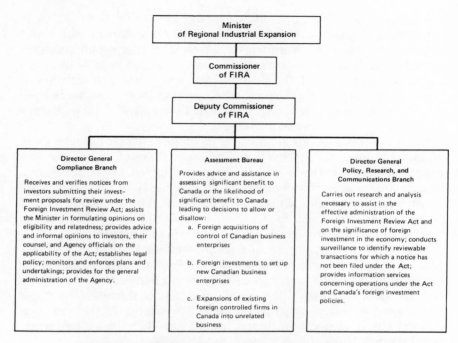

Figure 5-1   Canada's Foreign Investment Review Agency.

During and after the successful 1980 election campaign of the Liberal Party, Trudeau and his colleagues stated that FIRA needed to be strengthened in order to tackle the performance-related problems of inadequate research and development, export constraints, and limited autonomy in strategic decision making. The leader of the now defunct Ministry of Industry, Trade, and Commerce, Herb Gray, led the verbal onslaught against certain types of foreign direct investment and promised that the rules of the investment game would be changed. Most importantly, Gray pledged that periodic performance reviews would be made of large foreign firms already doing business in Canada, a task which was denied FIRA when it was first created. If implemented, the new policy would permit FIRA or some other agency in the Department of Regional Industrial Expansion to review retroactively the activities of foreign firms in Canada and to judge whether these firms have been good or poor corporate citizens in terms of their research-and-development allocations, export activity, distribution of subcontracts to indigenous Canadian firms, and other criteria. Firms found to be delinquent could be ordered to comply with certain tailor-made standards, and, as mentioned in Chapter 4, failure to comply might eventually lead to heavy fines, the loss of government contracts, or even in extreme cases, forced divestiture of assets.

In order to deflect some criticism lodged by foreign investors and the U.S. government against FIRA, the Trudeau administration moved to create a new interagency Committee on Industrial and Regional Benefits (CIRB) and an Office of Industrial and Regional Benefits to administer CIRB's policies and to monitor company compliance. CIRB is to deal with major private-sector projects of more than 100 million dollars and is to assist companies in the identification of suitable Canadian suppliers, to ensure fair participation by Canadians in contract bidding, to report on a regular basis compliance and noncompliance by firms with stated government objectives concerning industrial benefits, and to provide a satisfactory "debriefing" when Canadian bids have not been accepted.

Federal officials have also voiced their long-term commitment to the eventual publicization of takeover proposals and to the establishment of a government fund which would provide grants and loan guarantees to Canadian firms wanting to repatriate their assets or compete against foreign firms for acquisitions and mergers. Undoubtedly, foreign-controlled firms would be very leery about giving out confidential information concerning takeover bids which would then be publicized by a Canadian government hoping to find a suitable Canadian firm as a "white knight" bidder. Such a policy, if implemented, would certainly deter a fair number of direct investment proposals by foreign-based companies.

Foreign firms also insist that performance requirements established by Ottawa insinuate unjustly that foreign companies are less responsible corporate citizens than domestically-owned enterprises. In spite of this criticism, FIRA is stepping up its efforts to exact "undertakings" from potential foreign investors, and Ottawa may eventually give the green light for similar "undertakings" to be assigned to existing foreign investments. These undertakings, which are a form of performance requirements, are a set of tasks which must be accomplished by a subsidiary of a foreign firm within a specified time frame. These undertakings may include the training and hiring of a certain number of Canadian workers, export quotas, a mandate for the use of Canadian contractors or suppliers whenever economically feasible, minimum research-and-development expenditures, the establishment of secondary or tertiary facilities, the reinvestment of a certain percentage of profits in Canada, etc. FIRA will certainly be tough-minded in certain industries (such as the resource sector) and meek in certain others (such as the high-technology and major manufacturing sectors). For example, FIRA held up for a time Renault's takeover of American Motors, even though the great bulk of the assets of American Motors is concentrated in the United States. FIRA hoped to win concessions from Renault concerning more research-and-development activity in Canada, as well as the use of Canadian plants for the production of fuel-efficient cars and parts. Although not available for public scrutiny, the ultimate agreement probably provided FIRA with some gains, but the agency could only push so far because Renault held the ultimate trump card of threatening to close down major facilities in Canada, thus depriving thousands of Canadians of jobs. From the scattered information which is available, FIRA has also seemed to be quite willing at times to renegotiate undertakings when economic circumstances have made it very difficult for foreign-controlled firms to meet the agreed-upon objectives.

Because FIRA is already in place and because the review process is so secretive and decisions can be so arbitrary, the Canadian government can easily tighten investment restrictions in the future with a minimum of rhetoric and fanfare. Each phase of the process can become more detached, more deliberate, and more politically defensible. Tighter scrutiny can be given to the capitalization of proposed projects with preference assigned to investment requests which use a minimum of local market financing. New foreign investment in certain extractive industries can simply be given a cold shoulder, and foreign banks will continue to be very limited in terms of the expansion of full-service banking activities in Canada.[13] Conversely, enterprises willing to accept a minority position in joint ventures and to hire Canadian managers and employees will often be accorded red-carpet treatment. Specified levels of research-and-development activity, exporting, and utilization of Canadian suppliers and contractors can also be mandated.

In effect, the restriction policies pursued by the Canadian government now and in the future will undoubtedly be replicated to one degree or another by governments around the world. Consequently, the Canadian investment guidelines should be scrutinized very closely by multinational corporations and international investors in general. Likewise, the Canadian government should not lose sight of the fact that it must maintain an investment climate which is attractive enough to entice the tens of billions of dollars of foreign capital needed to expand and modernize the economic base and provide employment opportunities for the current and future generations of Canadian workers. Federal officials must also be concerned with the impact which investment policies might have on the Canadian consumer. The pricing accord reached by Alberta and the federal government in September 1981 may lead to a tripling of oil prices and a doubling of natural gas prices by 1986. Through the special revenue taxes and a diminution in foreign competition, the Canadianization policies pursued by the Trudeau government will also take a toll on the consumer's pocketbook, a very risky political proposition. Foreign investors in Canada must also be permitted by Ottawa to make a reasonable profit and to carry forth with activities which will keep their enterprises internationally competitive. The very complex challenge facing both national governments, such as the one in Canada, and multinational corporations is to attain the proper mixture of restriction and incentive policies which will permit the attainment of both selected national and international business goals.

CANADA'S INCENTIVE POLICIES

Lost in the glare of publicity accorded to the NEP and FIRA restriction policies is the fact that both the federal and provincial governments continue to offer major incentives for certain types of foreign direct investment. For example, the federal government's Department of Finance offers a broad range of incentives, including investment tax credits, research-and-development grants, accelerated capital cost and inventory allowances, special rates for corporate manufacturing and processing profits, special small-business tax rates, and employment tax credits.

In an effort to encourage foreign investment in economically depressed areas, Ottawa established in 1969 the Department of Regional Economic Expansion (DREE). During the period of its operation, DREE provided close to a billion dollars in grants, loan guarantees, and other types of incentives to both domestic and foreign investors willing to establish manufacturing facilities in various regions of the country, including the populous Montreal metropolitan area. As an illustration of what DREE attempted to do, during the fiscal year ending March 31, 1981, DREE ascertained that more than 700 investment-proposal applications were eligible for special incentives in the Montreal region alone. These successful applicants would be entitled to grants of up to 25 percent of the costs for a new project, excluding land, and 20 percent for large-scale expansions. The minimum investment would have to be 200,000 dollars, and priority would be accorded to modern rapid-growth industries. With the major bureaucratic reorganization announced by Pierre Trudeau in January 1982, the functions once carried out by DREE have now been transferred to the new Department of Regional Industrial Expansion and the revitalized Ministry of State for

Economic Development. Within this modified institutional framework, regional grants will still be accorded a top priority by the government in Ottawa.

   Provincial governments also provide a wide array of incentives, particularly for high-technology and export-oriented enterprises. In 1978, both the provincial government of Ontario and the federal government in Ottawa provoked the ire of Washington when they joined together to offer Ford a major incentive package to build an engine plant in Ontario which was originally expected to go to Ohio. In return for a 68-million-dollar incentive package (two-thirds of which was provided by Ottawa and one-third by Ontario), Ford pledged a capital expenditure of 535 million dollars and direct employment of 2600 workers and insisted that 2000 additional jobs would be created in feeder industries and another 2600 jobs in commercial and service industries. Ford also asserted that once on line, the new plant would bring an improvement of 150 million dollars per year in Canada's balance-of-trade account and provide 60 million dollars annually in corporate, personal, local property, sales, and duty taxes.[14] The provincial government in Toronto understandably wanted the new jobs, and the Liberal government in Ottawa easily perceived the political dividends which would accrue from having a major new industrial facility in the electorally important region of southern Ontario. As for Ford officials, they were very pleased with the lucrative incentive package and announced publicly the acceptance of the Canadian offer the day before a U.S. delegation was to arrive in Ottawa to protest Canada's incentive policies.

   Several provincial governments, especially the one in Quebec, were also upset with this incentive package. From their vantage point, Ontario, which already provides one-half of all the manufacturing jobs in Canada and continues to outdistance the other provinces in attracting new industries, did not warrant massive assistance from Ottawa. Officials in the federal government reminded Quebec City that in 1977 DREE had provided 75 percent of an 86-million-dollar grant which would go to General Motors if it were to build a 400-million-dollar aluminum-casting plant in Quebec. Although offering tentative approval for the project, General Motors has postponed the construction of the aluminum-casting facility, and Quebec officials still adamantly insist that Ottawa continues to give preference to major direct investments earmarked for Ontario.

   Federal officials are aware of this criticism emanating from various parts of Canada and have at times seemed to go out of their way to convince foreign investors to accept incentives in economically depressed regions. As a case in point, Volkswagen announced in 1981 that it wanted to convert an idle plant in Barrie, Ontario, into an automobile-parts facility. The plant would be VW's first in Canada and would cost 102 million dollars (Canadian). Once the plant was operational, at least 500 direct jobs and 2000 spin-off employment opportunities would be created. VW officials did not initially ask for a direct grant from the Canadian government but instead requested that Volkswagen be recognized as a designated vehicle importer with a duty-free status. This would be the same status accorded to North American automakers under the Canada-U.S. Auto Pact, except VW would be exempted from the requirement to assemble cars in Canada. Thus, in return for manufacturing auto parts in Canada, VW asked Ottawa to reduce the 13.75-percent duty it had traditionally paid for importing its cars into Canada from assembly plants in the United States. By approving such an agreement, Ottawa might be able to entice other automakers to Canada by stipulating that the more Canadian-made auto parts they used, the less duty they would pay on their vehicles exported to Canada.

Although the VW proposal would provide thousands of jobs without the need for a major incentive package from Ottawa, domestic political pressures persuaded federal officials to attempt to alter the deal with the German-based automaker. Ottawa requested that VW strongly consider building a new plant in high-unemployment areas such as Windsor, Ontario, or Montreal, an action extremely perplexing to and vehemently opposed by city officials in Barrie. In order to induce a change in VW's plans, federal officials reportedly offered to provide 50 million dollars or more in grants for the construction of a new facility.

Eventually, Volkswagen and the governments of Canada and Ontario reached a compromise which would permit VW to place the auto-parts manufacturing plant in Barrie. Federal officials agreed to VW's request that commencing in August 1983 the company's automobiles and light truck products would be allowed to enter Canada duty-free. In return, VW pledged to add "Canadian value" in parts, labor, and administrative outlays equal to at least 25 percent of the total costs of its cars and light trucks sold in Canada. In addition, even though it had not initially sought any direct funding agreement, VW was awarded a 9.2-million-dollar grant from the provincial government of Ontario.

The Canadian government has also established two programs to encourage research spending by both domestic and foreign-controlled firms. The defense productivity program provides research assistance in the defense arena, and the enterprise development program in the manufacturing sector. During 1981, 110 grants worth 143 million dollars (Canadian) were authorized in the defense sphere, and 98 million dollars (Canadian) in grants were made available in the manufacturing sector. Ottawa has been especially interested in attracting high-technology projects and has at times criticized the United States for impeding the transfer of technology across the border and for frustrating the development of a high-technology, export-oriented industrial sector in Canada. To buttress their allegations, Canadian officials point to a 1979 U.S. Treasury Department decision to impose countervailing duties on the import of a Canadian-produced Honeywell optical-sensing system. This verdict by the Treasury Department was justified solely on the grounds that the research and development needed to produce the optical-sensing system was largely subsidized by the Canadian government. In spite of this confrontation between Washington and Ottawa, there is no indication whatsoever that the Canadian government will cut back on its research incentive programs.

THE INCENTIVE AND RESTRICTION POLICIES OF THE PROVINCIAL GOVERNMENTS

As will be discussed in the next chapter, subnational governments now have a broad range of restriction and incentive policies directed at foreign investors. Nowhere is this more apparent than among the Canadian provinces.

As previously mentioned, Canada has one of the most decentralized federal systems in the world, with the provincial governments exercising a wide range of policymaking powers. Regionalism has also been a very strong factor in Canada's historical evolution, and Canadians continue to have a very weak sense of national identity. Moreover, the presence of two major ethnic groups has caused its share of problems. Lingering in the back of many French Canadian minds is the fear that the 6 million or so French-speaking North Americans will eventually be swallowed up and assimilated by the 240 million English-speaking people who inhabit the continent. Quebec has increasingly been viewed by Francophones as the homeland for French-speaking people who desire to preserve their language and culture. A siege mentality has in some respects developed, with Quebec being viewed as an island sanctuary in a sea of English-speaking people. Consequently, what is viewed as good for Canada, which is dominated by English Canadians, is at times viewed by Quebecers as bad for their province. The struggle through most of the twentieth century to modernize and to find an acceptable amendment formula for the Canadian constitution clearly illustrates the differing perceptions and priorities of the Quebec provincial government and those of Ottawa and the remaining nine provinces.

Uneven economic development and the emergence of a heartland-hinterland syndrome have also attributed to occasional breakdowns in relations between Ottawa and the provincial capitals. Far too often, these governments have viewed their relations in zero-sum terms; in other words, the perception that if one level of government wins, the other must automatically lose. Moreover, the fact that more than 60 percent of the entire population resides in just two provinces, Ontario and Quebec, while 85 percent of Canada's developed oil and gas reserves are concentrated in Alberta, has not helped to mitigate the problem. Ontario is also far and away the dominant manufacturing, financial, and communications center in Canada, with Toronto playing a much more pivotal role in the Canadian system than do New York and Los Angeles combined in the U.S. system. In addition, per capita income levels and unemployment rates differ dramatically from province to province, with the Atlantic region in much worse shape than Ontario and the Western provinces. Furthermore, the government institutions in Ottawa are poorly equipped to articulate provincial interests and concerns, and the federal political party structures have lately deteriorated into regionally based organizations.

It may even be argued that in certain economic sectors the European Community, which is composed of ten distinct nation-states, provides for a freer flow of goods, services, capital, and human beings than does the Canadian confederation. Most provinces currently have preferential purchasing policies, and some show favor to local institutions in their securities laws. Some provincial statutes also mandate favoritism to local labor and make it extremely difficult for workers from other provinces to seek out local employment opportunities. Quebec law also stipulates that French must be the language used by large businesses in that province. Any enterprise not complying with this edict could suffer major civil penalties and forfeit its contracts with agencies of the Quebec government.

This economic and cultural Balkanization of Canada has done little to facilitate improved channels of communication between and among the national and subnational government units. Indeed, Quebec held an historic referendum in 1980 to determine whether or not it wanted to begin the formal process of separating from Canada. Although the sovereignty issue was soundly defeated by a 59-percent to 41-percent margin, there continues to be great resentment and suspicion among many French-speaking Quebecers concerning how well the English-speaking majority in the rest of Canada will treat them. Francophones make up four-fifths of the population of Quebec and there is a strong possibility of additional referenda in the province directed at the issue of political sovereignty.

In both Atlantic and Western Canada, there is also considerable resentment toward Ottawa and Central Canada (namely Ontario). Many people in these provinces perceive that their regions have been treated as hinterlands and that they have had to make major sacrifices, such as paying for historically high tariffs on manufactured products in order to build up the industrial base in Central Canada. Albertans have especially felt this way, and when the dispute over oil pricing could not be resolved with Ottawa, the provincial government in Edmonton ordered a phased curtailment of oil production. Associations soon sprung up in various parts of the province calling for Alberta's independence or for the four Western provinces to join together to form a new nation. Lacking the cultural and ethnic impetus found in Quebec, the separatist movement in Alberta never did attract widespread support, and the pricing agreement finally worked out by Edmonton and Ottawa in September 1981 helped to defuse the separatist issue. Nonetheless, resentment remains strong in the West and in other parts of Canada and an avowed separatist was elected to the Alberta legislature in a by-election held in early 1982.

Even Canada's new constitutional amendment formula illustrates the deep regional disparities existing in the nation. This historic agreement was hammered out between Ottawa and the nine English-speaking provinces, with the Quebec government refusing to concur with the constitutional changes. In addition, under the new constitutional amendment formula worked out without Quebec's approval, provincial governments not agreeing with the amendment will simply be able to "opt out" and ignore the provisions of the amendment within their own provinces. The opting-out clause will certainly chip away at a sense of national consensus and will make it difficult to establish uniform Canadian political, economic, and social standards.

In the arena of investment policy, some provinces have never approved of the Foreign Investment Review Agency and desire to have complete autonomy over investment decisions within their own areas of jurisdiction. FIRA officials recognize that they are not considered as kindred spirits in certain provinces and have labored diligently to seek provincial approval before passing along their investment recommendations to the federal Cabinet in Ottawa. According to FIRA's chief official, Ottawa and the provincial governments have only disagreed on 3 percent of the decisions rendered by the federal Cabinet.[15] Some provincial representatives take exception with this statement, but it is still very clear that if a foreign investor can gain the support of the local and provincial government for a new project, the chances are excellent that FIRA and the federal Cabinet will grant the necessary approval. Therefore, the strategy which should often be used in making a direct investment in Canada is first to garner support locally *before* submitting the necessary application materials to FIRA.

Support for investment restrictions differs dramatically from province to province. Ontario has provided the backbone of support for FIRA and for Canadianization. Because 10 percent of Ontario's work force is employed by foreign-owned firms, the Ontario government has even set aside a modest amount of money to provide loans to Canadians wanting to buy back firms from foreign owners.[16] As enunciated in the Quebec government's 1979 publication, *Challenge for Quebec*, provincial leaders in Quebec City would also seem on the surface to be rather nonreceptive to various types of investment, but a close reading of the situation shows that Quebec recognizes the role which foreign direct investment must play in the expansion of the province's economic base. Several other provincial governments are also somewhat hostile to foreign direct investment in selected extractive industries. On the other hand, the Atlantic region and parts of the West would heartily support most any type of investment which would provide jobs for local people. In addition, during times of economic difficulties, all provincial governments become much less selective toward direct investment proposals, recognizing that keeping people gainfully employed may well determine the government's success or failure at the next election.

Foreign investors must recognize, however, that provincial governments are more interventionist than state governments in the United States or their subnational counterparts in most other countries. Saskatchewan, which is home to 40 percent of the world's known reserves of high-quality potash, began the process of nationalizing a good share of that extractive industry in 1975.[17] Under the threat of expropriation, Asbestos Corporation, a subsidiary of General Dynamics Corporation of St. Louis, finally agreed in the latter part of 1981 to sell a majority of its stock to the Quebec government. Several of the provincial governments directly control significant parts of key extractive, insurance, and financial industries and often maintain monopolies over hydroelectric and other utility sectors. Saskatchewan, for example, has approximately thirty Crown (state-controlled) corporations. Quebec government holding companies have purchased a controlling interest in a large Canadian firm, Domtar, and have been seeking out large equity positions in other major private firms with significant operations in Quebec. Through the intermediary of the Ontario Energy Corporation, the Ontario government has also purchased a controlling interest in Suncor, a subsidiary of Sun Company of Radnor, Pennsylvania. Suncor holds valuable oil leases and operates Canada's first oil sands-extraction plant in Fort McMurray, Alberta. All of these examples underline the fact that provincial governments are not timid about intervening in the economic sector. Likewise, foreign investors can often anticipate that some of their major competitors for business in Canada will be enterprises partially or wholly owned by provincial governments.

Conversely, each and every provincial government desires to attract certain types of foreign direct investment. Every province provides incentive packages to foreign investors, as do several municipalities. When combined with regional industrial grants from the federal government, these incentive packages can be worth tens of millions of dollars to prospective foreign investors. Consequently, after narrowing down options in terms of employment, transportation, research, quality of life, and other considerations, foreign investors should not be shy in contacting each government in provinces where facilities could logically be constructed. Generally, significant incentive packages will be offered by one or more of these governments, especially in the manufacturing and high-technology sectors. The Quebec government has even agreed to modify its revered Bill 101 language law in order to permit children of temporary residents in Quebec to attend English schools, regardless of the parents' language background. This modification was prompted entirely by Quebec's desire to entice more foreign businesses to establish facilities in the province.

LESSONS FOR THE FUTURE?

As a host country for foreign direct investment, Canada falls somewhere between a Third World and an advanced industrial nation. It shares in common with Third World countries an economy which is dependent on resource exports and manufacturing imports. Likewise, its future economic prosperity is integrally tied to further resource development. In most respects, however, Canada is undeniably an advanced industrial society with a modern and high-powered economic infrastructure. Its people enjoy a very high standard of living, and on a per capita basis, Canada is one of the foremost aid contributors to the developing world. In addition, Canadians did not experience the long and bitter colonial era which has prompted many governments in the Third World to be inherently suspicious of foreign investment activity.

Because of their high living standards, Canadians may well be willing to accept certain restrictions on future foreign direct investment, even if this might entail somewhat higher consumer prices and a somewhat slower pace in creating jobs. Such an enviable option, of course, is not really available to many developing nations because of the impoverished conditions facing many of their people and their devastatingly high unemployment and underemployment rates. Yet even in Canada, a threshold exists beyond which federal and provincial governments should not tamper with incoming direct investment. The Canadian voters have consistently shown in polls that they believe that high inflation and unemployment rates are of much more serious concern than foreign investment. Consequently, any governmental policies perceived by the electorate as bringing about too much inflation and unemployment or making Canadian industry less competitive internationally could cause problems for the incumbent government at the ballot box.

It is estimated that Canada will need anywhere from 250 billion to more than a trillion dollars in foreign financing over the next two decades in order to develop its resource, manufacturing, and high-technology sectors.[18] Approximately 80 to 90 percent of this amount will likely come from American investors. The Canadian governments at both federal and provincial levels can be expected to enact policies which will favor the procurement of these funds through debt and portfolio investments and through foreign partners accepting minority stakes in joint ventures. Nonetheless, a good share of this amount will continue to be in the form of direct investment. As a result, Ottawa and its provincial counterparts must implement laws which will make the investment climate in Canada healthy and stable enough to attract such investment. Unfortunately, the NEP, the tightening of FIRA provisions, and other interventionist policies carried out by Ottawa have brought into question the continued expansion of Canada's market economy. This has been manifested by the fact that Canadian direct investment in the United States tripled during the 1970s and on a per capita basis, there is now more Canadian direct investment south of the border than American investment in Canada. In 1979, 1.7 billion dollars left Canada in the form of direct investments in the United States, whereas only 675 million dollars in new U.S. direct investment entered Canada. In 1981, 10.2 billion dollars (Canadian) in net direct investment flowed out of Canada, a record high.[19] Furthermore, the overall net outflow of capital from Canada, which averaged 2 billion dollars annually during the 1970s, jumped to almost 10 billion dollars annually during the early part of the 1980s. With these trends in mind, the Canadian federal government cannot afford to become complacent about foreign direct investment in a complex era of interdependence in which intense competition still exists among host nations for most types of direct investment. The government must also recognize that policies which are aimed at frustrating foreign investors may also cause problems for domestic investors, who in turn will seek better alternatives outside of Canada.

In the extractive sector, foreign investors should expect in Canada and in other nations rich in natural resources some severe limitations. A typical successful investment in the future may well be patterned after the one which the Northwest Energy Corporation of Salt Lake City recently proposed to Ottawa. Northwest Energy applied to federal officials for permission to set up an exploration and production company in Alberta. The Utah-based firm gained strong support among key Alberta officials and then agreed to enter into a joint venture with two Canadian companies which would hold a majority interest. In addition, Northwest promised that at least two-thirds of the board of directors and a majority of the officers would be Canadians. The company also pledged to give preferential treatment to Canadian workers and suppliers of goods and services. A large percentage of any future profits would also be earmarked for reinvestment in the Canadian economy.[20] Not too surprisingly, Ottawa reacted favorably to the proposal during a period when it was turning down many others in the resource sector.

Overseas investors should also anticipate greater direct involvement by governments in resource-related industries. Petro-Canada, the state-owned company, has been very active in the oil and gas industry and may soon emerge as Canada's largest petroleum company. Governments can also be expected to show some favoritism toward state-owned enterprises and will also change some of the rules of the game governing direct investment in the extractive industries. Canada's NEP, particularly provisions giving special exploration and development incentives to domestic-controlled firms, and the granting to the Crown of a retroactive 25-percent share in most oil leases on federal land is a classic case of a government suddenly changing in midstream the rules of the game for foreign direct investment. In addition, the new Canada Oil and Gas Act will also afford many Canadian energy companies the option of squeezing out foreign shareholders.[21]

Although foreign investors will certainly face problems in Canada's extractive sector, the manufacturing and high-technology spheres will continue to offer many favorable opportunities. Firms will be expected to comply with certain research and development, export, employment, and supply standards. More emphasis will also be placed on convincing multinational corporations to go along with world product mandates. These mandates would provide the subsidiary of a foreign firm in Canada the right to assume responsibility for the research and development, product design and production, and the marketing and distribution of a particular product or service for the whole North

PROFILE OF A HOST NATION—CANADA **103**

American continent or even the world.[22] These restrictions, however, should more often than not be offset by favorable market opportunities and attractive investment-incentive packages. Indeed, potential inves-. tors must be aware that each province has its own economic and indus- trial development strategy and that investment barriers found in one province might not be present at all in a neighboring province. Fur- thermore, in order to maintain economic prosperity, to rationalize the structure of Canadian industry, and to remain globally competitive, the Canadian government's bottom-line policies, divorced from rhetoric, will be to maintain an open door to many types of foreign direct in- vestment. Canada's place within the highly competitive and interde- pendent North American economic setting will certainly necessitate a fairly lenient investment policy in the nonextractive sectors.

As for how the United States should react to the NEP and Canadiani- zation strategies, the best policy seems to be a combination of jawbon- ing, quiet diplomacy, and minimal substantive retaliation. Without a doubt, Canada has not complied with the spirit of the "national treat- ment" provision in the OECD Declaration on International Investment and Multinational Enterprises. This provision stipulates that foreign firms will be treated in a host nation in the same fashion as domestic companies. The NEP rule that provides incentives solely to Canadian- controlled firms certainly negates the OECD regulation, and the United States could justifiably decide to appeal through proper OECD channels.

A subcommittee of the U.S. Congress has already passed retaliatory legislation which would place a moratorium on foreign purchases of more than 5 percent of U.S. companies holding mineral leases on fed- eral lands. This action was intended specifically to rebuff Trudeau's Canadianization strategy and to thwart Seagram's attempted takeover of Conoco, Nu-West's effort to gain a substantial foothold in Cities Services, and the combined quest of Elf Aquitaine and the Canada Development Corporation to take complete control of Texasgulf. An- other subcommittee recommended that foreign investors be forced to comply with Federal Reserve Board credit rules prohibiting investors from borrowing more than 50 percent of the cost of an investment. This action was specifically directed against Canadian investors who had borrowed from Canadian banks close to 100 percent of the purchase price for the takeover of U.S.-based firms. Other retaliatory recommen- dations have included tightening the provisions of the Auto Pact and the Defense Production Act which guarantees contract work for Cana- dian firms. Access for Canadian firms and agencies to U.S. bond mar- kets could also be limited, and a proliferation of "Buy American" policies at both the federal and state levels could be injurious to Canadian firms which export to the American market.

Because of the vast differences in the size of the two economies and Canada's dependency on trade connections to the United States, there is no doubt that Washington could cause major problems for Ottawa. Certainly, the imposition of margin requirements which already apply to U.S. investors would be an acceptable policy alternative for Washington. However, the other retaliatory proposals would go against America's commitment to the unimpaired movement of direct investment. Moreover, any restrictions imposed on Canadian investments in the United States would probably work to the advantage of Ottawa. Canadian federal officials have been quite upset with the amount of investment going out of the country, insisting that Canadians should be patriotic enough to give top priority to building up the home economy. However, political support for any Canadian government would be jeopardized if constraints were placed on the investment activities of Canadian firms and individuals. Consequently, some leading figures in the Canadian government would be very pleased to see the United States retaliate and impose certain limitations on Canadian investors which Ottawa, for political reasons, cannot do itself.

Canada is not discriminating directly against U.S. investors, and the investment climate in the nonextractive sectors of the Canadian economy is still generally quite good. Therefore, both on sovereign and pragmatic grounds, the U.S. government should not overreact to changes being instituted in investment policy north of the border. Indeed, what is happening in Canada will likely occur in many other host nations in the future. The keen desire to be master of one's own economic destiny will certainly prompt many nations to impose certain investment limitations. On the other hand, the necessity of remaining competitive and well integrated in the increasingly interdependent global economic and resource system can be expected to temper the excesses of host nation restriction policies and leave many market sectors open for foreign direct investment participation. Thus, for international investors, the task at hand is to cast aside sensationalistic headlines and tough rhetoric and recognize that in most host nations investment opportunities will continue to be quite attractive. The ability to identify the major actors having an impact on foreign investment decision making and to make allies among key personnel at the local and regional governmental levels who want more jobs for their constituencies will greatly improve the chances that a proposed investment will be accepted by political and governmental leadership circles.

REFERENCES

[1] In Herbert Byleveld's "The Canadian Dollar: Where From and Where to Now?" *Canadian Business Review*, Winter 1980, pp. 35–41, the author contends that the Canadian dollar has been particularly strong against the U.S. currency in periods when the United States was actively involved militarily and Canada was not.

[2] U. K. Ranga Chand, "Pressure on Research and Development," *Canadian Business Review*, Winter 1980, p. 42.

[3] Ibid., pp. 42–43.

[4] Herman P. Bones, "Are Foreign Subsidiaries More Innovative?" *Canadian Business Review*, Summer 1979, p. 16.

[5] This quote from CBC President Al Johnson appeared in the *Vancouver Sun*, June 14, 1977, p. 2. For a more detailed look at the very complex Canada-U.S. relationship, see Earl H. Fry, *Canadian Government and Politics in Comparative Perspective* (Washington, D.C.: University Press of America, 1978, pp. 179–204).

[6] President Richard Nixon in 1972 and Canada's External Affairs Minister in 1975 both publicly stated that the special relationship should be considered as a thing of the past, although the two nations would continue to be staunch allies.

[7] *Financial Post*, August 23, 1980, p. 8.

[8] The Canadian Ownership Rating (COR) is computed by using the formula

$$\mathrm{COR} = \frac{R + (R/B \times S)}{I}$$

where: I = the total ownership interest issued or deemed to be issued and outstanding in a particular ownership class.

B = the aggregate of the following ownership interests in that class:
    (1) Any block representing more than 0.5 percent of the total ownership interests, excluding all ownership interests with foreign addresses.
    (2) At least 50 percent of the ownership interests, after excluding all interests having foreign addresses, which may be extended beyond 50 percent at the option of the applicant.
    (3) All blocks of ownership interests, identified above, ranked in order of magnitude beginning with the largest block.

R = The Canadian beneficial ownership of B.

S = The ownership interests of the class after deducting those with foreign addresses and those included in B.

A thorough explanation of the very complicated National Energy Program is found in Earl H. Fry (ed.), *Energy Development in Canada: The Political, Economic, and Continental Dimensions* (Provo, Utah: Brigham Young University Center for International and Area Studies, 1981).

[9] Ibid.

[10] Speech by Gorse Howarth, Commissioner of FIRA, to the Canadian-American Society, San Francisco, February 9, 1981.

[11] Ibid. Between 1974 and the fourth quarter of 1981, FIRA claimed to have received 2965 applications for the setting up of new businesses in Canada or for acquisitions of existing firms. Of this number, only 288 requests were rejected.

[12] See, for example, some of the written testimony submitted to the hearings of the Subcommittee on Consumer Protection and Finance of the U.S. House of Representatives, August 19, 1980.

[13] For many years, foreign banks were prevented from offering full services in Canada, even though Canadian banking institutions have long enjoyed fairly open access to the United States. A fine case study of Citibank's efforts to penetrate the Canadian market is found in John Fayerweather, *The Mercantile Bank Affair* (New York: New York University Press, 1974).

Under new legislation implemented in 1981, eleven foreign banks will be permitted to offer full services in Canada, whereas previously they could only engage in commercial lending and leasing activities and could not call themselves banks. However, foreign banking operations in Canada will continue to be severely limited because the Canadian assets of all foreign banks will not be allowed to exceed 8 percent of the total domestic assets of Canada's eleven existing chartered banks. Moreover, because Canadian banks are barred from holding more than a 10-percent stake in most types of Canadian companies, several of the foreign banks which have agreed to offer full services will have to divest themselves of some of their equity holdings.

[14] A very interesting account of the Ford-Ontario episode is provided in David Leyton-Brown, "The Mug's Game: Automotive Investment Incentives in Canada and the United States," *International Journal*, Winter 1979–1980, pp. 170–184.

[15] Howarth, Canadian-America Society speech.

[16] The Ontario government buy-back arrangement has thus far been largely symbolic. Only 10 million dollars was set aside during the first year, and as an opposition party representative pointed out, at that rate Ontarians could buy out foreign firms in about 250 years.

[17] The nationalization of the potash industry in Saskatchewan is chronicled in Maureen Appel Molot and Jeanne Kirk Laux, "The Politics of Nationalization," *Canadian Journal of Political Science*, June 1979, pp. 227–258.

[18] This figure was given in an Ontario government report published in *The Wall Street Journal*, October 6, 1980, p. 32.

[19] *Toronto Globe and Mail*, March 10, 1982, p. 2. Approximately 5.3 billion dollars (Canadian) was used for the government-inspired patriation by Canadians of foreign-controlled energy firms. The other 4.9 billion dollars represented Canadian takeovers of firms outside of Canada. In 1980, Canadian net direct investment abroad was only 2.8 billion dollars.

[20] *Financial Post*, September 27, 1980, p. 8.

[21] *Toronto Globe and Mail*, March 10, 1982, p. B9. Canadian oil companies will now have the power to buy back, cancel, or reclassify shares held by foreign investors, even if the foreign investors do not want to give up their stock. With the approval of two-thirds of the shareholders, a company may also classify stock as "constrained" shares; in other words, for Canadians only.

[22] See Pierre-Paul Proulx, "North American Trade in a Changing International Trade Context: The Role of World Product Mandates," a paper presented at the *Financial Post*-Corpus-CP Conference on World Product Mandating, Toronto, October 5, 1981.

6 DIRECT INVESTMENT AND THE CHALLENGES OF NATIONALISM AND SUBNATIONALISM

BEYOND NATIONALISM?

Easily discernible within the context of the previous chapters is the constant theme that what seems to be rational in an economic and business sense is often viewed as irrational or impractical in the political domain. For example, Canadian businesses might be much more competitive internationally if they could be integrated within a much larger North American Common Market structure and could pursue specific world product mandates. However, political "realities" dictate that such an arrangement would be unacceptable because of the risk of forfeiting some of Canada's national political sovereignty. This same reluctance to give up some political sovereignty for the benefit of economic cooperation and rationalization has also drastically slowed the integration process in the European Community.

Excessive nationalism was a principal cause of World War II, a cataclysmic conflict which left over 35 million Europeans dead and the economies of the European nations in utter ruin. Statesmen such as Jean Monnet and Paul-Henri Spaak hoped that the bitter war experience would prompt the creation of some form of United States of Europe, a supranational group in which individual nations would relinquish some national sovereignty for the good of pan-European cooperation and development. A major step was taken in this direction with the establishment of the European Community in 1958, bringing together under one umbrella organization the European Coal and Steel

Community, the European Economic Community, and the European Atomic Energy Community. France, Germany, Italy, Belgium, Luxembourg, and the Netherlands were the initial signatories of the new pact, and by the early 1980s the United Kingdom, Ireland, Denmark, and Greece were also counted as members of this important regional organization. Initially, a customs union was set up among these nations to foster the free movement of goods, people, and capital while at the same time establishing uniform tariffs on imports. The group has also agreed to establish common policies in the spheres of competition, agriculture, transport, and world trade.

The European Community can boast of a large population base of 270 million people in an area only one-fifth the size of the United States. A Council of Ministers, Commission, Court of Justice, and popularly elected European Parliament are also in place and assigned the weighty responsibility of proposing and implementing policies which will be for the good of the Community as a whole, even if individual state interests might be compromised.

The European Community has been a landmark experiment in the post-World War II era in the sense that strenuous efforts have been made to subjugate national interests for the good of regional development. Multinational corporations have at times benefited greatly from this arrangement by being able to establish facilities in an ideal locale in one country and then having relatively open access to nine other national markets. However, many individual and corporate investors have also learned the hard way that national content standards, customs specifications, and similar nontariff barriers have made it difficult to service the market in one nation without building a facility and thereby creating jobs in that particular country. Furthermore, the quest to make investment standards consistent within the European Community as a whole has met significant resistance from a few national capitals, and progress in this domain has been sporadic at best. Similar attempts to establish regional investment criteria and common market ties in parts of Africa, Central America, Southeast Asia, and South America have been even far less successful than the European experiment.

Once again, it must be reiterated that economic and resource interdependency in the modern era has rarely been accompanied by political integration. Indeed, many national political leaders still share the sentiments of General Charles de Gaulle, who felt a personal repugnance toward any transfer of national sovereign authority. De Gaulle hoped for regional cooperation in Europe but insisted that ultimate decision-making authority must continue to reside in the nation-state. The former French leader asserted that in the long run alliances were inherently unstable and that nation-states must necessarily continue to be the common denominator in world affairs. Moreover, de Gaulle argued that an international system consisting of sovereign nation-states could be stable, especially if the nations were able to develop a second-strike nuclear capability and thereby deter any potential foreign aggressor.

Because the overarching unit of concern for political leaders will continue to be the nation-state, international businesses face some special challenges. For example, the protection of à nation's business community and the preservation of jobs will make it very difficult for transnational corporations to service many markets simply through exports, even though economy of scale and market efficiency would oftentimes warrant the exporting of products over direct investment. In addition, concern for job preservation, control of fiduciary services, local development of high-technology industries, healthy international trade and payments balances, and, certainly not least, the next election, will most likely spur greater government intervention in the market system. State ownership of key sectors of industry, banking, and insurance may be expanded, and foreign-controlled firms will face additional difficulties in securing government contracts. The rules of the game in other facets of competition between foreign-owned and indigenously controlled firms will also be slanted against the former group. Indeed, the "Japan Incorporated" syndrome which calls for close cooperation between government, business, and labor and selective discriminatory practices toward foreign investors will be the model adopted by many governments in the future, but with much less success than the Japanese have attained.

State-owned enterprises can also be expected to expand their own direct investment activities. American Motors (Renault), Texasgulf (Elf Aquitaine), Standard Oil of Ohio and Kennecott Copper (British Petroleum), and Santa Fe International (Kuwait Petroleum) are but a few large U.S. corporations which are now controlled by state-owned foreign enterprises. As illustrated in the Elf Aquitaine-Libya issue described earlier, national political and economic aspirations may occasionally make the decision-making and gcal-attainment processes in these large state-owned firms different from those of privately controlled multinational corporations. In effect, one can anticipate at times a liberal mixture of politics and economics in decisions rendered by the state-controlled foreign enterprises.[1] The government of Kuwait has already poured more than 6 billion dollars into U.S. equity purchases, and Saudi Arabia and Kuwait combined have 200 billion dollars or more in reserves to invest worldwide. Although used for investments which will offer a good return on their money, these Middle Eastern funds emanate from governments, not private investors, and therefore the goals and motivations of government agencies must be distinguished from those of business representatives.

Because of the strong nationalist sentiments, foreign investors must ascertain which institutions and actors have the most influence over decisions linked to investment policy. Once having identified these key access points, investors must then attempt to protect their own interests within the national setting. Such a task requires a great deal of sophistication about political processes and the day-to-day workings of executives, Cabinets, Parliaments, courts, bureaucracies, interest groups, and the attentive public.[2] Almost invariably, parliamentary bodies are dependent on the executive branch for policy options and thus serve as little more than policy refiners. In traditional parliamentary systems such as in the United Kingdom and Canada, the Prime Minister and Cabinet members can actually determine what will be enacted by Parliament as long as their party enjoys disciplined majority support in the popularly elected lower chamber. On the other hand, committees and subcommittees of the U.S. Senate or House of Representatives may at times have a substantial say over certain aspects of investment policies, whereas their counterparts in other nations will have little if any influence. In the United States, Mexico, and Nigeria, elected Presidents may have a tremendous influence over political decisions linked to investment, but the Presidents in Germany, India, and a host of other countries will wield minimal power. Access to high officials in Mexico's Institutional Revolutionary Party (PRI), which has dominated Mexican politics at both the national and regional levels for over half a century, could be quite productive, whereas representatives of leading parties in the United States, Canada, Australia, and many other countries would have much more modest influence on key decision makers. Bureaucracies tend to be very complicated in most nations, and only a few agencies or even individual bureaucrats will deal directly with investment issues. These bureaucratic units must be carefully identified, however, because their influence over day-to-day policymaking may be far greater than that of elected officials. In essence, elected officials establish the parameters within which policies may be implemented, but these parameters are usually so broad that members of the bureaucracy have a great deal of discretionary power in the actual implementation of investment-related decisions.

Above all, investors must face up to the challenge of political nationalism and make the best of what on the surface may seem to be an extremely difficult task. One must constantly remember that newspaper headlines and preconceived notions about investment restrictions may lead to distorted images about the overall investment climate. For certain types of investment, the climate may actually be better in a so-called Communist nation, or Mitterand's France, or Trudeau's Canada, or Mugabe's Zimbabwe, than in the United States, simply because lack of competition in the other nations offsets nationalist-motivated restrictions. Access points in political systems differ dramatically from country to country, and much advanced research will have to precede any decision to invest; but one common thread to be found from one end of the globe to another is a definite preoccupation with political nationalism.

SUBNATIONALISM AS AN INVESTMENT ISSUE

Subnationalism as a New Force in International Relations

The effort of the business community to decipher national political phenomena has been complicated further by the recent emergence of subnational governments as salient international actors. James Rosenau has pointed out that a new feature in the transformation of world politics is the growing coherence and importance of subnational groups and a corresponding increase in divisiveness within national communities. In looking at Quebec, Scotland, the Basque section of Spain, and other regions, Rosenau concludes that "sub-groupism" has become a strong rival of nationalism and that where the rights, welfare, and aspirations of subnational groups "were once strictly domestic matters, now they are an integral part of the global system, rendering its structures more volatile as well as adding to the tendency toward decentralization."[3]

In theoretical terms, through the first six decades of the twentieth century scholars generally depicted "international relations" as connoting interactions among nation-states. In effect, nation-states were perceived as the only significant global actors, and their interactions were fairly much compartmentalized into what Arnold Wolfers has labeled the "billiard ball" approach to international relations.[4] According to this perspective, every nation-state was perceived as an impermeable entity with a monolithic national government unit exerting full control over resource allocation within the national boundaries. Moreover, many scholars within the discipline of international relations accepted the premises that the line between domestic and international politics is clearly delineated and that national governments are guided by an easily discernible set of interests which above all safeguard the integrity and security of the nation-state.

Over the past two decades, literature in the field of international relations has shown a greater sensitivity for international phenomena which are not adequately explained by the state-centric emphasis of the

billiard-ball approach. For example, one model depicts relations between nation-states as representing one level of interaction and nongovernmental transactions a different level, with both levels linked in a
cobweb fashion to create a multitiered system of international interactions.

Scholars such as Keohane and Nye have gone one step beyond the
cobweb approach and have identified three basic types of interactions
within the international system. "Interstate interactions" pertain to
official exchanges between representatives of national governments.
"Transgovernmental interactions" are linked to "sets of direct interaction among sub-units of different governments that are not controlled
or closely guided by the policies of the cabinets or chief executives."[5]
The final category, which has been labeled "transnational interactions," deals with "the movement of tangible or intangible items across
state boundaries when at least one actor is not an agent of a government
or an international organization."[6]

The international activities of subnational governmental units, a
special variant of the transgovernmental-interaction typology developed by Nye and Keohane, represent a phenomenon which has thus far
been largely overlooked even in scholarly works devoted to the influence of internal pluralisms on international relations.[7] Subnational
government units, particularly in federal systems, generally possess a
constitutionally derived area of policymaking competency. On the
other hand, the division of authority between a central government
unit on the one hand and regional government units on the other is
often tinged with grayness and is at times subject to intense controversy, particularly if significant societal cleavages are found within
a nation.

Within an increasingly interdependent world setting, subnational
government units have certainly become better aware of the influence
which international actors such as multinational corporations may
have on the well-being of their constituencies. Consequently, as a result
of significant differences among subnational units in terms of economic development, class, ethnicity, political preferences, or even historical linkages to external entities, one or more subnational governments may well wish to pursue international policies which differ
significantly from policies preferred by the central government or
other subnational government units. These differences may therefore
lead to disparate pressures being placed on the central government in
terms of foreign-policy priorities or may even prompt the subnational
government units to establish their own international linkages.[8] Without a doubt, the mixture of increasing global interdependency, major
societal differences among subnational units, and constitutional am-

biguity concerning the international competency of subnational government units provides a great deal of impetus for such units to expand their international contacts. In the case of the democratically elected Parti Québécois provincial government, the forging of international linkages has been considered as a key facet in its quest to create a politically sovereign Quebec nation. Yet even for subnational government units with less ambitious goals, the expansion of their international activities further complicates the effort to determine what "policies" are being pursued by a "nation-state" abroad, particularly in view of organizational process, bureaucratic politics, and transnational considerations.[9] In effect, what are the implications of subnational government activities in the international sphere, and can national governments cope with the evolving "many voices" phenomenon in an interdependent world? More importantly for this study, what impact will subnational tendencies have on future international investment activities?

Let us now leave the often complicated and jargon-riddled domain of theories, models, and paradigms and look at the pragmatic application of subnational tendencies. The evidence of a vast increase in subnational interaction in the international arena is voluminous. In 1970, four American states had opened offices overseas for the purpose of attracting foreign investment and trade opportunities. Today, two-thirds of all the states have one or more offices abroad. State expenditures for overseas promotion quadrupled from 1976 to 1980, and the number of offices abroad mushroomed from nineteen to sixty-six during the same period.[10] When Volkswagen announced a few years ago that it was searching for a plant location in the United States, thirty-five states expressed a strong interest. Pennsylvania finally landed VW, but the bidding war among the states became so intense that the Pennsylvania state government had to muster together a 100-million-dollar incentive package for the German-based transnational corporation which is partially owned by the Bonn government. Sony was contemplating placing a new audiovisual-tape plant near Tallahassee, Florida, until company officials received a phone call from a representative of Alabama's Economic Development Office. This representative offered to pick up Sony officials in New York in time for breakfast, fly them to Alabama in a state jet, and then return them to New York in time for a late lunch. Alabama's state leaders offered to exempt Sony from property taxes, "use" taxes on plant equipment, and sales taxes on the building materials used in the construction of a plant. In addition, a regional industrial-development agency pledged to finance the construction of a plant by issuing revenue bonds. Sony, in turn, would pay the interest on the bonds and lease the facility from the industrial-development agency. Once the bond was retired, Sony could buy the plant at a very nominal price. The Japanese-based multinational finally decided to build its plant in Dothan, Alabama, and has expanded the facility several times over the past few years.[11]

Canadian provinces have engaged in the same type of heated competition for investment projects and have even occasionally been pitted against American states in investment bidding wars. Australia, which at times in recent years has attracted foreign investment at the rate of more than one billion dollars per month, has also seen state pitted against state and state governments in sharp disagreement with the federal government over investment and economic development priorities.[12] The state of Western Australia has placed full-page advertisements in foreign newspapers trumpeting the fact that the "time is ripe" to invest in a resource-rich state four times larger than Texas.[13] Kentucky touts itself in Canadian newspapers as Canada's "eleventh province," and New York proclaims to domestic and foreign investors alike that "the ninth economic power in the free world isn't a country" and that it has established a special hotline to service potential investors.[14] For South Carolina and certain other states, foreigners account for one-fourth to one-third of all new direct investment within their respective boundaries. Consequently, competition among regional governments for overseas investment has become extremely intense and at times assumes the proportions of a cutthroat, winner-take-all poker game.

Not only regional governments are involved in what has been termed a "civil war for foreign money"; municipalities have also entered the fray.[15] In an effort to provide more jobs for local people and to diversify its economic base, the South Carolina city of Spartanburg began actively recruiting foreign investors almost two decades ago. This campaign has paid big dividends, with more than forty foreign firms investing in excess of a billion dollars in the city and creating thousands of new jobs. Another American city, Danville, Illinois, was nosed out by an Indiana city in attracting a West German-owned factory because the latter city could offer better incentives for defraying the costs of unemployment insurance and worker's compensation. Altogether, sixty U.S. cities competed for this one factory. Danville is now prepared to offer stiffer competition in the future because it finally convinced the Illinois legislature to authorize local communities to offer up to one million dollars in tax abatements over a ten-year period.[16] In the autumn of 1981, the U.S. Conference of Mayors agreed to sponsor a five-day trade fair in Zurich, the first of its kind. Direct mailings containing advertisements and invitations were sent to 2000 potential investors in Europe and approximately eighty U.S. cities signed up to rent booths at the trade fair, ranging from huge New York City to diminutive Bastrop, Louisiana.[17] This intense competition among city governments and chambers of commerce to attract direct investment has also spread to Canada, Australia, Brazil, and several nations in Europe.

To enhance cooperative ties and facilitate economic linkages, certain subnational governments have also strengthened relations with their counterparts in other nations. This is particularly the case between the United States and Canada. Several New England governors now meet on an annual basis with the premiers of Eastern Canada and have established a broad range of institutional agreements. Representatives of Alaska, British Columbia, and the Yukon also meet on a regular basis, as do officials of several other provinces and border states. These cross-border exchanges have prompted the U.S. State Department to station an officer in Ottawa who is to monitor subnational linkages between the two nations. The overall thrust of U.S. states and municipalities abroad has also precipitated the establishment within the State Department of a Liaison Office with State and Local Governments. Representatives of this office help to monitor and coordinate the many one-on-one relationships established between officials of U.S. state and local governments and their foreign counterparts.[18]

Some subnational governments in nations other than the United States have also become much more interventionist in their own economic affairs. The Quebec government, for example, has purchased controlling interests in corporations in almost all important economic spheres. As mentioned in the previous chapter, the acquisition of Asbestos Corporation from General Dynamics was made under threat of expropriation. Two Quebec government agencies also joined together to purchase a controlling interest in Domtar, a Montreal-based pulp and paper giant. Reportedly, the purchase was made because the Quebec government had been very displeased with Domtar officials for transferring the head office of one subsidiary to Toronto and for refusing to participate in a salt-mine project subsidized by the provincial government.[19] Several other provincial governments in Canada and regional governments elsewhere have also assumed controlling interests in resource-based industries, hydroelectric projects, fiduciary-related services, and mass-transportation facilities. This trend toward more active regional government involvement in economic affairs presents some special challenges and concerns for foreign corporations and must be watched very closely.

Restriction Policies

Regional governments have their own special restriction policies and legal codes which may prove highly disadvantageous to unwary investors. For example, several subnational units are attempting to impose a unitary system of taxation on transnational corporations. Under such an arrangement, a corporation with one-tenth of its worldwide sales, payroll, and property in a certain subnational region would find that one-tenth of its overall income would be subject to taxation by that subnational government. Many transnational businesses have complained about the procedure and insist that regional governments should only be permitted to tax income earned within their areas of jurisdiction. Nevertheless, a handful of American states and subnational units in other countries have adopted the unitary accounting method for taxation.[20] Many subnational units are also turning toward high royalties and special severance taxes on the extraction of resources, an issue which has especially provoked animosities between resource-producing and resource-poor states and provinces in the United States and Canada. In addition, Maine and Wisconsin have plant-closing laws which penalize certain industries which cease operations within their borders. Legislatures in approximately twenty other American states are also considering laws which would mandate that companies: (1) publicly announce their intention to close plants from sixty days to two years in advance; (2) offer one week's worth of severance pay for each year of service rendered by an employee; (3) bear the expense for retraining and relocating affected workers; and (4) compensate impacted communities for the projected loss of tax revenues.[21]

Furthermore, each subnational unit may have its own special requirements concerning manufacturing standards, labor regulations, property usage, and consumer protection. As an illustration, the state of Maine has enacted implied-warranty laws which override any written warranty between a buyer and seller and insist that consumer goods must be of "fair, average quality," free of material defects and "fit for the ordinary purposes" for which the goods are used. Large automobile manufacturers have vehemently criticized the law as going beyond the bounds of reason and argue that present consumer protection provisions offered by the industry are adequate. In spite of these assertions, several other states have implemented implied-warranty laws similar to Maine's which apply to a broad range of product lines.[22]

Court systems in several subnational units are also being used increasingly to thwart takeover bids by overseas investors. Hobart utilized the Ohio court system as part of its successful strategy to fight off Canadian Pacific, and many other companies are now using local and regional courts in an attempt to block hostile takeover efforts.[23] French-based Elf Aquitaine was forced in its acquisition bid for Texasgulf to file lawsuits in the federal courts in Louisiana, Nebraska, and Utah in order to enjoin the use of those states' takeover laws to delay its tender offer.[24]

A checkerboard pattern of restrictions and incentives definitely exists among subnational units, and investors must carefully survey this very complicated situation. New York may disapprove of a takeover by Arab investors of a U.S.-bank holding company, whereas several other states would approve such a transaction. The Ontario provincial government may turn a cold shoulder to various types of investment proposals, while its neighboring provinces to the east and west would bend over backwards to entice the same investors. Some American states and Canadian provinces prohibit or severely limit foreign investment in agricultural properties, and the attorney general of Oklahoma even attempted to prohibit such investment in both agricultural and commercial land and to force the divestiture of previously owned foreign properties. On the other hand, many other states and provinces have no restrictions whatsoever toward the acquisition of property by overseas investors. Indeed, as will be illustrated in the next section, an investment which is prohibited by one regional government may well qualify for an incentive package in another.

Incentive Policies

Without a doubt, intense competition among subnational governments does permit international investors the opportunity to attract a wide array of incentive-package offers. In order to provide jobs, diversify and modernize their economic bases, and keep the electorate satisfied, local and regional officials have pieced together some lucrative incentives for overseas corporations. As an example, Lazzaroni, an Italian confectionery company, was being priced out of the American market because of escalating freight rates and increased production costs in Italy. Consequently, the firm made a decision to build a new facility in the United States and was immediately courted by several states. Because of its large sales volume in the New York City region, Lazzaroni leaned toward establishing its plant in the Northeast and was not disappointed by what the International Division of the New York State Department of Commerce offered in the way of incentives. This state government agency arranged for the entire cost of Lazzaroni's 2.3-million-dollar building project to be financed by long-term, low-interest, tax-exempt bonds sold to area banks under the auspices of a quasi-governmental industrial-development agency. Lazzaroni will also have to pay only 50 percent of the normal local taxes assessed on its 6.5-acre site and will receive a ten-year abatement on state taxes.[25]

Thus, a wide variety of incentives, including tax breaks, loans, outright grants, free training of workers, free site selection and site-preparation services, and research-and-development subsidies, are now provided by many subnational governments to job-creating foreign investors. The state of Georgia, for example, offers these types of services and promotes many missions overseas to publicize the trade and investment opportunities in that state. Georgia's well-financed Department of Industry and Trade also operates international offices in Bonn, Brussels, Tokyo, and Sao Paulo. As of the beginning of the 1980s, twelve foreign governments had opened trade offices in Georgia and forty-one had consulates or honorary consulates in the Atlanta area. Twenty thousand new jobs have been created as a result of 1.3 billion dollars in foreign direct investment emanating from twenty-eight different countries. Foreign investors had opened 348 facilities in Georgia at the beginning of the decade, and 100 of these were major manufacturing plants.[26] The sweepstakes to attract new investment has now spread to most state units, and a few have enjoyed the same measure of success as Georgia. Figures 6-1 and 6-2 illustrate some of the incentives available to investors on a state-by-state basis.

Many U.S. state governments also provide special assistance to municipalities in order to attract new industries and businesses. Figure 6-3 indicates some of the community-development assistance programs sponsored by these state governments. Both the federal and state governments in the United States are also promoting enterprise zones in major urban areas. The idea of enterprise zones was first proposed in Great Britain in 1978 by Sir Geoffrey Howe. In 1980, the British Parliament approved the creation of eleven such zones, with government support committed for a minimum of ten years. One zone each was earmarked for Scotland, Wales, and Northern Ireland, and eight for England. The zones range in size from 125 to 1000 acres and provide special incentives for investors willing to build facilities within a zone.

As of early 1982, eight U.S. state legislatures had also passed enterprise zone laws and legislation was pending in most other state legislative chambers. A great variety of incentives are available to investors, ranging from a 1000-dollar grant in Connecticut for each job created in the zone to a credit on corporate income and school taxes in Florida.[27] A federal program introduced by the Reagan administration in Congress in 1982 would provide businesses located in specially designated urban zones with a 75-percent reduction in corporate income taxes for operations within the zone and the elimination of capital-gains taxes. Tax credits would also be available for wages paid to low-income employees. In addition, the U.S. Commerce Department's Economic Development Administration and the U.S. Department of Housing and

	Privately Sponsored Development Credit Corporation	State Loans for Building Construction	State Loans for Equipment, Machinery	City and/or County Loans for Building Construction	City and/or County Loans for Equipment, Machinery	State Loan Guarantees for Building Construction	State Loan Guarantees for Equipment, Machinery	City and/or County Loan Guarantees for Building Construction	City and/or County Loan Guarantees for Equipment, Machinery
Alabama	•								
Alaska	•	•	•						
Arizona	2					•7	•7		
Arkansas	•					•	•		
California	•3	•				•	•		
Colorado									
Connecticut	•	•	•	•	•	•	•	•	•
Delaware		•	•	•		•	•		
Florida	•								
Georgia	•								
Hawaii		•	•						
Idaho	•								
Illinois	•	•	•						
Indiana						•	•		
Iowa	•								
Kansas	•								
Kentucky		•				•			
Louisiana	2	2	2			•6	•6		
Maine		•				•	•		
Maryland	•	•	•						
Massachusetts	•			•	•	•			
Michigan	2			•					
Minnesota	•	•	•	•6	•6				
Mississippi	•								
Missouri	•		•5						
Montana	•		•	•9					
Nebraska	•								
Nevada									
New Hampshire	•	•				•	•		
New Jersey		•	•			•			
New Mexico	2								
New York	•	•	•	•	•				
North Carolina	•								
North Dakota	•	•				•			
Ohio	•	•	•			•			
Oklahoma	•	•		•	•				
Oregon	•	•		•	•	•			
Pennsylvania	•	•8		•4	•8				
Rhode Island	•					•			
South Carolina	•								
South Dakota						•			
Tennessee		•							
Texas		•							
Utah						•			
Vermont	•	•	•						
Virginia	•					•1			
Washington	•			•					
West Virginia		•		•					
Wisconsin									
Wyoming	•								
STATE TOTALS	34	23	17	11	8	19	17	1	1
Puerto Rico	•	•				•	•		

[1] Activity is limited to ports authority in Georgia and to port districts in Oregon and Washington.

[2] Authorized but none is active.

[3] State-sponsored but privately operated nonprofit regional job development corporations may be established in low-income areas to provide loans to small businesses.

[4] Available through the Minority Business Development Agency.

[5] Loans also cover working capital, site improvements, and inventories.

[6] Permitted for processing products of agriculture, including forestry and timber production.

[7] Guarantee applies to Act 9 industrial revenue bonds up to $1 million.

[8] State and local program of participation in building construction.

[9] Authorized if a one-mill, multipurpose tax levy is approved by local voters.

Figure 6-1 U.S. state direct-loan programs. (U.S. Department of Commerce, *Attracting Foreign Investment to the United States*, 1981, p. III.4.)

	Industrial Buildings	Industrial Parks	Office Buildings	Warehouses	Recreational Attractions	Retail Merchandise Establishments	Medical Facilities	Pollution Control Systems	Purchase Land	Purchase Equipment, Machinery	Refinance Existing Facilities at Lower Interest Rates	Company May Buy Bond-Financed Plant on Installment Purchase	Installation of Utilities	Engineering Fees	Landscaping of Plant Site	Construction Financing	Legal Fees Associated with Project	Financing Fees	Debt Service Reserve
Alabama	•		•	•			•	•	•	•	•		•	•	•	•	•	•	
Alaska	•	•	•	•	•			•	•	•	•		•	•	•	•	•	•	
Arizona	•	•		•		•	•	•	•	•			•	•	•	•	•	•	
Arkansas	•		•	•				•	•	•	•	•	•	•	•	•	•		•
California								•		•				•					
Colorado	•		•	•	•	•	•	•	•	•	•		•	•	•	•	•	•	•
Connecticut	•		•	•	•			•	•	•	•	•	•	•	•	•	•	•	
Delaware	•							•	•	•	•		•	•	•	•	•	•	
Florida	•							•	•	•	•		•	•	•	•	•	•	
Georgia	•		•					•	•	•	•	•	•	•	•	•	•	•	
Illinois	•	•9	•9		•9	•10	•9	•	•	•		•11	•9	•	•	•	•	•	
Indiana	•	•	•	•	•			•	•	•		•1	•	•	•	•	•	•	
Iowa	•		•12	•				•	•	•	•		•	•	•	•	•	•	•
Kansas	•	•		•			•	•	•	•	•	•	•	•	•	•	•	•	
Kentucky	•	•		•				•	•	•	•		•	•	•	•	•	•	
Louisiana	•		•	•	•		•	•	•	•	•		•	•	•	•	•	•	•
Maine	•		•	•	•			•	•	•			•	•3	•3	•3	•3	•3	•3
Maryland	•	•	•	•	•		•	•4	•	•	•		•	•	•	•	•	•	
Massachusetts	•		•2	•				•	•	•	•		•	•	•	•	•	•	
Michigan	•	•		•	•		•6	•	•	•			•	•	•	•	•	•	•
Minnesota	•		•	•	•	•	•	•	•	•			•	•	•	•	•	•	•
Mississippi	•	•		•				•	•	•	•		•	•	•	•	•	•	
Missouri	•		•	•			•	•	•	•			•	•	•	•	•	•	
Montana	•	•	•	•	•	•	•	•	•	•			•	•	•	•	•	•	•
Nebraska	•	•		•				•	•	•			•	•	•	•	•	•	
Nevada	•		•	•				•	•	•			•	•	•	•	•	•	•
New Hampshire	•		•	•				•	•	•	•		•	•	•	•	•	•	
New Jersey	•	•	•	•	•		•	•	•	•	•		•	•	•	•	•	•	
New Mexico	•	•	•	•	•		•	•	•	•			•	•	•	•	•	•	
New York	•	•	•	•	•		•	•4	•	•	•	•	•	•	•	•	•	•	
North Carolina	•							•	•	•			•	•	•	•	•	•	
North Dakota	•	•	•	•	•			•	•	•			•	•	•	•	•	•	
Ohio	•		•8	•8	•8	•8		•	•	•			•	•	•	•	•	•	
Oklahoma	•	•		•5	•			•	•	•	•		•	•	•	•	•	•	
Oregon	•	•	•	•	•		•	•	•	•	•		•	•	•	•	•	•	•
Pennsylvania	•	•	•	•	•	•	•	•	•	•	•		•	•	•	•	•	•	•
Rhode Island	•	•	•	•	•	•	•	•	•	•	•		•	•	•	•	•		•
South Carolina	•			•				•	•	•			•	•	•	•	•	•	
South Dakota	•	•	•	•	•	•	•	•	•	•			•	•	•	•	•	•	
Tennessee	•	•	•	•	•	•	•	•	•	•			•	•	•	•	•	•	•
Texas	•							•	•	•			•	•	•	•	•	•	
Utah	•	•		•	•		•	•	•	•			•	•	•	•	•	•	
Vermont	•		•	•			•	•	•	•			•	•	•	•	•	•	
Virginia	•		•12	•			•	•	•	•			•	•	•	•	•	•	
Washington	•	•	•	•			•	•	•	•			•	•	•	•	•	•	
West Virginia	•		•	•5	•			•	•	•	•	•	•	•	•	•	•	•	
Wisconsin	•		•7	•	•			•	•	•			•	•	•	•	•	•	•
Wyoming	•		•	•	•			•	•	•	•	•	•				•		
Puerto Rico	•	•	•	•	•		•	•	•	•	•		•			•	•	•	•

[1]Applicable when existing facility is for an entirely new type of operation.
[2]In downtown urban revitalization districts only.
[3]Applicable if part of total project.
[4]Applicable to research facilities only.
[5]Permitted only if related to manufacturing operations.
[6]Applicable to any structure suitable for, intended for, or incidental to use as a factory, mill, shop, processing plant, assembly plant, fabricating plant, warehouse, research and development facility, engineering, architectural or design facility, or tourist and resort facility.
[7]Applicable if structure is a national or regional headquarters facility.
[8]Applicable only if facility is occupied by company obtaining bonds, not permitted for speculative buildings.
[9]Permitted if in a home rule community.
[10]Permitted in some circumstances.
[11]Permitted for medical facilities only.
[12]Limited to multistate, regional, or national headquarters buildings and operations centers.

Figure 6-2 U.S. state industrial revenue bond programs. (U.S. Department of Commerce, *Attracting Foreign Investment to the United States*, 1981, p. III.6.)

	Authorization for Local Redevelopment Agencies	Selected Development Loans and Grants		Preferential Siting
		General	Targeted	
	48	43	18	4
Alabama	X	X		
Alaska	X	X	X	
Arizona	X	X	X	
Arkansas	X	X	X	
California	X	X		
Colorado	X	X	X	
Connecticut	X	X	X	
Delaware	X	X		
Florida	X	X	X	X
Georgia	X	X		
Hawaii	X	X		
Idaho	X	X		
Illinois	X	X		
Indiana	X	X		
Iowa	X	X		
Kansas	X			
Kentucky	X	X		
Louisiana	X			
Maine	X	X		
Maryland	X	X		
Massachusetts	X	X	X	X
Michigan	X	X		
Minnesota	X	X		
Mississippi	X	X	X	
Missouri	X	X	X	
Montana	X	X		
Nebraska	X	X		X
Nevada	X			
New Hampshire	X	X		
New Jersey	X	X	X	X
New Mexico	X	X	X	
New York	X	X		
North Carolina	X	X	X	
North Dakota	X			
Ohio	X	X	X	
Oklahoma	X	X		
Oregon	X	X		
Pennsylvania	X	X		
Rhode Island	X			
South Carolina	X	X		
South Dakota	X	X		
Tennessee	X			
Texas	X	X		
Utah	X	X		
Vermont	X	X	X	
Virginia	X	X	X	
Washington	X	X	X	
West Virginia	X	X	X	
Wisconsin	X	X		
Wyoming	X	X	X	
District of Columbia				
Puerto Rico				

Figure 6-3 Community development assistance programs sponsored by U.S. state governments. (*U.S. Department of Commerce, Attracting Foreign Investment to the United States, 1981, p. III.28.*)

Urban Development also dispense grants and loans to domestic and foreign investors willing to establish facilities in certain urban areas. State and local governments are often given a great deal of discretionary authority on how these federal funds are to be allocated.

Many businesses, suspicious about quality-of-life considerations within the depressed areas and problems with economic infrastructure development, have thus far adopted a wait-and-see attitude toward the zones. On the other hand, some zones, benefiting from significant federal, state, and local government assistance and from swift local government action to change zoning regulations, redefine land-use requirements, and generally eliminate bureaucratic red tape, have offered incentive packages irresistible to a large number of businesses.

INVESTING IN A FRAGMENTED WORLD

Some of the world's best thinkers insist that we as human beings must begin to think in terms of the world as a "spaceship earth" or "global village." The development of ultradestructive nuclear weapons, the spread of pollution, and the growing vulnerability of national units to international economic and resource trends would all seem to warrant cooperation on a global scale. As one eminent author has concluded, "despite the inevitable parochialism of our attachments to national societies and cultures, the change most required is the gradual acceptance of the reality of a common experience, common dangers, and a common goal."[28]

In many respects, the nation-state is outmoded and drastically ill-equipped to cope with contemporary international and subnational pressures. Or put in other words, the nation-state "is neither large enough to plan on a global scale, where that is needed, as in environmental controls and resource allocation, nor small enough to be accountable to people where they live."[29] Economic and political trends within nation-states are also in constant turmoil. As Peter Drucker has surmised, there is "an increasing conflict between the fundamental trends in the economy, which push toward integration, and the fundamental trends in the world polity, which push toward fission."[30]

The so-called Southern tier of nations in the world expects that the Northern countries should be willing to make sacrifices on their behalf. Thus, the developing "have not" peoples of the world want to acquire some of the bounties already achieved by citizens in the advanced industrial "have" societies. Although some assistance will be forthcoming from the North, the developing nations should recognize that political realities will severely limit the amount of direct state aid headed in their direction. As long as people continue to maintain nationalist loyalties and perceive unemployment and poverty as existing within their own local milieus, it will be politically risky for government leaders to provide the amount of international economic assistance needed to improve the lot of people in distant developing countries.

On a worldwide basis, the maze of tariff and investment barriers erected by nations is irrational, as clearly illustrated by the beggar-thy-neighbor policies of the 1930s which helped to plunge the world into the Great Depression. Nonetheless, whether capitalist, socialist, or communist in orientation, nation-states will continue in the future to give top priority to nationalist pursuits, even when such priorities run counter to economic rationalization on a global scale.

Balkanization within nation-states will further complicate the task facing international investors seeking secure and profitable investment opportunities. Especially in investment matters, regions will occasionally be pitted against regions, states against states, counties against counties, and even cities against cities. All desire to build up their own local economies and provide employment opportunities for their local people, even if this must be accomplished at the expense of their counterparts elsewhere. Quite frankly, the "have" and "have not," "heartland-hinterland" syndrome often characterizes relations within states as well as among nations. For example, many Canadian provinces have always perceived that Ontario has received the lion's share of benefits from Canadian confederation. Some American states believe that economic benefits have gone disproportionately to California and New York, whereas some of their counterparts in Australia make similar comments about Victoria and New South Wales. Thus, subnational governments will venture out in a world of increasing economic interdependence and political fragmentation and attempt to control their own economic destinies. Leaders of subnational governments in Australia, Canada, Brazil, and the United States have already made many trips abroad in an effort to attract foreign investment, and they will be joined by many other governments in the near future. Some subnational units, such as Quebec, are also developing sophisticated agencies which resemble mini-state departments or ministries of foreign affairs. Rules and regulations governing direct investment are also becoming much more complicated at the subnational level. Because of this tendency, Dow Chemical has created a new position of manager of state regulatory affairs in order to keep track of business regulations implemented by the fifty American state governments. Other transnational corporations will surely take similar actions to keep on top of subnational investment codes and procedures around the globe.[31]

However, in spite of the political fragmentation, most national and subnational government units will continue to seek out direct investment opportunities. Consequently, investors must be prepared to do a great deal of research in order to comprehend the political complexities, idiosyncracies, and legalisms prominent at the national and subnational levels. They must then ascertain the access points to the governmental system and learn how to interact effectively within the system and to mesh their investment goals with those of the system. Through diligent research and legwork, astute investors will recognize that subnational units may provide very worthwhile investment opportunities within a national setting which is generally not so attractive, and vice versa. They will also learn that key allies at the subnational level may be able to persuade national-level agencies to provide the green light for investment proposals. Investors must learn the rules of the political game and comprehend that these rules do not begin and end in national capitals. The challenge is formidable, but those enlightened enough to decipher the political and governmental labyrinth at all levels and bold enough to act promptly will reap substantial investment rewards.

REFERENCES

[1] For an interesting look at this phenomenon, consult Douglas F. Lament, *Foreign State Enterprises* (New York: Basic Books, 1979).

[2] The "attentive public" is defined as the 5 to 10 percent or so of the electorate who keep well-informed about political events and make their opinions known to decision makers within the governmental system.

[3] James Rosenau, *The Study of Global Interdependence* (London: Frances Pinter, 1980, p. 87). He adds that "this fragmentation, of course, has contributed substantially to both the proliferation of macro units and the decline in governmental effectiveness. No less important, it has also altered the basic structures of world politics by bringing questions pertaining to the internal fabric of societies much more fully onto the global agenda."

[4] Arnold Wolfers, *Discord and Collaboration: Essays on International Politics* (Baltimore: Johns Hopkins Press, 1962, p. 19).

[5] Robert O. Keohane and Joseph S. Nye, "Transgovernmental Relations and International Organizations," *World Politics*, Vol. 27, 1974, pp. 39–62.

[6] Joseph S. Nye and Robert O. Keohane, "Transnational Relations and World Politics: An Introduction," in Keohane and Nye, *Transnational Relations* (Cambridge: Harvard University Press, 1972, p. xii). The authors lump transgovernmental and transnational interactions together into a category known as "transnational relations" in order to differentiate these two phenomena from the state-centric connotation of the term "international relations."

[7] For example, the subnational government dimension is either glossed over or ignored entirely in such important works as Keohane and Nye, *Power and Interdependence: World Politics in Transition* (Boston: Little, Brown, 1977) and Richard W. Mansbach, Yale H. Ferguson, and Donald E. Lampert, *The Web of World Politics* (Englewood Cliffs, N.J.: Prentice-Hall, 1976).

In his article, "'Foreign' Policies of U.S. Publics," *International Studies Quarterly*, June 1977, pp. 277–318, Chadwick F. Alger looks briefly at the activities of local and state governments in the international sphere. Other preliminary research on the topic is found in E. H. Fry and G. A. Raymond, *Idaho's Foreign Relations: The Transgovernmental Linkages of an American State* (Boise, Id.: Boise State University Monograph Series, 1978), and E. H. Fry, "Provincial Politics and Canadian Foreign Policy," in *Encounter With Canada*, Wayne Reilly (ed.) (Durham, N.C.: Duke University Press, 1980).

8 As Garth Stevenson explains in "The Distribution of Foreign Policy Making Power Between the Federal Government and the Provinces," a paper presented at the Canadian-American Relations Seminar, Harvard University, April 15, 1980, these differences among subnational units "may produce divergent tendencies in foreign policy which find expression either in divergent pressures brought to bear on the central government or even in demands for direct foreign involvement by the subnational units themselves."

9 The bureaucratic reference is linked to Graham T. Allison's typologies in *Essence of Decision* (Boston: Little, Brown, 1971) and the genre of bureaucratic literature which followed in the wake of this highly successful book.

10 *Business Week*, March 2, 1981, pp. 25−26.

11 *National Journal*, October 18, 1980, pp. 1746−1747.

12 *Toronto Globe and Mail*, August 17, 1981, p. B14.

13 One of these advertisements was placed in the *Christian Science Monitor*, July 27, 1981, p. B2.

14 *The New York Times*, October 13, 1980, p. D3.

15 *The Economist*, October 25, 1980, p. S14.

16 *The Wall Street Journal*, September 4, 1981, p. 40. The successful efforts of Columbus, Indiana, to attract foreign investors are chronicled in Ibid., September 22, 1982, p. 31.

17 Ibid., September 4, 1981, p. 40.

18 A good overview of the responsibilities of this new State Department office is found in a speech entitled "State and Local Governments as Partners in the International Community." This speech was made by W. Beverly Carter, Ambassador-at-Large for Liaison with State and Local Governments and is distributed by the State Department.

19 *Toronto Globe and Mail*, August 20, 1981, p. B1.

20 Wisconsin, Vermont, and California are among the American states which have adopted the unitary approach to taxation.

21 *Christian Science Monitor*, March 24, 1982, p. 13.

22 *The New York Times*, January 11, 1981, p. 23.

23 See, for example, Ibid., January 26, 1981, pp. D1 and D5.

24 *The Wall Street Journal*, June 29, 1981, p. 14.

25 *Salt Lake Tribune*, November 5, 1981, p. D5.

26 Jasper Dorsey, "Georgia's Industrial Revolution," *Sky*, September, 1979, pp. 14−18.

27 *The Wall Street Journal*, July 28, 1981, p. 29.

28 W. W. Rostow, *The World Economy: History and Prospects* (Austin: University of Texas Press, 1978, p. 657).

29 Richard J. Barnet, *The Lean Years: Politics in the Age of Scarcity* (New York: Simon and Schuster, 1980, p. 306).

30 Peter F. Drucker, *Managing in Turbulent Times* (New York: Harper and Row, 1980, p. 168).

31 *The New York Times*, June 1, 1981, p. D9.

7 | THE POLITICS OF INVESTMENT RESTRICTIONS

RESTRICTIONS—THE NATIONAL AND INTERNATIONAL PARAMETERS

Governments in host countries are now able to limit the strategic planning options available to the affiliates of multinational enterprises in ways which were inconceivable just a few short years ago. In most textbooks dealing with international economics, one is informed that restrictions on outward and inward direct investment are imposed by these governments in an overall effort to protect the domestic economy. In actuality, restrictions tend to be quite selective and are frequently implemented in order to placate certain powerful interest groups which have direct access to governmental decision-making circles. Indeed, because of their organizational abilities and influence, these interest groups can often exert overwhelming pressure for the imposition of protectionist measures, even though a numerically superior but fragmented general public desires the consumer benefits derived from the free movement of capital and goods. This imbalance in political influence is especially blatant in nations where public accountability is lax and where elected officials and key bureaucrats may have an economic stake in industries seeking protection from foreign competition.

International businesses are often hamstrung by these national restrictions and complain most vociferously about being excluded from activities in certain economic sectors. Moreover, they protest against growing national price controls, requirements for domestic product content and ownership, stipulations that labor be allowed more say in the day-to-day decisions of management, and formal or informal policies which favor indigenous businesses in the distribution of government contracts. For example, multinational firms are very disturbed by a Japanese takeover law which first requires the unanimous approval of the board of the company to be acquired. The same disquietude is in evidence as a result of the Singapore government's deliberate policy to force up wages in order to sway foreign direct investment into highly skilled and capital-intensive industries. On the other hand, host governments worry about the linkage of multinational enterprises to home countries, the shifting of profits and tax liabilities through intracompany transfers, and the overall impact which such firms may have on locally owned competitors. For these host nations, the all-consuming desire of multinational corporations to maximize profits on a worldwide basis may run counter at times to the government's all-consuming quest to protect the economic well-being and political integrity of the individual nation-state, or at least influential actors within the nation-state.

A fair number of scholars argue that an international code for direct investment is needed, a code which will determine the rules of the game for governmental and international business conduct similar to what the General Agreement on Tariffs and Trade (GATT) attempts to do for international trade and the International Monetary Fund (IMF) strives to do for global monetary transactions. Certain international organizations have recently been in the forefront of efforts to develop such a code of conduct which would be fair both to the transnational enterprises and the countries receiving the foreign direct investment. In particular, the UN Commission on Transnational Corporations has been attempting to elaborate an investment code since 1977, with many members of the Group of 77 (the developing countries) lobbying extensively for very stringent investment guidelines with mandatory penalties for noncompliance.

In 1976, the Organization for Economic Cooperation and Development (OECD), which represents advanced industrial societies around the world, ratified a Declaration on International Investment and Multinational Enterprises, and it reaffirmed its support for this document in mid-1979. As a leading member of this organization, the United States has resisted the imposition of harsh government restrictions on direct investment and has insisted that national governments should neither promote nor discourage inward or outward investment. The United States has consistently approved of guidelines or codes which (1) are voluntary, (2) do not discriminate against multinational enterprises in favor of "national" companies, and (3) are balanced to include references to the responsibilities of governments as well as multinational firms and to all enterprises whether privately controlled, state-directed, or managed by a board composed of both private investors and state representatives. Policymakers in Washington view the OECD document as generally constructive and well-balanced but believe that the OECD should put more pressure on member governments to desist from offering subsidies to entice certain categories of foreign investors, particularly those in the automotive and high-technology fields. The United States has also expressed some sympathy toward the efforts of the special UN Commission but fears that the implementation of strict mandatory controls exercised by national governments over multinational enterprises might well dry up direct investment activities in the developing countries. In effect, the United States and many of its compatriots in the exclusive club of advanced industrial nations favor few restrictions on the activities of transnational corporations and individual international investors. In marked contrast, many developing nations favor major governmental limitations on direct investment activity in host countries and are working to secure support for such restrictions in the UN Commission on Transnational Corporations and in a formal declaration favoring a New International Economic Order (NIEO).

Appendix I provides an extensive survey of investment-restriction policies currently on the books in approximately sixty nations accounting for more than 90 percent of all foreign direct investment activity. The list is primarily based on information provided by questionnaires which were sent out to these governments by the author in the latter part of 1981. Of course, the laborious process of translating each government's penchant for legalese and jargonese into plain English was needed before the chart could be compiled in its final form.

This chapter will supplement Appendix I and illustrate how political tendencies and concerns impact upon the process of imposing restrictions on direct investment. Moreover, the list in the appendix cannot show which restrictions in reality are ironclad and which may be more or less circumvented. As an illustration of the incongruity which can at times exist between written statues and actual practices, one government official informed the author during a recent lecture tour to Southeast Asia that he wished that lawyers and executive officers of U.S.-based enterprises would not take restriction laws promulgated by his government so seriously, because these laws could often be ignored or modified. This government representative added that these laws had been put into effect in the first place to provide some outward harmony and consistency to investment regulations within a regional association of Asian nations and also to demonstrate to the electorate that the national government was not a pushover for powerful multinational enterprises. Yet he went on to insist that his government's leaders recognized the political and economic dividends associated with developing the nation's fragile economic infrastructure and in creating desperately needed industrial jobs. Consequently, the political rhetoric and statutes linked to inward direct investment would remain tough, but the behind-the-scenes accommodation of such investment activity would be quite generous. Later discussions with representatives of multinational corporations doing business in the country substantiated this official's point of view.

On the opposite side of the coin, the author lectured in a neighboring country which had fairly lenient investment restrictions on the books but had developed a reputation among international businesses for changing the rules of the game once the investment was made. The problems encountered by foreign investors were exacerbated even further by in-fighting among bureaucratic agencies claiming special jurisdiction over aspects of investment activity and demanding that these investors comply with often contradictory rules. Because the bureaucracy was so entrenched and changes in government through coups and other such tactics so commonplace, it was extremely difficult for the top government leaders to bring any semblance of order and consistency to the regulation of the business community.

Consequently, restriction laws or the lack of such laws may provide only a rough approximation of what investors will face; therefore, they must embark upon sophisticated project-specific risk forecasting before carrying through with an investment. Investors will face politicians and key bureaucrats in many Third World countries who believe that the Japanese example of achieving modernization and technology transfer through licensing agreements and minimal direct investment is the road to follow. As a result, they might adopt an obstructionist approach to many types of direct investment proposals. On the other hand, many will also attempt to emulate the Singapore example which brought rapid modernization and an improved standard of living through inward direct investment by large transnational enterprises. These government officials will attempt to work closely with foreign investors, and few major investment restrictions will be listed in government statutes.

Investors may also learn the hard way that their lawyers can provide only a cursory or even distorted view of the restriction climate in a given nation. Some nations deemphasize legal contracts, litigation, and an adversary-oriented legal perspective, a tendency which is both foreign and alarming to many American- and European-trained lawyers. Perhaps the variance in legal systems is best exemplified by the American and Japanese cases. The United States, with a population of 230 million people, has a very complicated legal structure which provides employment opportunities for 500,000 lawyers. In contrast, the 120 million Japanese generally frown upon adversary-type relations and have a much less sophisticated legal system which can function quite adequately with only 15,000 lawyers.

National restrictions on inward and outward direct investment have been with us at least since the time of the Hanseatic League in the fourteenth century and will continue to plague international business in spite of the growing interdependence of the global economy.[1] Louis Rukeyser, when asked if he was bullish on America's financial future, epitomized the feelings of many business representatives toward political and governmental circles by responding that he was definitely optimistic but warning that his optimism was guarded because "we have seen over the last twenty years the infinite capacity of politicians of both parties to louse up an otherwise healthy economy."[2] However, like it or not, those politicians and government officials, no matter how enlightened or dim-witted, will continue to play a key role in the success or failure of international investment projects. Moreover, as Henry Kissinger pointed out repeatedly in his halcyon days as an academician but seemed to ignore once in office, elected officials and key bureaucrats tend to focus on the short-run and have a habit of reacting to events and constituency pressure rather than engaging in creative long-term planning, tendencies which may occasionally wreak havoc with the investment strategies of businesses. Consequently, as a direct result of these political tendencies, businesses must understand the ins and outs of the politics of investment restrictions, even in faraway lands, and then develop their own contingency plans.

THE RESTRICTION GAME

The OECD Code on International Investment and Multinational Enterprises insists that foreign investors are generally entitled to receive the same treatment from national governments as that accorded to domestic investors and businesses. Nonetheless, active discrimination toward foreign investors exists in the advanced industrial nations covered by the OECD code as well as in the vast majority of developing countries. Furthermore, in spite of the widespread publicity given to the efforts of Margaret Thatcher, Ronald Reagan, and a few others to implement supply-side economics and to limit governmental activity in the economy, the trend in most countries continues to be toward greater state intervention in the economic sector. Moreover, as the activities of Canada's Foreign Investment Review Agency and Australia's Foreign Investment Review Board cogently illustrate, a government's scrutiny of foreign investment proposals can be very secretive, very arbitrary, and at times very frustrating for international businesses.

Because multinational enterprises are mobile and nation-states are not, it has been commonplace to consider that an international business can overcome many restrictive barriers simply by threatening to take its facilities, jobs, and revenues elsewhere. This image of maneuverability and flexibility so often attributed to multinational corporations has always been overemphasized, for once a major capital investment has been made in a certain country, it becomes a very painful economic proposition simply to pull up roots and depart. Furthermore, the company would have to give up its trained work force and forfeit any goodwill it had developed in the host nation, calling into question any future investment and trade linkages with that country. For example, when Coca-Cola withdrew from India because it refused to comply with a government order to divulge its secret formula to Indian investors, the company found it had also lost the option of exporting its product to the Indian market.

Increasing international business competition and easier access to technology through licensing arrangements may also be tilting the investment game in favor of national governments. As an example, many small and medium-size firms in the United States have for decades been perfectly content to service their local markets and not worry about expanding either nationally or internationally. However, with the trend toward mergers and acquisitions and the dramatic upsurge in foreign direct investment activity in the United States, these firms now find that their localized markets are being invaded by both large U.S.-based conglomerates and foreign competitors. For the sheer sake of economic survival, some of these smaller enterprises now recognize that they must seek out new markets overseas and become transnational in their orientation. With the proliferation of such small and medium-size multinational enterprises and with growing competition from firms headquartered in the developing, nearly industrialized, and even Soviet bloc countries, host nations may be acquiring greater bargaining leverage in implementing investment restrictions. For example, because a half dozen companies may be seeking a certain direct investment opportunity today whereas only one or two may have competed a decade ago, the host government could feasibly mandate stringent regulations concerning local equity participation, reinvestment of profits, types of technology transfer, etc. Three or four of these firms may reject these stiff government restrictions, but the other two, in their eagerness to acquire new market opportunities, may reluctantly agree to abide by these regulations. The degree of competition among multinational enterprises for new direct investment opportunities will vary appreciably from industry to industry, but the trend through the 1980s and 1990s may well be toward greater bargaining leverage on the side of national governments. Nonetheless, these governments should never lose sight of the fact that they must permit a foreign enterprise to make a profit in the host market or they will risk losing direct investment altogether.

As illustrated in Appendix I and in Figure 7-1, restriction policies may vary dramatically from country to country. Generally, however, economic sectors either wholly or partially closed to foreign investors include defense, utilities, transportation, communications (including media), banking, insurance, and other financial institutions, certain natural resources, and farm and ranch land.[3] Beyond these specific sectors, one encounters a wide variety of both official and unofficial restrictions which require careful scrutiny before an investment is made. In France, for example, an interdepartmental committee examines all but the smallest investment proposals and then makes recommendations to the Cabinet. In spite of Treaty of Rome provisions to the contrary, this committee even screens many applications coming from investors within the European Community itself.[4] The French government will occasionally veto investment proposals, as it did in the summer of 1980 when Billerud-Uddeholm of Sweden attempted to acquire 80 percent of Société Lafarge-Emballage, a packaging affiliate of Lafarge, S.A., a cement group.[5] In line with the French government's customary practices, no detailed explanation was given for the veto. The French government also does its best to reserve export and research-and-development subsidies for home-grown firms and to award government contracts to local enterprises. Moreover, government officials generally concede that they favor a "French solution," meaning a domestic sale, over foreign takeovers.[6] When an American liquor concern sought to buy Chateau Margaux, the government blocked the deal because of the damage it might cause to "national prestige." Eventually, this Bordeaux winery was sold to a French supermarket chain at an appreciably lower price.[7] IBM has long complained that French government pressure is responsible for its loss of major government and private sector contracts. Executives of the American-based company claim that the government consistently favors granting contracts to CII-Honeywell Bull, which is controlled by French interests. However, IBM has made few official protests to the government, claiming that, as they say in the French Foreign Legion, "things could always get worse."[8] On the other hand, when a French government committee blocked the Sperry Corporation's French subsidiary from delivering a 5.6-million-dollar computer ordered by a French steel mill, Sperry sued. The case eventually went to arbitration, and Sperry was awarded 1.2 million dollars in damages. This may well

1. Government monopolies not open to overseas investors.
2. 51 to 100 percent mandatory local ownership.
3. Screening and prior approval for projects.
4. Limits on repatriation of profits.
5. Export controls.
6. Limits on foreign ownership of land.
7. High income tax on profit remittances.
8. Antitrust legislation.
9. Price controls.
10. Strict licensing arrangements.
11. Rigorous exchange controls.
12. Investments required to be above a minimum amount.
13. Raw materials must be purchased domestically.
14. Very high duties, taxes, and levies.
15. No tax treaties.
16. Complicated value-added tax provisions.
17. Managing director and large percentage of members of the board must be nationals.
18. Government option to purchase percentage of stock.
19. Only leasehold land available.
20. Percentage of total production must be exported.
21. Ineligibility for soft loans and cash grants.
22. Limit on amount of stock held by single investor.
23. Joint ventures only.
24. Nonnationals required to obtain national status within a number of years.
25. Local office in host country required.
26. Nationalization.
27. Expropriation.
28. Ethnic-group ownership stipulations.
29. Boycott and antiboycott provisions.
30. Investment to be channeled through specific financial institutions.
31. No transfer of capital for portfolio investment.
32. Mandatory investment in secondary industries.
33. Government delays in processing investment applications.
34. Medium- and long-term financial credit prohibited for alien investors.
35. Minimum and maximum lengths of time for investments.
36. Mandated percentage of capital to come from abroad.
37. Penalties for invalidating agreements.
38. Visa and work-permit limitations.
39. Mandated research-and-development stipulations.
40. Extensive use of local suppliers.
41. Takeover bids require prior approval of company to be acquired.

Figure 7-1 Types of investment restrictions.

have been the first time a U.S. company had gone to court over such an issue, and observers will be watching closely how Sperry's sales will do in the future and whether other foreign firms will also seek redress within the French court system.

In overall perspective, many U.S. companies seeking to establish a base in France believe that it may be preferable to be a minority partner in a joint venture with a local company, in spite of French government assertions that 85 percent of all foreign investment proposals were accepted in the pre-Mitterand era.[9] Such an arrangement would qualify the U.S. firm for special grants, loans, and subsidies, and as a Sperry representative has suggested, "it's better for an American company to get 49 percent of the profits and dividends than to be shut out of the market entirely."[10] This recommendation will be increasingly true for other national markets as well, although each investment option being considered by a company must be viewed on a case-by-case basis and should take into account the industry involved, the specific project under consideration, and the region in a country where a facility would be located.

The equity participation issue is of major importance to many national governments, with some permitting foreign investors to assume a controlling interest in an enterprise for only a limited number of years. The Andean Pact nations require under Decision 24 that foreign subsidiaries must have at least 51-percent local ownership and corresponding management participation by the late 1980s (1993 for Bolivia and Ecuador) in order for these ccmpanies to continue to enjoy the liberalized trade concessions available within the regional market. However, special concessions are available to foreign firms which export a high percentage of their production outside the Andean region. In addition, several of the Andean Pact members have been bending the Decision 24 regulations when it suits their economic purposes.[11]

Under Malaysia's New Economic Policy, the bumiputras, or ethnic Malaysians, must be given at least a 30-percent stake in all companies by 1990, with Malaysians who do not qualify as bumiputras limited to a 40-percent stake and foreigners to a 30-percent stake.[12] Such "fade out" or limited forced-divestiture policies will certainly proliferate in the years ahead, with wholly owned subsidiaries most vulnerable to government restrictions, and joint ventures with foreign investors holding a minority position least vulnerable. Furthermore, as Stephen Kobrin has insightfully pointed out, disinvestment policies are not simply a manifestation of economic nationalism, reflecting national pride, an antiforeign bias, or political opportunism.[13] Rather, disinvestment is a policy instrument intended to achieve specific national political-economic objectives by increasing government control over the activities of certain investors and businesses. As a consequence, forced divestment is generally very selective, and transnational enterprises can certainly take substantive action to limit their exposure to such government policies. In particular, firms which hire a large number of people but produce in any given country only one phase in an integrated international production network may not be very vulnerable to forced divestment. A government pushing for a divestiture under such circumstances would risk losing all of the jobs, because it could be effectively cut off from the global production network. Moreover, firms which export a large part of their production, which have access to closely guarded technological innovations, or which are able to make a decent profit as a minority shareholder in a joint venture will often be exempted from divestiture policies. On the other hand, international firms involved in extractive industries, or in any of the targeted economic sectors listed at the beginning of this chapter, will face major difficulties in the future in their efforts to maintain a controlling interest in their overseas subsidiaries.[14]

International investors must also recognize that restriction policies which are implemented by obscure sectors of the bureaucracy and which often receive little publicity may have a much more dramatic impact on the profitability of foreign operations than the specter of forced divestment à la Mitterand's France. Environmental-protection standards and rules aimed at preserving endangered species in the United States have literally cost individual investors hundreds of millions of dollars and precipitated in some cases the complete abandonment of once profitable business ventures. Extensive wage and price controls, such as were in effect for several years in Canada, Brazil, and several other countries, may also cause overwhelming difficulties for certain businesses. Export performance requirements also seem to be proliferating. Mexico, for example, obliges foreign automakers to offset 50 percent of their import activity through exports of cars and car parts. Local content standards and consumer-protection codes may likewise lead to major problems, and an increasing number of governments are also pushing for parent firms to assume greater liability for the actions of their subsidiaries. Belgium, France, Norway, and Switzerland are among the countries that now have laws attempting to safeguard the interests and assets of local subsidiaries against disadvantageous decisions rendered by their parent companies. Shareholders of these subsidiaries may now file suits in an effort to show that parent company decisions are contrary to the best interests of the subsidiary. Moreover, some national governments in Europe and elsewhere are beginning to define a parent company's financial obligation much more broadly, and regulators are attempting to apply the principle of "economic unity" to transnational enterprises both in their antitrust litigation and in their efforts to thwart alleged tax evasion through intracompany transfers.

William Brock, the Reagan administration's Special Trade Representative, once commented that "Japan carefully targets certain industries, pumps in investment, and surrounds them with protectionism until it is ready to unleash them on the world."[15] Although few if any countries are able to keep pace with the Japanese international trade machine, they all share Japan's concern with protecting local enterprises and local jobs, regardless of global economic and resource tendencies which indicate the marketplace inefficiency of such parochial perspectives. High unemployment rates and recessionlike conditions will undoubtedly intensify some aspects of parochialism. For example, the Dutch court system refused for a time in 1981 to permit Ford to close down an unprofitable plant in the Amsterdam region, claiming the loss of jobs was more important than Ford's profit-and-loss motivations. At a time when nearly one in ten workers in Europe is without a job, the linkage between union issues and politics becomes much stronger in many countries on the Continent and international firms encounter strenuous opposition in implementing worker-furlough or plant-closure strategies.

Thus, concern for the *patrie* and political loyalties cemented in the nation-state will continue to produce a plethora of restriction policies which will plague all international investors and prove to be financially fatal to more than just a few. Within this increasingly complex and hostile regulatory environment, investors will have to be highly selective in terms of investment targets and flexible enough to adapt some of their overall goals to the specific needs and objectives of political and economic leadership circles in the host nation. Some international businesses will conclude, and rightfully so, that profits cannot be made through direct investment in certain countries and thus will rely on exporting, licensing, and other related types of arrangements to service these nations. In most cases, however, direct investment will continue to be a profitable proposition and many firms will be able to maintain effective control over the subsidiary's decision-making process, even when its equity position is less than 50 percent in a joint venture.

PLAYING THE RESTRICTIONS GAME

The Political Dimension

The United States has long been considered as one of the least restrictive havens in the world for foreign direct investment. Yet even in America, foreign investors are prohibited altogether or severely restricted in terms of investment activity in industries linked to defense, maritime trade, aviation and aeronautics, communications, and selected energy-resource sectors.[16] As mentioned previously, the Kuwait Petroleum Corporation was allowed to acquire most of the assets of California-based Santa Fe International, but one of Santa Fe's subsidiaries was forced to forfeit its government defense contracts and its files were purged by federal officials. Some opponents of the takeover even argued that the entire transaction should have been voided by Washington because of the sensitive defense-related activities of this one subsidiary.[17]

Governments at the state and national levels in the United States also impose significant product-liability and equal-opportunity-employment standards. For example, a few American employees have sued Japanese subsidiaries, claiming that they are being discriminated against because they receive only one annual bonus, whereas Japanese employees of the firm almost invariably receive two bonuses on a yearly basis. In addition, at least seventeen American states have imposed "Buy American" restrictions on certain types of government purchases, following in the footsteps of the federal government's own Buy American Act of 1933. The U.S. Securities and Exchange Commission also requires that any firm purchasing more than 5 percent of the stock in a publicly listed U.S. corporation disclose this acquisition and fill out forms providing some very sensitive information about the firm's operations. Direct investments made in the United States might also subject foreign firms to the restrictions of the U.S. Trading With the Enemy Act and to other related restrictions. The Trading With the Enemy Act allows the President of the United States to regulate and control transactions with countries considered to be hostile to the United States. This law certainly has extraterritorial implications and has caused numerous problems for multinational enterprises and for U.S. relations with certain friendly countries. For example, several years ago a French subsidiary of U.S.-based Fruehauf contracted to sell equipment to the French firm Berliet, which in turn was providing parts for trucks to be sold to China. Washington ordered Fruehauf to direct its subsidiary to terminate the deal, but Berliet refused to annul the contract. The three French directors of Fruehauf France sued the other five directors and asked that the contract be honored. The French courts subsequently ruled that the contract must be honored because failure to do so would imperil the subsidiary's existence and risk the loss of jobs. In another instance, Washington attempted to prevent Ford and General Motors cars and trucks manufactured in Argentina from being shipped to Cuba. When the Argentine government threatened to nationalize the production of the subsidiaries and then sell the vehicles to Cuba, the U.S. government backed down.[18] The federal government also began proceedings against Gulf Oil for allowing Gulf of Canada to take part in a worldwide uranium cartel that was organized with the blessings of the Canadian government during the mid-1970s. Federal authorities may also prosecute U.S.-based firms for permitting their overseas subsidiaries to honor the Arab boycott toward trade with Israel, even though the boycott may be quite legal in the countries where the subsidiaries are located. In spite of the fact that some of these examples indicate that disruptions were temporary, multinational corporations must be concerned about the rather liberal intervention of the U.S. government into the international trade and investment sphere in an era of vacillating tensions between the two superpowers. Moreover, as the Siberian natural gas pipeline episode has poignantly illustrated, the imposition of U.S. government restrictions can wipe out years of careful international trade and investment work on the part of firms within the United States.

Furthermore, the United States has often been described as being mired down in a maze of antitrust regulations, although conditions have generally improved over the past decade. Antitrust laws are intended to prohibit anticompetitive mergers, monopolization, price-fixing, and restrictive agreements between manufacturers and dealers. Aspects of antitrust rules and fair business practices have also been used time and time again in federal and state courts in an attempt to frustrate foreign acquisitions of American firms. After years of court battles, Sandoz of Switzerland finally backed off from its campaign to acquire control of McCormick, the spice company. In a 1980 settlement, Sandoz agreed to sell some of McCormick's nonvoting shares back to the American company and to refrain for five years from any further attempts to acquire the firm. McCormick had waged a long and bitter campaign in the U.S. federal court system, claiming that, among other things, Sandoz had improperly influenced the price of McCormick shares.[19] Brascan, Canadian Pacific, and Seagrams are only a few of the foreign firms which, like Sandoz, considered that they had made successful takeover bids in the United States only to be frustrated by decisions rendered by some branch of the federal or state governments.

Whether in the United States or elsewhere, investors must understand the types of restrictions which they might encounter and the decision-making processes which produce these restrictions. As an example, bills coming out of the U.S. Congress often have provisions (called riders) which have little if any relationship at all to the main body of the bill. Subcommittees of Congress are often responsible for steering these riders through the legislative process, and rarely do the activities of these subcommittees receive much attention from the media or the public at large. Nonetheless, in 95 percent of the cases, the actions of the subcommittees are upheld by full committees, and the actions of the full committees are supported 90 percent of the time by the entire House of Representatives or the Senate. Consequently, if one can ascertain how a subcommittee is going to vote, there is a 90 percent likelihood of predicting how the House or Senate will act upon a specific piece of legislation.[20] Of course, major compromises are made at times in conference committees which iron out differences in legislation passed by the two chambers. It is also very difficult to implement legislation which might pique members of the executive branch. Nevertheless, it remains a fact of life that if legislation can be successfully introduced and passed at the subcommittee level, its chances of becoming law are excellent.

McCormick and other U.S. firms which have been targets of foreign takeovers have actively lobbied at the subcommittee level for protection. In particular, pressure has been placed on subcommittees to implement reciprocity provisions and establish margin requirements for stock transactions. As a concrete illustration of this process, one well-known U.S. cereal company perceived that it was a takeover target for a large Canadian conglomerate. The U.S. company hired a well-known Washington law firm to orchestrate a strategy which would dissuade this Canadian suitor. One of the tactics utilized was to gather together a number of U.S. companies that were facing a similar predicament or were unhappy with how the Canadian government had treated their own investment proposals. A member of the U.S. Congress was then asked to sponsor subcommittee hearings on investment reciprocity, and the law firm provided a list of prominent business, legal, and academic representatives who would be willing to testify in favor of such reciprocity. Indeed, several interest-group organizations exist in Washington which specialize in providing such expert witnesses at a moment's notice. The subcommittee hearings were eventually held, and witnesses argued that Canadian investors in the United States should be subject to the same privileges and restrictions south of the border as are accorded to U.S. investors in Canada. In other words, as long as the Foreign Investment Review Agency (FIRA) was in place in Canada, certain restrictions should be placed on Canadian direct investment in the United States. Because of executive-branch opposition, the bill in this case was never implemented but did receive widespread attention in Canadian business circles. Moreover, through the subcommittee hearings and court action, the U.S. cereal company was able to indicate to the Canadian suitor that it wanted no part of a takeover bid and was prepared to spend millions of dollars in legislative, judicial, executive, and media circles at both the national and state levels to make life miserable for this foreign investor. The message seemed to hit home because the Canadian suitor soon turned its attention to other U.S. takeover targets.[21] In effect, any foreign investor seeking a hostile takeover in the United States or most any other nation will face failure, criticism, and ill-feeling unless that investor understands the linkage between investment-restriction policies and political processes.

The task facing international businesses in trying to mitigate the impact of investment restrictions is, of course, extremely arduous. In the United States alone, 80,000 distinct government units are currently in existence, and these units can be further subdivided into hundreds of thousands of departments and agencies and almost 10 million individual employees. Moreover, a foreign-based enterprise will encounter 15,000 lobbyists entrenched in Washington, D.C. and thousands more spread around the world's capitals or regional centers. Some of these lobbyists will share a common interest with the foreign enterprise, but others will do their best to place impediments in the way of the overseas competitor.

Once the foreign investor has engaged in extensive research and understands the political processes and pertinent organizations and actors impacting upon restriction policies, the next step is to ascertain whether allies should be garnered initially at the national level or at the local level. In rare cases, some initial lobbying at the international or regional echelons may bear some fruit, which helps to explain why a large number of multinational firms have stationed representatives in Brussels, the headquarters for the European Commission and the European Community bureaucracy. In a great number of instances, however, extensive legwork should be done initially at the local level. By convincing local governmental and business leaders of the benefits to be derived from a new investment or acquisition, valuable allies will be made in the quest to minimize the imposition of restriction policies. To be insensitive to the concerns of key people at the local level could lead to disaster, such as occurred with the abortive bids of Mobil for Marathon Oil and Canadian Pacific for Hobart. Allies at the community and state or provincial levels will then help drum up support among their representatives in national governmental bodies, who in turn can help open doors to key decision makers in the bureaucracy. Strong grassroots support may be the key factor in the ultimate approval of an investment proposal or in the imposition of very mild investment restrictions. Attention paid to local political and governmental figures may even become more important in the future if the current emphasis on government decentralization in the United States, France, Belgium, the United Kingdom, and several other countries is fully implemented.

The Bureaucratic Dimension

A sophisticated understanding of policymaking processes and the standard operating procedures of both agencies and individual bureaucrats will also be necessary if a foreign firm is to successfully steer an investment proposal through the governmental labyrinth. In many respects, it is bureaucrats and not elected officials who will be the key people involved in the formulation and implementation of restriction policies. For example, Franklin D. Roosevelt has been widely considered as a very forceful American President, but one of his former aides once commented: "Half of a President's suggestions, which theoretically carry the weight of orders, can be safely forgotten by a cabinet member."[22] This assistant went on to say that if the President asked a second time about a particular issue, a Cabinet member could say that the matter was being investigated. If the President asked a third time, a wise Cabinet member would then make sure the President was given at least part of what he was requesting. The aide sagaciously added, however, that the President rarely asked three times.[23]

John F. Kennedy, on several different occasions, reportedly made the following comment to friends offering policy suggestions to him: "Well, I agree with you, but I'm not sure the government will."[24] In one of the transcripts from his notorious White House tapes, Richard Nixon clearly revealed his frustration with the government bureaucracy. Nixon complains in a conversation with George Schultz, then Director of the Office of Management and Budget, that "we never fire anybody. We never reprimand anybody. We never demote anybody. We always promote the SOB's that kick us in the [expletive deleted]."[25] The President even recalled a specific incident in which an unnamed official of the Small Business Administration in San Francisco bucked the White House. Nixon contends that "this fellow deliberately did not—I read the memorandum—he did not carry out an order I personally gave. I wrote the order out [unintelligible]. And, the SOB did not do it."[26]

The bureaucracy has thus been singled out at times for blunting the power and policy-formulation capability of elected officials. As Max Weber surmised several decades ago: "Under normal conditions, the power position of a fully developed bureaucracy is always overpowering. The 'political master' finds himself in the position of the 'dilettante' who stands opposite the 'expert,' facing the trained official who stands within the management of the administration."[27] Chief executives even have problems mastering their own executive organizations. One scholar has depicted the American chief executive as facing in the executive branch a "mammoth bureaucracy, slow in responding to his purposes, unimaginative in the face of momentous problems, laboring mightily to bring forth a mole."[28] Henry Kissinger has asserted that "placating the staff then becomes a major preoccupation of the executive."[29] He further insists that in a bureaucratic system, serving the machine becomes a more absorbing occupation than defining its purpose and adds that decision makers are inevitably transformed into arbiters rather than leaders.[30]

The bureaucracy has been described as a "giant amoeba" which "slurps along, a shapeless blob, following the path of least resistance. It pushes out in every direction, and its substance flows into the bulges."[31] A psychiatrist compares the bureaucracy to a "great white marshmallow," in which individuals forfeit their own identity in order to comply with a certain type of organizational behavior.[32] The rules that commonly become paramount in the existence of a bureaucrat include maintaining tenure, spending all allocated appropriations, keeping one's superior from being embarrassed, keeping the program moving, and maintaining a stable and well-circumscribed constituency.[33]

It is these rules which should be kept in mind by the foreign investor, whether the investment is contemplated in the United States or in Upper Volta. When resistance is encountered in one bureaucratic domain, the emphasis may have to be shifted to winning approval in a higher echelon of the bureaucracy. Bureaucrats in general do not like to rock the boat and certainly do not want to incur the wrath of their immediate superiors. Consequently, an obstinate individual or subunit of a particular agency will quite often fall in line if pressure is exerted from higher up. Of course, any appeal to higher echelons should be supported by the enthusiastic endorsement of the local and regional allies.

If resistance is solid within an entire department, the investment proposal may have to be restructured and then submitted to a new agency altogether. For example, some proposals which were initially viewed with disfavor by French and Canadian screening agencies eventually gained approval when the investors decided to place investments in specially designated regions and thereby garnered the support of the government agencies which administered these special programs.

Furthermore, once an investment has been successfully made, the transnational enterprise cannot afford to become complacent. As discussed earlier, the investment rules of the game tend to change rather dramatically in certain countries. As an illustration, one firm was invited by the Malaysian government to build a plant and provide products for the local market. Once a substantial investment had been made by this firm, it was informed that the government had altered plans from a vague "consideration of exports" to requiring that 75 percent of the plant's output be exported.[34] After Peugeot had expanded its 100-million-dollar assembly plant, the Nigerian government informed the French automobile manufacturer that it would have to import all of its components and supplies through the underutilized port facilities in Lagos. Under this arrangement, the parts would have to be trucked over 500 miles of poor roads and the overall process would be much more expensive and time-consuming than the previous method of daily cargo flights from France directly to the Nigerian plant. Nevertheless, Peugeot decided to comply with the host government's request.[35] International firms must also recognize that in various countries politics and government service are viewed by many people as very lucrative businesses and easy ways to quick money. Both through hindering the operations of foreign subsidiaries and abetting illegal market operations, these officials can do great damage to even the most sophisticated investment strategies. For example, Teijn Limited of Japan had to put its Nigerian subsidiary into receivership in 1981 because it could no longer compete with smuggled goods which had allegedly entered the African nation with the assistance of certain well-placed customs officials.[36]

Moreover, the imposition of wage and price controls and similar constraints, even though not aimed specifically at foreign investors, may have a catastrophic impact on the financial health of the foreign-owned subsidiary. Consequently, the multinational enterprise must lobby individually and as part of industry associations and be involved in political activities at least to the same extent as political action committees (PACs), which funnel corporate contributions for political campaigns, are in the United States.

COPING WITH FUTURE RESTRICTIONS

Investment restrictions will become more onerous in the future, and a far greater number of strategic choices made by the affiliates of multinational enterprises will be linked to national and local government regulations rather than simply to the interplay of market forces. In particular, transnational enterprises can expect both an increase in the screening of investment proposals and periodic reviews of the subsidiary's performance record once a direct investment has been made. Moreover, this screening and review process will continue to be very arbitrary and subject to pressure from influential local business groups which do not want foreign competitors to have unimpaired entry into their home markets.[37] This problem may be further exacerbated by the dramatic increase in state-owned enterprises. The most severe challenges by far will be faced by extractive industries, with businesses providing financial, defense, communications, transportation, and utility services also experiencing major restrictions. Fewer difficulties will be encountered by the high-technology sector and by mobile, labor-intensive businesses which have an integrated production network spread over several countries. The World Bank's International Center for the Settlement of Disputes or a commission linked directly to the United Nations may become more active in the future in resolving disputes between multinational enterprises and host governments. Most of the time, however, host governments will insist that their own national adjudication processes be used in order to resolve investment-related conflicts.

On the other hand, most if not all nations will continue to actively solicit foreign direct investment and will be very careful not to regulate themselves out of the investment game. Although showing clear preference for the transfer of technology through licensing arrangements and for foreigners to take a minority position in joint ventures, national governments in most advanced industrial and nearly industrial societies and in many developing countries will continue to welcome a wide range of foreign-controlled subsidiaries.

To succeed in this highly complicated milieu of investment restrictions, international businesses must learn explicitly how political and bureaucratic networks work and how regulations are adopted, modified, and eliminated. They must also carefully identify the key political, bureaucratic, and interest group actors involved in the regulatory process. In addition, they should appreciate the fact that the formulation of public policy may differ dramatically from the implementation of such policy. In other words, a wide range of investment restrictions may have been enacted into law by executives and legislatures, but the bureaucracy may have great latitude in selectively implementing and enforcing these restrictions. Conversely, bureaucratic agencies can cause great grief for foreign investors even when national legal statutes are devoid of investment restrictions. Furthermore, provisions which treat foreign and domestic businesses equally, such as environmental-protection, product-liability, and equal-opportunity standards, may have a greater impact on the success or failure of a foreign-controlled business venture than those restrictions which are aimed specifically at overseas investors.

Parent governments should also recognize that their business community must be given the latitude to "do as the Romans do" when competing for investment opportunities in other countries. Certain provisions contained in America's Foreign Corrupt Practices Act and in similar documents enacted by a handful of other nations should be universally applied and cannot be compromised for the sake of business expediency. Nevertheless, competition has become so intense that businesses must have the flexibility to interact with political, bureaucratic, and business representatives in ways which are perfectly acceptable within the given nation's cultural framework, even though such conduct might be considered reprehensible from the parent country's cultural vantage point. Ideally, international standards will be enacted in the future which will carefully spell out what is acceptable and unacceptable in interactions between business and governmental representatives. Until that distant day, however, laws and traditions in host countries will have to determine the general parameters for government-business linkages.

To be good corporate citizens within a host country, multinational enterprises must understand the major goals and concerns of the attentive publics at both the local and national levels and then harmonize and dovetail investment objectives with these special aspirations and needs. In this respect, overseas affiliates should not be hesitant to publicize accomplishments that coincide with the country's particular interests. The nurturing of local grassroots contacts will also be crucial in determining the success or failure of the foreign investment. As discussed in an earlier chapter, subnationalism is a key facet of contemporary national and international relations. An alienated community group may doom an investment proposal even though the national governmental apparatus has given the green light for the project. To illustrate this point, the refusals by cantonal governments in Switzerland and prefectures in France to grant work permits have at times stymied direct investment projects already approved at the national governmental level. As one author has pointed out, "permission by the central governments does not mean freedom to go ahead with an investment even in unitary states."[38] Conversely, enthusiastic support at the local and regional levels may often be enough to open what were once closed doors at the national level. In order to provide local jobs and diversify and expand the local economic base, political, bureaucratic, and business elites will often back the investment proposal of a foreign firm even when the overseas investor is facing stiff resistance from state-owned enterprises. From their point of view, it is preferable to have a foreign firm in their community which provides direct economic benefits to local citizens than to preserve the ascendant position of a state-owned company which does not offer such local benefits. To be quite succinct, in spite of the dearth of literature dealing with the subnational dimension, local linkages may well be the key to winning or losing the investment-restrictions game. Nonetheless, a foreign investor must also pay close attention to the national political and bureaucratic echelons and make sure that an adversary relationship does not evolve between its local supporters and national elite groups. Allies are desperately needed at both levels in order to keep restrictions at a minimum and thereby enhance the economic vitality of the business enterprise.

REFERENCES

[1] Because of growing competition from foreign competitors, the Hanseatic League implemented increasingly severe investment regulations in the latter part of the fourteenth century in a vain effort to reserve investment privileges exclusively for its own members.

[2] *Christian Science Monitor*, December 30, 1981, p. B5.

[3] A. E. Safarian, "Policy on Multinational Enterprises in Developed Countries," *Canadian Journal of Economics*, November 1978, p. 644.

[4] Ibid., pp. 644–646.

[5] *The Wall Street Journal*, August 8, 1980, p. 17.

[6] Ibid., April 7, 1980, p. 24.

[7] Ibid.

[8] Ibid.

[9] Ibid.

[10] Ibid. Prior to the nationalization of its facilities in France in 1982, ITT complained that the French government had consistently refused to give any orders to its French subsidiary, Compagnie Générale des Constructions Téléphoniques, and had refused to give a trial order for ITT's most advanced systems. Orders from the French postal service had also gone exclusively to subsidiaries of two French-owned companies, Compagnie Générale d'Electricité and Thomson-CSF. See *Business Week*, September 29, 1980, p. 58.

[11] *The Wall Street Journal*, March 26, 1982, p. 31.

[12] *Asian Wall Street Journal*, September 9, 1981, p. 1.

[13] Stephen Kobrin, "Foreign Enterprise and Forced Divestment in LDCs," *International Organization*, Winter 1980, p. 85.

[14] As an illustration of the vulnerability of extractive industries, the Venezuelan government recently assumed a majority interest in a joint venture with Reynolds Metals. In upping its stake from 28 to 50 percent, the government complained that Reynolds had been reluctant to invest capital in Venezuela and thus the people of Venezuela would best be served by having government representatives determine the future policy priorities of the joint venture. See *The Wall Street Journal*, January 20, 1981, p. 26.

[15] *Christian Science Monitor*, May 12, 1981, p. 1.

[16] For detailed information concerning U.S. government restrictions, consult Sarkis J. Khoury, *Transnational Mergers and Acquisitions in the United States* (Lexington, Mass.: Lexington Books, 1980, pp. 91–142), and Earl H. Fry, *Financial Invasion of the U.S.A.* (New York: McGraw-Hill, 1980, pp. 44–57).

[17] Santa Fe's subsidiary, C. F. Braun, was forced to withdraw from defense-related nuclear work after the firm was acquired by the Kuwaiti state-owned corporation.

[18] Stephen J. Kobrin, "The Political Environment," in *The Cultural Environment of International Business*, Vern Terpstra (ed.) (Cincinnati: South-Western Publishing, 1978, pp. 231–232).

[19] *The Wall Street Journal*, October 9, 1980, p. 20.

[20] A. Lee Fritschler and Bernard H. Ross, *Executive's Guide to Government: How Washington Works* (Cambridge, Mass.: Winthrop, 1980, p. 78).

[21] The author was asked to participate in the hearings sponsored by the Subcommittee on Consumer Protection and Finance of the U.S. House of Representatives and was also able to observe rather closely the unfolding of the U.S. cereal maker's strategy to thwart the takeover bid by the Canadian company.

[22] Richard Neustadt, *Presidential Power* (New York: Wiley, 1964, p. 22).

[23] Ibid.

[24] Roger Hilsman, *The Politics of Policy-Making in Defense and Foreign Affairs* (New York: Harper & Row, 1971, p. 1).

[25] *Salt Lake Tribune*, July 20, 1974, p. 6.

[26] Ibid.

[27] Max Weber, "Essay on Bureaucracy," in *Bureaucratic Power in National Politics*, Francis Rourke (ed.) (Boston: Little, Brown, 1965, p. 11).

[28] Louis Koenig, *The Chief Executive* (New York: Harcourt, Brace & World, 1964, p. 405).

[29] Henry Kissinger, "Domestic Structure and Foreign Policy," in *International Politics and Foreign Policy*, James Rosenau (ed.) (New York: Free Press, 1969, p. 265).

[30] Ibid., pp. 264–265.

[31] Jack Anderson and Carl Kalvelage, *American Government . . . Like It Is* (Morristown, N.J.: General Learning Press, 1972, p. 59).

[32] Matthew Dumont, "Down the Bureaucracy!" in *Politics/America*, Walter Dean Burnham (ed.) (New York: Van Nostrand, 1973, p. 167).

[33] Ibid.

[34] *Business International*, January 9, 1981, pp. 9–10.

[35] Yves L. Doz, Christopher A. Bartlett, and C. K. Prahalad, "Global Competitive Pressures and Host Country Demands," *California Management Review*, Spring 1981, p. 63.

[36] *Business Week*, February 22, 1982, p. 51.

[37] In Safarian, "Multinational Enterprises," p. 647, the author concludes that formal investment-review mechanisms in Australia, Canada, and Japan are very ad hoc and arbitrary: "The fact is that clearly defined objectives in this area of policy, accompanied by explicit and consistent criteria and enforcement procedures, are notable by their absence."

[38] Ibid.

8 ⊖ THE POLITICS OF INVESTMENT INCENTIVES

THE LURE OF INVESTMENT INCENTIVES

Literally billions of dollars in investment incentives are currently being distributed by national, regional, and local governments around the world. As illustrated in Figure 8-1 and Appendix II, these incentives come in a wide variety of forms and may provide funding for 50 percent or more of the initial start-up expenses of an international enterprise and 10 percent or more of the costs of operating the business over a ten- to twenty-year period.

Competition among national and regional governments to attract certain types of foreign direct investment can be extremely intense, as exemplified by the recent bidding war in Western Europe to entice the Ford Motor Company to build a new automobile-assembly plant. Governments in France, Austria, Ireland, Spain, Germany, and Portugal were the chief bidders vying to convince Ford that their specific country was the ideal location to construct this 800-million-dollar plant which would employ 8000 workers. Austria eventually offered 300 million dollars in incentives, and the French government may have raised the ante to as high as 440 million dollars, providing Ford would build the plant in the economically depressed region of Alsace-Lorraine. In July 1982, Ford announced that it would build the plant in Portugal and would release details about the incentive package offered by the Lisbon government early in 1983. As documented earlier, Ford was also successful in pitting Canadian provincial and U.S. state gov-

1. Import-duty concessions
2. Tax concessions
   a. Primary producers
   b. Equalization of tax payments
   c. Acceleration of depreciation allowance
   d. Capital gains
   e. Double-taxation agreements (corporation and personal)
   f. Energy conservation
   g. Customs-duty exemptions
   h. Credits on approved projects
   i. Relief from transfer taxes
   j. Office equipment for business start-up exemptions
   k. Employing nationals
   l. Real estate tax exemptions
   m. Credits for modernization
   n. Dividend-tax exemptions
   o. Credits for "pioneer industries"
   p. Incentives for management of enterprises
   q. Tax holidays for investment in underdeveloped areas
   r. Duty reduction on export of manufactured goods
   s. Tax exemptions for interest paid on foreign loans
   t. Credits on fixed assets
   u. Partial to full waiver of local taxes
3. Low-interest loans for start-ups
4. Land grants
5. Subsidized transportation
6. Industrial land subsidies
7. Subsidized assistance for essential services
8. Banking secrecy and anonymity guarantees
9. Export financing
10. Interest subsidies
11. Credit guarantees
12. Preferential entry for imported foreign capital
13. Interest rate rebates on loans
14. Government guarantees to secure credit
15. Interest-free advances to finance research and development
16. Equal treatment with local investors
17. Unimpaired capital and profit remittances
18. No time limit for foreign direct investment activity in host nation

Figure 8-1 Types of investment incentives.

19. Incentives for reinvestment of profits in host nation
20. Capital assistance
21. Market-rate loans
22. Prohibition on confiscation and nationalization
23. Public free-trade zones
24. Risk guarantees
25. Job-training subsidies
26. Open-door negotiations based on merits of project
27. Patent-rights allowances
28. Low-cost, prefinancing loans
29. Leasing incentives
30. Capital-equipment subsidies
31. Assistance in feasibility and marketing studies
32. Assistance in land and labor search
33. "Unconditional" capital subsidies
34. Partial government loan underwriting
35. Special incentives for hotel construction and other specialized projects
36. Cash grants for fixed assets
37. Fiscal incentives regarding carry-back/carry-forward losses
38. Guarantees against exchange rate losses
39. Exemptions on import of raw materials and semimanufactured items
40. 100 percent exemptions where manufacturing for 100 percent exports
41. Antidumping protection
42. Government competition protection
43. Government advisory services
44. Subsidized factory premises rental
45. Cash grants for moving costs
46. Housing allowances for personnel
47. Company-merger incentives
48. Investment-credit guarantees
49. Protection of trademarks, patents, and copyrights
50. Exclusive licenses
51. Guarantees against price controls

ernments against one another in the late 1970s and finally received close to 70 million dollars in grants from the Canadian and Ontario governments for the establishment of an engine plant in that province.

The lure of investment incentives may appear at times to be over-powering, but international investors must take time to reflect on the motivations for such incentive policies. Certainly, competition is one major reason for the dramatic increase in investment inducements. Whether nation is pitted against nation, or region against region, gov-ernments want to bring to their own specific areas of jurisdiction the jobs, technology transfer, and other beneficial parts of the so-called package which accompanies direct investment. The government in Taiwan, for example, desires to transform the island's economy from labor-intensive, low-value product industries to high-technology pro-duction. The establishment of an industrial park, which caters ex-clusively to high-technology firms and which also doubles as a foreign trade zone, represents one substantive step towards achieving this goal. In order to attract Flow Industries, a Washington-based company which is a world leader in the production of water-jet cutting equipment, the Taiwanese government built the entire plant and then leased it to the American firm at very favorable rates. Flow Industries was also ex-tended a five-year tax holiday, and government agencies put up 49 per-cent of the capital required for the project. Because of the foreign-trade-zone stipulations, the firm is also permitted to import materials and parts duty-free and then export its production to other nations along the Pacific Rim.[1]

Consequently, just as the export subsidy war has heated up in recent years, so has the investment-incentive battle. Simply for the sake of remaining in the incentive ball game, nations which already have highly attractive market systems are now offering investment sweeten-ers. In certain respects, the incentive war is ludicrous, especially in federal systems of government. For example, the United States is such an attractive investment haven that there is no need for the present to offer significant incentives. Nonetheless, because the American federal system consists of one national government, fifty state governments, and thousands of county and municipal governments, the subnational units are offering billions of dollars in incentives for the sake of enticing foreign investors to their specific locales. Under such conditions, international investors are in the very enviable position of being able to pick and choose their opportunities in a very lucrative market and then being afforded the privilege of demanding major investment conces-sions. An understanding of political and governmental operations at the national and subnational levels will be extremely important if the foreign investor is to maximize the advantages offered by incentive packages.

The second motivation for governments to offer investment incentives is to attempt to offset conditions within the host country which are worrisome to multinational enterprises. Great Britain has offered enticing incentive opportunities in an attempt to bring new industries to strife-ridden Northern Ireland. Administrations in Jamaica, Uganda, Peru, China, and several other countries have also sweetened the incentives pot in an effort to overcome the checkered reputations which previous governments in those nations had earned among multinational businesses. High unemployment, worker militancy, poor transportation and communications facilities, unstable governments, and various other weaknesses in the economic and political infrastructures may also prod governments to bolster investment inducements.

When such conditions exist, the foreign investor cannot afford to be blinded by what may well be a highly lucrative incentive package. The merits and demerits of the investment climate must be carefully weighed with incentives given a low priority on the list of relevant factors. The government's consistency or lack of consistency in applying investment regulations once the project is underway will undoubtedly be a crucial consideration. Above all, the firm's ability to generate a consistent profit under a variety of political and economic conditions which have existed in the nation in the past or which are likely to occur in the future must serve as the acid test for whether or not an investment should be made. Once the firm has carefully scrutinized these basic factors, incentives which offer a hefty commitment of government funds for start-up expenses and which permit unimpaired repatriation of profits and liberalized transfer-pricing arrangements may then be added to the overall equation and perhaps allowed to tip the scale in favor of the direct investment.

In China, for example, the administration in Beijing agreed in 1979 to give unprecedented privileges to foreign investors in special trade zones located near the border with Hong Kong. Well over one billion dollars in direct investment poured into these zones in the first three years of their existence, with investors especially attracted by Beijing's liberalized attitude toward trade and investment and by low labor and land costs. On the other hand, the long-range profitability of such ventures may still be quite questionable because of uncertainties associated with the stability of national and provincial leadership groups; tenuous legal rights; bureaucratic infighting; inadequate shipping facilities; the lack of local managers, technicians, and skilled workers; limited access to China's domestic market; and other considerations.[2]

The third major reason for piecing together incentive packages is to attempt to resolve serious disparities in regional economic development. Within the political context, voters in the "have not" regions will generally shy away from supporting incumbents who have done little to improve the material lot of their districts. More ominously, nations which have pockets of underdevelopment interspersed with regions of relative prosperity may risk major civil strife, especially when severe ethnic, religious, or ideological cleavages already exist within the country.

Once again, investors must proceed with caution before committing to projects in depressed regions, and incentives must take a back seat to factors such as development of transportation and communications, access to markets and raw materials, availability of skilled and reliable labor, and so on. On the other hand, the preoccupation of certain governments with regional disparities would seem to offer especially attractive investment opportunities, particularly in several advanced industrial nations. For example, the willingness to establish a facility in specially designated regions in France and Canada may not only produce millions of dollars in incentives but may also be the critical factor in determining whether or not the investment will be approved by screening agencies in those two nations. Incentives available in enterprise or free-trade zones in Great Britain, the United States, or a host of other nations may also be extra frosting on the cake for investors already convinced that profitable market opportunities exist in those countries.

SELECTING AN INVESTMENT PACKAGE

The investment-incentive war has never been as intense as it is today, and problems may be on the horizon because government inducements definitely distort both competition and the interplay of market forces. Moreover, because the stakes have become so high in this cutthroat poker game, sore losers in the incentive battle may be tempted to retaliate through the imposition of trade barriers and other forms of protectionism. Nonetheless, the specter of future difficulties for the international trade and investment community has not for the moment deterred governments from anteing up huge sums of money in a concerted effort to ensnare foreign investors.

Examples of government largesse are plentiful. France has designated half of its territory as being eligible for special incentives and annually doles out a billion dollars or more for inducements. Under current criteria, investors willing to construct a food-processing plant in Alsace-Lorraine or the Pas-de-Calais regions could receive a grant from the French government for as much as 75 percent of initial start-up costs.³ For investing in the Mezzogiorno, the underdeveloped southern region of Italy, or in Sicily and Sardinia, the government in Rome will provide companies with outright grants ranging from 45 to 56 percent of initial costs and financing at as low as one-third of the Italian prime rate. Soft loans, exemptions from corporate taxes for up to ten years, subsidies for employer-paid health and pension plans, free technical advice, training for top and middle management, and a host of other incentives are also doled out by Rome. It is estimated that Italy has dispensed over 2 billion dollars annually during the past decade for investment incentives, although the results have not been overwhelming. To be more precise, Italy's incentive programs have been plagued by poor planning and coordination on the part of national and regional bureaucracies. Moreover, too many subsidies have been dispensed to capital-intensive industries in underdeveloped regions which have a desperate need for thousands of new jobs.

On a more optimistic note, Ireland has certainly achieved far greater tangible results from its incentive programs than have the vast majority of its neighbors in Europe. Ireland's Industrial Development Authority (IDA) periodically takes its show on the road to Chicago, New York, Tokyo, and other major cities, promising to provide a mixture of tax incentives, high depreciation write-offs, and low plant and labor costs. In 1981 alone, the IDA negotiated for 150 new and expanded ventures with U.S. companies, projects which would entail 700 million dollars in capital and the creation of 15,000 new jobs.⁴ Its trump card is the unimpeded entry which foreign firms based in Ireland will enjoy to the affluent markets of the European Community. Moreover, the IDA has developed a good reputation for assisting firms with their problems (such as poor telephone service and industrial-gas interruptions) after the investment has been made. Industrial output has increased dramatically in Ireland over the past decade, and thousands of jobs have been created by foreign enterprises. For the most part, these foreign firms have been pleased with both the incentive packages and the overall business climate in the Irish Republic, although they have expressed some concern about balance-of-payments and currency-stabilization problems.⁵

Knowing how incentive policies are formulated and implemented and identifying the key political and bureaucratic actors involved in the process can lead to highly advantageous contractual arrangements for multinational enterprises. Indeed, contacts with individuals and bureaucratic agencies involved in incentive programs may be the key to gaining access to once closed markets, with millions of dollars in inducements thrown in to sweeten the investment agreement. For example, IBM has at times experienced its share of problems with Canada's Foreign Investment Review Agency, but by working directly with departments involved in doling out investment incentives and by agreeing to build a facility in Quebec, IBM not only recently gained approval for a new investment project but also received 6 million dollars in nonrepayable grants from agencies of the Canadian government. The same strategy has also been used quite successfully in France. Even in Mexico, which has often been perceived by foreign firms as hostile to their investment proposals, agencies involved in dispensing incentives have at times been the key to a successful entry into that country. For those firms willing to export most of their production and locate within 12 miles of the U.S. border, Mexico's Border Industrial Development Program will provide major incentives, including unimpeded and untaxed importation of machinery and raw materials. Other government agencies can also exempt exporting firms from the Mexicanization of their equity and management, a provision which helped to entice Ford and Chrysler to Mexican soil. Through selling stock to banks or utilizing other types of stock transfers, even firms which Mexicanize 51 percent of their holdings can ensure that they maintain day-to-day control over management decision making. Moreover, such firms then become eligible for grants which may include a 25-percent investment-tax credit, a 20-percent employment-tax credit, 30-percent discounts on energy costs, and other benefits.[6]

International investors should also recognize that incentives for overseas direct investment are offered at times by parent governments as well. In December 1979 the Japanese Diet passed liberalized foreign exchange laws which facilitate foreign direct investment ventures by Japanese firms. The Tokyo government also provides very generous investment guarantees and financing arrangements for certain types of direct investment projects. Likewise, the U.S. government provides incentives for overseas investment through special tax provisions; OPIC insurance; the Export-Import Bank; bilateral friendship, navigation, commerce, and tax treaties; the Hickenlooper and Gonzalez amendments; and low-interest loans for projects in certain developing nations. In order to ensure that their home-based firms remain internationally competitive, many other governments in advanced industrial nations are offering similar types of incentives.[7]

As can be readily seen in Appendix II, there are currently an unprecedented number of incentive packages available from host and parent governments alike involving literally billions of dollars in benefits. Therefore, sound business judgment dictates that firms engage in a great deal of research and ascertain both the pre- and postinvestment performance records of governments offering such investment entice-ments before making the final commitment to proceed with a project.

GOVERNMENT INCENTIVE POLICIES IN PERSPECTIVE

It is quite easy for international firms to get caught up in the euphoria of the investment incentive war now being waged by national and subna-tional governments, but incentives must be kept in perspective. In almost all cases, government incentive policies should rank far below market, labor, resource, energy, transportation, communications, qual-ity of life, and other criteria used in making an investment decision. For example, Singapore offers a well-developed economic infrastruc-ture, a favorable geographic location, a stable political climate, a lack of corruption, a highly probusiness environment, an educated work force, and preferential access to the high-growth ASEAN market. An invest-ment in Singapore may thus be much more advantageous in the long run for a foreign firm than an investment in a neighboring nation which lacks many of these features but is willing to furnish a lucrative incen-tive package.

Companies must also be wary about how the courts may react to various elements contained within the incentive package. For example, in order to attract new direct investment and thereby reduce its high unemployment rate, the government of Belgium enacted a law which permitted most foreign executives residing in the country to exclude from 10,000 to 30,000 dollars of their income in calculating their taxes. Belgian courts subsequently ruled that it was illegal to grant personal income-tax concessions to foreign business representatives working in Belgium. Consequently, the tax changes meant that multinational firms would have to dole out at least 30 percent more in compensation to their non-Belgian employees. General Electric, Gulf Oil, Sheraton Hotels, and Borg-Warner Chemicals have already vacated Brussels be-cause of high costs, and the court decision, which was, of course, op-posed by the Prime Minister and the Cabinet, could well prompt other firms to move to neighboring nations within the European Commu-nity.[8]

As described in the previous chapter, firms must also understand the ins and the outs of the political process which result both in investment restrictions and investment incentives. Incentives are implemented by elected officials at the national and regional levels to placate powerful interest groups and to improve their own reelection chances. Pork-barrel tactics are also quite common, with one elected official supporting benefits for the influential constituents of another official in order to gain backing for the interests of his or her own powerful constituents. Furthermore, once the decisions have been rendered by lawmaking bodies, the bureaucracy then enjoys a great deal of latitude in implementing the new policies. In particular, foreign firms must cultivate contacts in incentive-granting agencies and allow these agencies to become their advocates in negotiations with elected officials and other bureaucratic departments. With the enthusiastic support of these granting agencies, firms may well gain access to previously closed markets, be accorded generous incentives, and be exempted from certain investment restriction policies.

An understanding of local and regional policymaking processes is also crucial for investors seeking special incentives. Multimillion-dollar incentive packages are now being dispensed with what at times seems to be reckless abandon by governments in U.S. states, Canadian provinces, German Länder, and their subnational counterparts in other countries. A foreign enterprise showing a willingness to establish facilities in specially targeted areas of nations may well reap a bonanza in investment incentives from national, regional, and municipal government units. For example, a decision by a high-technology firm to construct a plant in Montreal would likely result in millions of dollars in grants, low-interest loans, and other inducements from the governments in Ottawa, Quebec City, and Montreal. A foreign manufacturer willing to establish a facility in a free-enterprise zone in Miami would also be eligible for a variety of grants from the U.S. Department of Housing and Urban Development and the Economic Development Administration of the U.S. Department of Commerce, as well as from the state government of Florida, the government of Dade County, and the city government of Miami. When site-location flexibility is available to a foreign investor in a particular country, careful research and extensive legwork aimed at the local and regional government levels will generally pay huge dividends. And ironically, some of the most lucrative incentive packages are now being offered by governments in countries which, even without incentives, would offer extremely attractive market opportunities for foreign investors.

REFERENCES

[1] *Christian Science Monitor*, February 11, 1982, p. 10.

[2] *The Wall Street Journal*, June 5, 1981, p. 29 and *Business Week*, January 11, 1982, p. 50.

[3] *Business Week*, August 6, 1979, p. 41.

[4] *U.S. News and World Report*, February 8, 1982, p. 50.

[5] *Christian Science Monitor*, May 5, 1981, p. 21. A few foreign firms have not been able to make a profit in Ireland. For example, Wrangler, the maker of jeans, has pulled out of the Irish Republic. On the whole, however, the mix of investment incentives, relatively low labor costs, and unimpaired entry to the affluent European Community market has proved to be quite beneficial for most foreign firms.

[6] *The Wall Street Journal*, May 12, 1981, p. 27.

[7] See Craig M. Watson, "Counter-Competition Abroad to Protect Home Markets," *Harvard Business Review*, January-February, 1982, pp. 40–42.

[8] *Business Week*, February 22, 1982, p. 50.

2001 AND BEYOND: THE FUTURE OF INTERNATIONAL INVESTMENT

9

AN ESCALATING POLITICALIZATION OF INVESTMENT ACTIVITY

In February 1982 the French government enacted the most extensive program of nationalization in France since the end of World War II. This new program boosted state control over industrial output from 12 percent to 16 percent and eliminated all major sources of private credit, including the legendary Rothschild banking group. In all, five major industrial enterprises, thirty-nine banks, and two financial holding companies were nationalized under the new law. In addition, formal charges of fraud were brought against the chairman of the Banque de Paris et des Pays-Bas (Paribas) because he had transferred considerable assets of the bank to a Swiss subsidiary before the nationalization law had been enacted.

With the government's takeover of Thomson-Brandt, Saint-Gobain, Rhone-Poulenc, Pechiney Ugine Kuhlmann, and Compagnie Générale d'Électricité, foreign-owned firms face more difficulty than ever before in securing contracts from both the burgeoning government sphere and dwindling private sector. Employment, balance of payments, and other considerations will also be used by government representatives to rationalize "Buy French" policies. Moreover, foreign firms such as American-based Honeywell and ITT and German-based Hoechst AG face the specter of losing their French subsidiaries altogether in the second wave of nationalizations.

What occurred in France in 1982 will be repeated sporadically in many other countries over the next few decades. From 1958 until 1981, France had been governed by a moderate-conservative coalition of Gaullists and centrists who vehemently rejected an extensive new campaign of nationalizations. Fearing the consequences of rising unemployment and tired of the patrician practices of President Giscard d'Estaing, the French voters finally opted for a change in 1981 and swept Socialist Party leader François Mitterand into the presidential seat at the Elysée Palace. The voters later reconfirmed their support for Mitterand's regime by providing the Socialist Party and its allies with a working majority in the Chamber of Deputies. As a result, the French presidency, prime ministership, cabinet, and major chamber of parliament were all headed by members of the same party, thereby providing Mitterand with the opportunity to steer his ambitious economic plan through France's rather complicated and cumbersome decision-making system.

In spite of their worries associated with rising unemployment and inflation and major disparities in the distribution of income, it is not at all clear that the French voters wholeheartedly supported the major revamping of the economic sector which was finally enacted by Mitterand and his colleagues. The voters were simply disenchanted with the previous administration and recognized that Mitterand's coalition was the only viable alternative to the moderate-conservative alliance which had dominated French politics since the inception of the Fifth Republic in 1958. A similar disenchantment with a corruption-prone administration and a desire for a change brought the Parti Québécois (PQ) to power in 1976. The PQ government then proceeded to accelerate the trend toward expanding the public sector and bringing more industrial groupings under direct state control, policies which have received a very mixed reaction from the Quebec public as a whole. The voters have generally agreed, however, that the PQ has brought "clean" government to the province and that it is concerned with the rank-and-file Quebec citizen, perceptions which helped to reelect the government in 1981.

The crucial point to be drawn from these examples is that the voters in advanced industrial societies do not generally want a major restructuring of their economic systems which will lead to severe limitations on market activity. On the other hand, they will tolerate certain national government solutions to economic problems and, for the sake of change, will periodically elect regimes which will carry government intervention in the market sector far beyond what the voters originally intended. Eventually, the governments of François Mitterand in France and René Lévesque in Quebec will give way to moderate-conservative administrations which will decry the massive government intrusion into the economic sphere and attempt to dislodge the state from certain economic activities. Post-World War II history has shown, however, that this dismantling of state activity rarely if ever restores the economic order which existed prior to the leftist government's ascendancy to power. Government intervention in the market systems of the advanced industrial world is thus a cyclical process, with administrations pinpointed along a political spectrum ranging from Mitterand, Lévesque, and Clement Attlee on the left to Margaret Thatcher and Ronald Reagan on the right. A majority of the postwar governments in the Western democracies have, of course, been moderate-centrist with only occasional swings leftward and rightward. Nonetheless, the pendulum drift from liberal to moderate to conservative government and then back has in the long run edged government systems toward greater intervention in the economic sectors. In other words, when conservative governments do come to power, they are unwilling or unable to eliminate all the interventionist policies enacted by earlier liberal regimes, policies which by this time the electorate has grown accustomed to. In the developing nations, the swing from left to right can often be much more extreme (such as the shift from Frei to Allende to Pinochet in Chile) and the moderating influence of centrist groups is less pronounced.

Thus, a survey of government economic policies from 1945 until the present clearly substantiates that government intrusion in the economic sector is generally at an all-time high in both developing and advanced industrial societies. Moreover, because of a gradual change in the public's attitude toward social-welfare policies over the past four decades, what is considered today as a moderate or even conservative approach to government interaction in the market system would have been perceived as quite radical in 1945. When these tendencies are combined with the public's acceptance or at least acquiescence to "national" solutions to economic problems, it is not difficult to predict that the international investment arena will become even more politicized in the decades ahead. Furthermore, one must remember that this pendulum swing from left to right and back again will most likely be accentuated because so many problems in an age of complex global interdependence cannot be adequately resolved by national or subnational governments. Only international cooperation can bring about workable solutions to nuclear proliferation, pollution, technology transfer, currency stabilization, inflation, unemployment, and a host of other problem areas. Unfortunately, international linkages will be slow to develop, and dissatisfied voters, frustrated with negative political, economic, and social trends which they feel should be rectified by their incumbent home governments, will simply turn to opposition parties as a panacea for relief. Geopolitics will also be impacted because as ruling parties or coalitions change, so may alliances. Radical shifts in international and regional alliances undertaken recently by Ethiopia, Somalia, Zimbabwe, Jamaica, and other countries may become more commonplace in this new age of complex interdependence.

In general, international investors can expect the following trends to prevail in the decades ahead:

1. *Resource and Energy Sectors* Businesses can anticipate that investment restrictions will be the most onerous in the extractive industries especially in times of relative economic prosperity. Many foreign enterprises will have to be satisfied with minority positions in joint ventures, and host governments will pressure these firms to establish secondary industries to complement their extractive activities. In addition, energy-importing nations may have to pledge involvement in various investment projects within the energy-rich countries in order to secure steady sources of raw materials, a practice already in vogue in Saudi Arabia and Mexico. Moreover, nations which have already achieved high standards of living and which have fairly diversified economic bases, such as Canada and Australia, will substantially expand restrictions on foreign involvement in their resource and energy sectors. Likewise, within the next decade, the United States will most likely tighten up on foreign access to energy and raw-material sources, although existing direct investments in these sectors will be protected under a grandfather clause.

2. *High Technology Sector* Multinational enterprises engaged in high technology activities will enjoy the most bargaining leverage vis-à-vis host governments, although parent governments will continue to make it difficult at times to transfer highly sensitive technological innovations and data. Host government investment incentives will far outweigh restrictions in this sphere as nations attempt to keep pace with the rapid changes in technology.

3. *Manufacturing Sector* Investment restraints and incentives in the manufacturing sphere will differ dramatically depending upon local employment conditions and on competition provided by indigenous or state-owned enterprises. Multinational corporations can best protect themselves from onerous restriction policies by being good corporate citizens and showing tangible support for the host nation's societal and economic advancement. Retaining strict control over the distribution and marketing network for the subsidiary's

products will also diminish the chances that a multinational enterprise will face severe host government restrictions.

4. *Other Sectors* Foreign firms engaged in infrastructure activities considered crucial to national security, such as public utilities and mass communications, or sectors impacting upon the control of the economy, such as banking and insurance, will be increasingly vulnerable to government restrictions.

COPING WITH THE POLITICS OF INTERNATIONAL INVESTMENT

To a limited extent, negotiations currently being pursued on an international scale may mitigate some of the excesses of national political restrictions on investment and trade activity. Efforts to formulate international codes of conduct for both multinational enterprises and host and parent governments may eventually bear some fruit. In particular, discussions now underway within the Organization for Economic Cooperation and Development and the European Community will result in some substantive policies for the advanced industrial societies. On the other hand, discussions within the United Nations, which are punctuated by major differences between the nations of the North and South, will lead to few significant agreements and will be impeded further by the lack of enforcement provisions. The Group of 77, out of frustration over lack of progress in the North-South dialogue and in the implementation of a New International Economic Order, may seek to impose rather harsh limitations on the activities of multinational corporations. Such restrictions, which would definitely present new challenges for the international business community, would be counterproductive in terms of denying these nations much-needed jobs, capital, technology, management, and marketing expertise. Moreover, the Group of 77 is far from being a monolithic organization, and there would be enough defections to make the uniform enforcement of any stringent code virtually impossible.

Bilateral and in some cases multilateral agreements may also help to standardize rules of the game designed to eliminate bribery, kickbacks, unethical political contributions, and other questionable political activity. Even in this case, however, agreements will generally be among a few of the advanced industrial nations and will have only a minor impact on business-government linkages.

To say the least, the world is still years away from formulating an investment agreement which would parallel what GATT has done for trade and the IMF for monetary transactions. Yet in spite of the growing politicization of the investment sector and the continued reliance on national or even subnational solutions to major economic problems, prospects will continue to be quite good for many international investors through the duration of this century and well into the next. However, the firms which prosper will have to show as much political acumen as financial genius in their decision-making processes. They will also have to cast off their ethnocentric biases and stereotypes about the political arena in order to compete effectively in an economically interdependent but politically fragmented world. They must learn that gaining political and governmental allies at the subnational level may be much more important than national-level contacts in determining the success or failure of an investment project. Furthermore, hobnobbing with high elected officials in grandiose palaces or at luxurious dinner parties may be much less productive than getting down in the trenches in the everyday working environment of rather obscure elements of the bureaucracy. These top elected officials may have a great deal to say about highly publicized nationalization and expropriation policies, but it is the bureaucrats who will make the key day-to-day decisions about procurement, credit, tax, energy, labor, environment, tariff, antitrust, consumer protection, product liability, and a myriad of other investment-linked issues. Although monumental investment tragedies à la post-Shah Iran will certainly occur in the future, the health and vitality of most multinational corporations will in the long run be affected much more profoundly by micropolitical decisions and actions taken at the bureaucratic and local levels than by spectacular macropolitical changes ushered in by revolution and conventional wars.

As aptly illustrated by the billions of dollars in investment incentives being thrown around by hundreds of national, regional, and local governments, direct investment is still a very prized and sought-after commodity. For perhaps the first time in human history, almost every nation on earth is actively seeking direct investment from abroad in an effort to create jobs and to modernize and expand economic infrastructures. For example, the Communist nations alone represent a potential market of at least 1.5 billion consumers. China's Four Modernizations Campaign is a radical departure from the policies of previous Communist administrations because there is now an implicit emphasis placed on the development of light industries and consumer goods. This same shifting of priorities is also evident in certain Eastern European countries. Although fraught with many dangers, direct investment in the Eastern bloc has almost unlimited potential, and one can anticipate that Communist regimes will become less ideological and more pragmatic economically as exposure to Western values and products intensifies. It seems quite a paradox to many Westerners that over the past few years Gulf has continued to pump oil in Marxist Angola, with its field operations protected against guerrilla raids by Cuban troops. What is seemingly such a paradox today may well become the norm for tomorrow.

Furthermore, never before have technological innovations been introduced so rapidly, with today's incredible achievement being rendered obsolete by new products and processes brought to the marketplace tomorrow. Under such circumstances, most governments must continue to seek direct investment to survive economically and technologically in a highly competitive and interdependent international business environment. Consequently, a golden age of international investment may be in the offing, but opportunities and pitfalls will vary dramatically on an industry-to-industry and nation-to-nation basis.

Multinational corporations, which already account for about one-half of the world's present industrial output, must adapt to the changing times by engaging in very sophisticated political risk analysis. This analysis must be project-specific and take into account developments and idiosyncrasies not only at the national level but at the regional and local grassroots levels as well. Risk analysts employed by these multinational firms must also be adept in identifying key actors in interest groups, elected bodies, and bureaucracies and have a comprehensive knowledge of policymaking processes at all echelons of government. In an age of rapid expansion of state-owned enterprises and state responsibility for social-welfare functions, international investors will face many political challenges in the future, but proper planning and a thorough understanding of the politics of international investment can ensure the successful operation of most overseas projects.

THE CHALLENGES FACING THE UNITED STATES

The Corporate Dimension

As documented in the first two chapters, the golden age of international investment will not be dominated by U.S.-based multinationals nearly to the extent which occurred between 1945 and 1970. Indeed, the decline in U.S. industrial and financial leadership has been quite precipitous. In 1960, 111 American companies were situated among the top dozen world leaders in thirteen major industrial groupings, giving U.S. firms 71 percent of the leadership positions. This number has dwindled to 91 (58 percent) in 1970 and to 72 (46 percent) at the beginning of the 1980s. In the mid-1950s, U.S. banks accounted for 50 percent of the total assets of the top 100 banks in the world. By 1980, this figure had declined to 15 percent.

Much of the problem facing American enterprises may certainly be traced to corporate management. For far too long, corporate leaders have been content to rest on their laurels, harboring erroneous assumptions that it would not be difficult to maintain the international ascendancy which their companies have enjoyed since 1945. Many of these captains of industry forget that because of the massive devastation and shedding of blood which had occurred in Europe and Asia during the 1939 to 1945 period, America inherited by default the enviable position of being the *only* great industrial power on the globe, with all other nations at the time being light years behind.

Remarkable changes have transpired since the end of World War II, and America may still be leading going into the stretch, but the rest of the pack is beginning to catch up and is taking dead aim on the perennial frontrunner. Corporate management ranging from Fortune 500 enterprises to small local firms must abandon its parochial outlook. All too often, large corporations have shifted away from international divisions in favor of global-product groups directed from the United States. Although making some sense from a management point of view, this shift has often resulted in a declining interest in foreign operations and a diminishing concern for what is occurring at the national and subnational levels in many overseas countries.[1] Consequently, managers stationed in the United States are prone to view political and governmental occurrences abroad through an American frame of reference, a situation which could lead to major investment fiascoes. As Raymond Vernon astutely points out, U.S.-based managers of global product divisions may in their training and outlook be "as American as the Dallas Cowboys and apple pie."[2] Vernon adds that unlike the international specialists which they replaced, these new U.S.-based managers may shrink away from unfamiliar problems, ranging "anywhere from transacting business in pesos to wrestling with Belgian labor laws."[3]

As for the smaller firms which have been perfectly content to service the U.S. market and are extremely ignorant and/or suspicious of exporting and investment activity, they will soon learn that an international perspective must be adopted just for the sake of survival. These smaller American enterprises must anticipate much greater competition for regional markets from large American conglomerates and from an increasing number of foreign businesses. Because of the attractiveness of the U.S. market system, direct investment will continue to pour into the United States over the next two decades and competition will stiffen. Moreover, many of these small and medium-size U.S. firms already provide products and services which may be in great demand around the globe. As affluent as the U.S. market is, 95 percent of the world's population live outside America's borders, and tremendous business opportunities are available overseas. The willingness and ability to expand abroad and compete head-on with foreign businesses may well become the key factor in the ultimate survival of many small and medium-size firms in the United States.[4]

Management must also adopt longer time horizons for investment overseas and should not be at the mercy of stockholders clamoring for steady increases in dividend payments. Nissan, for example, was actively involved in the U.S. market for ten years before turning a profit. Markets must therefore be carefully cultivated and government and bureaucratic representatives overseas convinced that American firms are willing to make long-term investments in local economies and to link their own profit ambitions to an overall improvement in the nation's economic picture.

American firms must also recognize that much can be learned from management and technological breakthroughs developed overseas. The Japanese have done fabulously well in adapting technology obtained from the United States and Europe to product lines which appeal to a large number of consumers. American businesses should be able to achieve the same results. Moreover, the working relationship which has evolved between Japanese management and labor should provide valuable lessons for U.S.-based enterprises. Although the data base is still somewhat limited, surveys involving U.S. firms which have been acquired by Japanese investors indicate conclusively that American workers much prefer the new Japanese management over the previous American management. An improvement in management-worker relations in the United States would go a long way toward developing the pricing, quality, and after-sales servicing which are so necessary to catapult U.S.-made products back to the top of the line in international markets. Unless U.S. corporate management wakes up and accepts this new challenge at home and abroad, a major new force in international industrial and financial development will be represented by foreign-controlled enterprises in the United States.

The Government Dimension

Without any doubt, the relative decline in America's economic position worldwide is partially attributable to other nations picking themselves up by the bootstraps in the postwar period and working long and hard to become more competitive. On the other hand, a part of America's competitive problem is directly linked to the deliberate policies of foreign governments to discriminate against American firms. In other words, the politics of international investment is alive and well and an international economic system based primarily on market forces has long since gone into hibernation. Paraphrasing George Meany once again, international trade and investment activity has degenerated into a guerrilla war, and the United States is consistently allowing itself to be ambushed.

Even in an international system which would permit relatively unimpaired international investment activity and guarantee "national" treatment for foreign corporations, the U.S. business community would have its hands full competing with the large number of multinational enterprises now headquartered in Western Europe, Japan, the Soviet bloc, and the nearly industrialized countries. Such competition, however, would be extremely healthy for consumers, and American companies have the capability and wherewithal to do admirably well. Unfortunately, decisions being rendered by governments abroad are stacking the deck against the American competitors. Whereas foreign firms enjoy almost unimpeded access to U.S. markets, American investors face significant roadblocks in many nations, beginning with America's closest neighbors to the north and the south and then extending across the Atlantic to Western Europe and across the Pacific to Japan.

As both the world's number one direct investor and number one host nation for direct investment, the United States is in the pivotal position of being able to push strenuously for some major changes in the rules of the game governing international investment. Federal officials in Washington must begin to recognize that constant statements supporting a market-oriented international economic system, relatively free from government intervention and nationalist constraints, are not producing major policy changes in national capitals around the world. Nor is the practice of jawboning foreign governments for imposing investment restrictions prompting a significant modification in policies. Foreign direct investment activity is at an all-time high in the United States in part because the American government has instituted fewer investment restrictions than any other major industrial society in the world. In effect, the home governments of those corporations which are making the most significant direct investments in the United States generally do not even come close to providing the same opportunities to U.S. investors in their home markets. And ironically, an increasing percentage of investment activity in the United States is attributable to state-owned enterprises which do their best to place political barriers in the way of American firms trying to compete with them on a head-to-head basis back in the home country.

For the sake of moving the international economic system toward a greater market orientation, government leaders in the United States must begin to put some bite into their complaints about investment restrictions. Formal protests to GATT and the OECD over discriminatory investment policies must become more vigorous and more numerous. The economic might of the United States must also be used occasionally to show discriminating nations that America can compete very effectively in a protracted subsidy's war. For example, the Ex-Im Bank in 1981 provided a loan to the Ivory Coast for power equipment with a twenty-year payment period instead of the ten years prescribed by OECD export-credit guidelines. The president of the bank stated that "we did it to be ornery," but the real reason was to show major nations involved in subsidizing exports that the United States could be a formidable competitor and that such subsidies must be toned down dramatically.[5] Repeated instances of "orneriness" may be needed in order to truly convince other countries about the destructiveness of trade and investment restrictions and incentives. At the annual economic summit meetings of the great powers, the President of the United States must also speak plainly and bluntly behind closed doors concerning the U.S. resolve to take substantive action if investment barriers are not gradually eliminated. The leader of the American people may even have to threaten as a last resort to push for investment-reciprocity legislation. A limited reciprocity bill would mandate that the laws, regulations, and government practices in a foreign investor's home country should be no more restrictive toward foreign direct investment than the U.S. federal government is toward such investment in the United States. If a certain major restriction does exist in another country, then foreign investors from that country would be subject to the same restriction in the United States. If the restriction were subsequently to be removed by the foreign government, then the restriction would no longer be applied to that nation's investors within the American market. This new provision should be aimed specifically at developed nations within the OECD and would be implemented on a case-by-case basis.

Although hopefully such a drastic action can be avoided, a reciprocity law would nonetheless illustrate in a substantive way America's commitment to free trade and capital mobility and show the U.S. consternation toward growing protectionism and discrimination in the advanced industrial segment of the globe. Indeed, such a law would be a clarion call to other developed nations, particularly Japan, to cast aside their complacency and to begin to push vigorously for a workable investment code. The United States should also be prepared to meet on a bilateral basis with other nations to hammer out investment codes which will go beyond the limited agreements achieved by the OECD in theory but often neglected in practice. In essence, the United States in the short run may have to be actively engaged in the guerrilla war of international investment in order to ensure American companies an equal opportunity to secure overseas investment opportunities. In the long run, however, the U.S. government must remain committed to a market-oriented international economic system, which of course will never be devoid of political maneuvering. Nonetheless, such a system is most conducive to this new era of complex interdependence and will provide the best results in modernizing and expanding national economies around the world and in improving the standard of living of humankind. Foreign investors should thus for the most part continue to enjoy "national" treatment and a "most-favored-nation" status within the American market, and the U.S. government must strive diligently to ensure similar privileges for American investors overseas.

REFERENCES

[1] Raymond Vernon, "Gone are the Cash Cows of Yesteryear," *Harvard Business Review*, November-December, 1980, pp. 153–154.

[2] Ibid., p. 154.

[3] Ibid.

[4] See Craig M. Watson, "Counter-competition Abroad to Protect Home Markets," *Harvard Business Review*, January-February, 1982, pp. 40–42.

[5] *Business Week*, October 12, 1981, p. 44.

APPENDIX I: RESTRICTION POLICIES

ARGENTINA

Approval needed from executive branch in:
  Defense industries   Education
  Energy   Banking
  Communications
Investments in excess of 20 million dollars need approval from President
Few if any investments permitted in automotive industry
Repatriation only possible after three years (or longer term if so fixed) and only
  if laws are adhered to
Special tax levied on profits remitted annually when amount exceeds 12 per-
  cent of the total value of the foreign investment

AUSTRALIA

Restrictions in:
  Banking
  Nonbank financial intermediaries and insurance companies
  Broadcasting
  Newspapers
  Civil aviation
  Real estate (exceptions possible)

Investment reviewed by government in:
    Uranium—75 percent Australian   Fishing
        equity   Forestry
    Mining (other than uranium)
    Agriculture
    Pastoral activities
Export controls on:
    Coal   Petroleum products
    Iron ore   Tin
    Bauxite   Salt
    Aluminum   Uranium
    Petroleum   Materials of nuclear significance

AUSTRIA

Prevention of excessive foreign ownership in:
    Banking   Tourist trade
    Insurance   State monopolies
Increased tendency to keep foreigners from acquiring land or even ownership
    of apartments

BELGIUM

Regulations in:
    Brewing industry
    Industries handling rags
    Industrial activities considered to be hazardous, injurious to health, or un-
        pleasant, i.e., explosives factories, dumps, quarries, mines
Licenses or prior authorization required in:
    Flour products
    Various food items
    Alcoholic beverages
    Animal feeds
    Fertilizers
    Instruments for weighing, measuring, counting
    Precious metal products
    Diamonds
    Small arms and ammunition
    Pharmaceutical/phytopharmaceutical products
    Electric power and gas
    Petroleum products
If foreign contribution is goods and equipment, authorization must be obtained
    from Institut Belgo-Luxembourgeois du Change (IBLC)
Approval of Minister of Finance needed for real-property and business-entity
    ownership

Each company is required to deposit in a special account all salary payments exceeding a certain amount, and the biggest wage earners must invest 10 percent of their income in Belgian companies or government bonds

BOLIVIA

Andean Pact Decision 24 generally enforced
Applications must first be submitted to National Investment Institute
Investments in public sector must first be submitted to National Projects Committee
Investments approved or disapproved according to following criteria:
  Final destination of product
  Saving and generation of foreign currency
  Level of technology
  Production costs
  Financial conditions of investment
  Size of investment
  Project's economic effects
  Use of domestic raw materials

BRAZIL

Up to 60 percent income tax on remittances of profits
51 percent Brazilian ownership required in various sectors
Ownership or operation of the following industries prohibited:
  Airlines and coastal shipping   Fishing companies
  Newspapers   Lotteries
  Radio or television stations   Most of the computer industry
Building permits required
Antitrust legislation
Government administers price controls on virtually all industrial products
Strict licensing agreements often make technology transfer nonprofitable
Rigorous exchange controls
Repatriation and remittances can be controlled, reduced, and even prohibited
  in periods of serious imbalance in international payments
Corporate income-tax rate is 35 percent
Excessive profit tax, capital-gains tax, dividends tax, etc.

CANADA

Review of all new proposals by FIRA
Several provinces regulate foreign ownership of land
National Energy Policy requires that the oil and gas sector be at least 50 percent
  Canadian-owned by 1990 (see Chapters 5 and 6)

CHILE

Foreign investor must bring in capital within:
  Eight years—mining investments
  Three years—all others
Capital cannot be remitted to another country until it has been in Chile at least
  three years
Foreign Investment Committee's approval needed for:
  Investments over 5 million dollars
  Government and public-service sector activities
  Communication-media services
  Activities performed by foreign-state or foreign-public institutions
Restrictions in:
  Petroleum
  Petroleum by-products
  Nuclear energy

CHINA

In a joint venture, the proportion of the investment contributed by the foreign
  participant shall in general not be less than 25 percent
Technology and equipment must be advanced and appropriate to China's needs
Raw materials must be purchased from Chinese sources whenever possible
Representatives of foreign enterprises, organizations, etc., must register with
  authorities if they are carrying out economic activities and if they stay longer
  than six months

COLOMBIA

Prior authorization required
No foreign investment in:

Drinking-water supply	Insurance
Sewage	Other financial institutions
Electric light and power	Domestic transportation
Sanitation and cleaning	Advertising
Telephone	Commercial radio and television
Postal services	Newspapers
Telecommunications	Magazines
Partial real property	Domestic marketing
Commercial banks	

Yearly transfer of profits limited to 20 percent or less of initial investment
Permission required for reinvestment of profits
Andean Pact Decision 24 generally enforced

COSTA RICA

Duties and taxes on imported goods very high:
    Capital goods, 5 to 15 percent
    Imported goods not produced locally, 10 to 50 percent
    Imported goods produced locally, 100 to 150 percent
45 percent income tax on incomes in excess of one million colón
Private monopolies prohibited
Some land areas reserved for ownership by nationals
Ministry of Economy can enforce price controls
State monopolies in:
    Utilities   Petroleum refining
    Communications   Alcohol production
    Railroads   Insurance and banking
No foreign ownership in mass media

DENMARK

Agriculture and real estate restrictions

ECUADOR

No foreign investment in:
    Advertising   Newspapers
    Broadcasting stations and television   Magazines
Andean Pact Decision 24 generally enforced

EGYPT

Investment in following fields require prior government approval:
    Industrialization
    Mining
    Energy
    Tourism
    Transportation
    Reclamation of barren land—long-term tenancy not exceeding fifty years
    Housing/urban development
    Banks—Egyptians must control at least 51 percent of capital
    Construction—50 percent Egyptian capital

EUROPEAN ECONOMIC COMMUNITY

See individual member country

FEDERAL REPUBLIC OF GERMANY

Investors must notify Finance Office and pertinent municipal authorities about projects

Some preference given to local enterprises in awarding of government contracts

FINLAND

No foreign investments in:

Mining	Commercial banking
Forestry	Foreign-currency trading
Wood processing	Insurance-company funding
Pulp-paper products	Shipping and aviation facilities

Strict government standards in activity linked to:
Auditing
Credit information

Managing director and two-thirds of board of directors and supervisory board must be Finnish (some exceptions permitted)

No foreign ownership of real property without permission

Restrictions in:
Radio and television broadcasting
Postal and telegraph services
Most trade in alcohol and denatured spirits

Finnish national must be the responsible manager in:

Hotels and restaurants	Real estate
Newspapers and magazines	Trade

FRANCE

All investments subject to review, generally on a case-by-case basis

Stringent restrictions in:
Military-equipment industry
Broadcasting
Petroleum
Chemicals
Mines
Aircraft
Explosives
Railroads
Water
Electricity
Fertilizers
Banking
Insurance

Paris—Special permission necessary from Ministry of Environment

Transfers between France and foreign countries strictly regulated in:
Nuclear power
Pharmaceuticals
Transportation
Defense equipment
Certain industrial and financial sectors currently subject to nationalization

GABON

New companies must grant 10 percent of their capital to government
Government retains right to purchase up to 25 percent of company's stock
Mining—government can purchase up to 60 percent of firm's capital
Companies must be headquartered in Gabon and must reinvest portion of profits in the country
Foreign-owned concerns must give Gabon citizens management responsibilities as soon as possible
Prior declaration to Ministry of Finance required

GREECE

Minimum investment to be in excess of 150 million drachmas
Repatriation of not more than 6 percent of capital (foreign exchange used may not exceed 8 percent of foreign-exchange receipts)
Items imported to aid investment (i.e. machinery, instruments, tools, etc.) will be exempted from import duties, but must be reexported within three months of completion of work (otherwise exemptions not valid)
All investments must be approved
Capital not repayable until one year after enterprise begins
Land and real property in frontier areas may not be acquired by aliens

GUATEMALA

Prior approval by National Export Promotion Center
Importation of raw materials and agricultural raw materials already produced in Guatemala prohibited (possible exceptions)
Gasoline not exempt from customs duties, taxes, etc.
All companies must register with the Mercantile Registry

HONG KONG

The Crown owns all land in Hong Kong; therefore, businesses conduct enterprises on leasehold land

INDIA

Investment of over 40 percent of capital requires government permission
When 51 percent equity is held by foreign investor, 10 percent of total production must be exported
Some industries allow only foreign technical collaboration

INDONESIA

All foreign investment must be in joint ventures
At outset of venture, 20 percent must be held by Indonesian entrepreneurs
Within ten years the Indonesian share participation must increase to at least 51 percent

IRELAND

Nonmanufacturing companies are liable to corporation tax on their profits at a rate of 45 percent (reduction in that rate has been proposed)
10 or 25 percent value-added tax is applied to most goods at each stage of production until purchased by the consumer
30 percent capital-gains tax
A 5 to 60 percent capital-acquisition tax on gifts and inheritances
Income-tax rate of 60 percent for individual's income in excess of 4000 pounds

ISRAEL

Limitations in:
  Communications
  Air/water transport
  Banking
  Exploitation of land or other natural resources

ITALY

Transfer of earnings or profits limited to 8 percent per year
Capital not able to be repatriated until two years following investment
Investments of over 8 million dollars need government approval
Authorization needed in:
  Insurance   Banking
  Air transportation   Tobacco (state monopoly)
  Ship/aircraft industries
Government permission needed on investments and expansion which are more than 19 million dollars
Certain industrial sectors not eligible for soft loans/cash grants
Petroleum is the only industry with some exploration restrictions on percentage of foreign ownership

IVORY COAST

Prior registration with government required

JAPAN

Permission required for all investments
No 100 percent foreign investment in:
    Agriculture, forestry, fishing   Oil
    Mining   Computers
    Petroleum, including refining   Medicines
    Leather/leather products
Banking and insurance are regulated industries
No single investor may own more than 10 percent of investment without approval
Corporate income tax of 42 percent
Takeover bids first require unanimous approval of the board of company to be acquired

KOREA (SOUTH)

Minimum investment 500,000 dollars
Foreign equity limited to 50 percent or less (some exceptions)
Foreign investment admitted only in:
    Large-scale facilities which cannot be built and operated by local means
    Metal production
    Machinery production
    Electric and electronic-products production
    Export-oriented projects for which overseas markets cannot be effectively explored by nationals
    Projects contributing to development and utilization of domestic resources
    Chemical industries (no factory construction in Seoul)

KUWAIT

Foreign investment only permitted in joint ventures with at least 51 percent Kuwaiti ownership

LUXEMBOURG

Prior approval required from Ministry of the National Economy and Middle Classes

MALAYSIA

All investors must register with government, which will determine government participation level

15 percent withholding tax on royalty payments
British investments must receive approval from Prime Minister's office
Bumiputra (native Malaysian not of Chinese origin) participation levels mandated for all projects

MEXICO

Government monopoly in:
  Petroleum and hydrocarbons
  Basic petrochemicals
  Radioactive minerals and generation of nuclear energy
  Electricity
  Railroads
  Telegraphic and wireless communications
No foreign investment in:
  Radio and television
  Urban and interurban automotive transportation
  Domestic air and maritime transportation
  Forestry
  Gas distribution
Foreign control not to exceed share of capital
Investment *must* benefit nationals
New foreign equity not to exceed 49 percent of total equity (but 100 percent
  ownership allowed in "in bond" industries, i.e., assembly of components for
  export)
Foreign ownership limited:
  Mining—34 percent
  Manufacture of automotive parts/secondary petrochemical products—40
    percent
Prohibition of foreign ownership in land along seacoast and borders
Mexican ownership necessary in:
  Banking
  News dissemination
  Domestic transportation
  Land settlement
  Forest- and marine-products exploitation
Investment must be complementary and not competitive with Mexican industry
Registration of all contracts involving transfer of technology is compulsory
Regulations dealing with inventions and trademarks are very restrictive

MOROCCO

Agricultural land may not be owned by foreigners
50 percent Moroccan ownership required in order to be eligible for incentives
Tax-exemptions decrease in the Casablanca industrial belt in order to promote
  development throughout Morocco
Small percentage of profits must be reinvested in Morocco

Generally, a company's board chairman and a majority of its directors must be Moroccans

NETHERLANDS

Investment in heavily populated western and center provinces is subject to a levy (i.e., Randstad)
Bonuses not given for investment in land
Minimum investment levels in each calendar year necessary to receive bonuses

NEW ZEALAND

Approval required for more than 25 percent equity participation
Consent for loans exceeding 300,000 dollars required
All remittances require the consent of the Reserve Bank
Special restrictions on land ownership
Registration required for incorporation

NIGERIA

Strict foreign-exchange-control regulations
Government authorizes remittance of dividends as they are declared
Permission by government required for investment
Investment must be shown to be beneficial to Nigeria
Whenever possible, jobs should be filled by Nigerians

NORWAY

Licenses and concessions must be obtained for productive and manufacturing activity
No foreign ownership in:

Inland and coastal shipping	Grain
Aircraft	Broadcasting
Banking	Railroads
Insurance	Other public sectors
Operation of domestic airlines	

All oil companies must use Norwegian equipment and services (when competitive in all respects)
Special permission needed for ownership of real estate
VAT levied at 20 percent on both domestic and imported goods

PAKISTAN

Strict limits on remittance of profits
Permission required for importation of some machinery

Permission required to set up industries in:
  Cement
  Sugar
  Vegetable oil
  Cotton spinning and ginning
  Other government-specified industries
Government approval required for location and sponsorship of an industry
Registration and license required for importing goods
No foreign investment in petrochemicals

PANAMA

Government may issue quotas intended to:
  Prevent excessive imports of products
  Protect domestic industry against unfair international competition
  Assure national consumers of a supply of products when domestic produc-
    ers unable to provide for needs of domestic market

PHILIPPINES

Partnership with more than 3000 pesos in capital must register with the Se-
  curities and Exchange Commission
Investment of over 30 percent capital equity needs approval
Investment can be 100 percent in pioneer areas of economic activity
Exploitation of natural resources must be 60 percent Filipino
Banking—70 percent Filipino
Investment houses—majority of voting stock Filipino
Retail trade—100 percent Filipino
Private land—60 percent Filipino
Public land—60 percent Filipino
Shipping—75 percent Filipino
Coconut industry—majority Filipino
Non-Philippine national must attain status of national within thirty years
Incentives withdrawn if paid-up capital is at least 500,000 pesos
Foreign investment in nonpioneer agricultural areas limited to 40 percent
95 percent of a company's employees must be Filipinos
Local raw materials must be given preference over imports

PORTUGAL

Foreign investment subject to authorization and registration with Foreign In-
  vestment Institute
Foreign investment not allowed in public sectors:
  Defense industries   Banking
  Public utilities   Insurance
Approval for foreign investment granted only when investment is for techno-
  logical improvement, increased productivity, etc.

SAUDI ARABIA

Approval needed from Foreign Investment Committee
Foreign firms must have local office in Saudi Arabia
75 percent Saudi employees required within five years
Real estate ownership for personal use or investment only granted by royal
approval (factories and housing for employees may be owned if investment
project is approved)
Private ownership of land for resale or speculation is prohibited
Retail/wholesale trade restricted to wholly Saudi-owned firms
Private banks—60 percent Saudi ownership

SINGAPORE

Registration required for all companies (fee included)
51 percent Singaporean ownership in:
  Retail trade
  Hotels
  Property

SOUTH AFRICA

No guarantee of equity capital
Pretoria Witwatersrand Vereeniging (PWV) region subject to a black/white ratio
requirement
New direct investment is normally only permissible by means of transfer of
funds to South Africa through banks and/or investors providing plant/
technical know-how
Repatriation of profits (which represent current profits) must be financed from
cash funds, not from local borrowing, and be based on actual business activities in South Africa
Companies which are owned 25 percent or more by nonresidents and which
have availed themselves of exchange-control authority to take local loans in
any form are subject to exchange-control permission to repatriate profits

SOVIET UNION

U.S.S.R. is a planned economy, and the state owns and directs use of all productive resources.
Trade with major Western nations often linked to a barter system

SPAIN

Reciprocity required
Prior authorization for governments of official entities of foreign sovereignty
required
If nationalization occurs, right to investment lapses

50 percent holdings allowed for most companies
40 percent holdings allowed for shipping and airline company
25 percent holdings allowed for public-service company
15 percent holdings allowed for newly founded banks

SUDAN

Only Sudanese citizens allowed to engage in wholesale or retail activities
Foreigners not normally allowed to buy land from Sudanese nationals (only if
  land was previously foreign-owned)

SWEDEN

Ownership of real estate severely restricted
Generally high taxes—40 percent state, 28 percent local
Permission from Riksbank to import capital to establish or acquire more stock
  in a business required
Riksbank does not normally agree to transfer of capital for portfolio invest-
  ments
Consent of Riksbank needed for repatriation of capital
No foreign investment in:
  Air-transport facilities
  Ownership of Swedish vessels
  Manufacture of war materials
Existing law allows workers to take part in negotiations on any company deci-
  sion directly affecting them

SWITZERLAND

Temporary/permanent residence permit only valid in one canton at a time
Establishment of foreign-owned corporation must be approved by national
  bank

TAIWAN

Prior approval of Investment Commission required

TANZANIA

In most major and basic industries, it is government policy to acquire a share of
  at least 50 percent

THAILAND

Industry-by-industry specifications, but most industries open to foreign investment

Some industries require dominant Thai investment of 51 percent
Limitations in:
   Foreign ownership of land
   Natural resources, i.e., minerals and forest reserves
   Real property

TRINIDAD/TOBAGO

Priority government participation in:
   Natural resources
   Agriculture
Government prefers 51 percent local ownership in joint ventures
No foreign investment in:

Distribution	Insurance
News media	Furniture industry
Public utilities	Boat building
Commercial banking	

Each new investment treated on a case-by-case basis
Generally foreigners may not own property

TUNISIA

After receiving approval, investor must begin operations within one year
Importation of used equipment requires permission
Equipment older than five years not permitted
Cost of used equipment should not be more than 30 percent of new value
Annual tax on license to do business is 1 percent of total sales, due every three
   months

TURKEY

Normally investments under 50 million U.S. dollars, with equity ratio between
   10 to 49 percent, are acceptable
Above 50 million dollars, special permission needed
Over 50 million dollars, can set own ratio of equity
Investment not to be less than 2 million U.S. dollars
Joint ventures preferred
Investment is preferred in:

Electronics	Hydroelectric and power projects
Telecommunications	Petrochemicals
Machinery	Synthetic fibers
Metal products	Iron and steel
Manufacturing	Automobiles (particularly engines)
Forestry and paper products	Agricultural machinery

Delay in processing applications common

UNITED ARAB EMIRATES

Prior government approval for projects
Local equity participation varies from industry to industry

UNITED KINGDOM

Permission or prior approval from Exchange Control Authorities needed to
   qualify for later repatriation of profits

UNITED STATES

Federal government restrictions in:
   Coastal and inland shipping
   Air and rail transportation
   Hydroelectric power
   Defense-related functions
   Atomic energy
   Telecommunications
   Certain resource-extraction sectors
State government restrictions (which are not uniform and must be considered
   on a case-by-case and state-by-state basis):
   Banking   Securities
   Insurance   Land ownership
See Chapters 2 and 6 for further details

URUGUAY

Authorization needed in:
   Electricity   Intermediary financial activities
   Hydrocarbons   Railroads
   Basic petrochemicals   Telecommunications
   Atomic energy   Radio
   Strategic mineral exploitation   Press
   Agriculture and livestock   Television
   Meatpacking plants
Prohibited activity:
   Banking
   Transferring to Uruguay of funds in excess of 5 percent of paid-up capital
      and reserves
   Effecting of any investment resulting in control over local corporations
   Holding of stock in local corporations other than investment corporations
   Investing in real estate or mortgages in Uruguay
   Investing in local public debt in excess of 20 percent of paid-up capital
   Transferring to Uruguay funds from realization of foreign assets
   Offering stock for public subscriptions

Partaking in financing of public utilities
Holding (for more than one year) stock in excess of 30 percent of total capital stock issued in each of two or more foreign corporations that are principally engaged in the same industry in their country of domicile
Invested capital cannot be repatriated before end of third year after date of location contract
Use of internal medium- and long-term financial credit prohibited
No tax treaties

VENEZUELA

Restricted industries include:
Telephone
Mail
Telecommunications
Water and sewage
Electricity
Defense
Television
Radio
Newspapers and magazines in the Spanish language
Domestic transportation
Publicity
Professional services
50 percent corporation tax for net income in excess of 4.6 million dollars (subject to exchange rate fluctuations)
Up to 10 percent municipal tax on gross sales
20 percent dividend-remittance tax
75 percent of labor force must be Venezuelan citizens
Special regulations in:
Insurance
Commercial banking
Other financial institutions
Extractive sectors
No foreign acquisition of nationally owned stock
Within fifteen years of establishment, company must be no more than 49 percent foreign owned
Andean Pact Decision 24 generally enforced

YUGOSLAVIA

Foreign participation not to exceed 40 percent
Foreign partner cannot acquire ownership or property rights
Major decisions need approval of Worker's Council
No investment smaller than 10 percent of equity in project
Minimum investment of 262,000 dollars (subject to exchange-rate fluctuations)

Foreigner is usually not chosen to be managing director (law is vaguely worded)

Foreigner cannot engage in:

Insurance

Retail and wholesale trade

Communal, social, and similar services

Foreign investments must be long-term investments (minimum five years—maximum twenty years)

Foreign investor prohibited from indefinite participation in joint venture's income

Up to 50 percent of foreign exchange earned by exports can be transferred abroad to foreign partner

Joint venture contract determinant of foreign investor's legal rights

ZAIRE

Minimum investment of 500,000 zaires

If all promoters are foreign, at least 80 percent of total funds must come from abroad

Loans toward the investment shall not exceed 70 percent of the total

Sum total of loans due in at least five years shall not exceed 30 percent of investment amount

Investment must benefit economy and people

Penalties exist for invalidating agreements

Enterprise agrees to allot profits set aside to making new expansion or modernization investments in Zaire (profits set aside must be declared)

Government approval needed:

Energy mining

Forestry

Transportation

State has ultimate ownership of land and retains mineral rights

Government desires that at least 40 percent of investment should be available to Zairians

ZAMBIA

Prior government approval required for projects

Government requires submission of annual audited balance sheet showing company's activities

APPENDIX II:
INCENTIVE POLICIES

ARGENTINA

Duty-free entry of capital equipment
Preferential tariff concessions available within framework of Latin American
   Integration Association
Special concessions may be available on case-by-case basis to encourage mod-
   ernization of plants and equipment

AUSTRALIA

Equal treatment with local investors
Importation of materials, plant, and equipment for manufacturing receives con-
   cessional rates of duty
Mining:
   Special crude-oil pricing policy
   Special income-tax reductions
   Levy reduction on exporting coking coal
Income-tax concessions available to primary producers:
   Equalization of income-tax payments
   Depreciation allowance
No capital-gains tax
Double-taxation agreements
Subsidies for job training/retraining
Tax concessions for some energy-conservation expenditures

Export incentives:
  Development grants
  Expansion grants
Regional incentive programs/industrial development:
  Loans
  Grants
  Subsidized transport
  Cheap industrial land
  Subsidized charges for essential services

AUSTRIA

Equal treatment with local investors
Limited tax liability for nonresidents
Thirty-one double-taxation agreements
Banking secrecy/anonymity guaranteed
Government incentives include:
  Accelerated depreciation   Export financing
  ERP-fund loans   Low-interest start-up loans
State and local government incentives include:
  Interest subsidies   Credit guarantees
  Land grants   Partial waiver of local taxes

BELGIUM

No restrictions on importation of foreign capital
"General Aid Law"—stimulation of economic expansion or introduction of
  new productive industries, incentives include:
  Interest-rate rebates on loans
  Government guarantees to back credits
  Financing new investments
  Real estate tax exemption
  Interest-free advances to finance research and new product development
Regional aid subsidies especially in:
  Chemicals   Recovery of waste products
  Ferrous and nonferrous metals   Certain textile products
  Electronics
VAT reduced to zero when:
  New investor
  Investment meets certain labor-creating criteria
  New investment exceeds past investment

BOLIVIA

Special customs privileges
Preferential tax treatment

Special depreciation allowances
Generally unimpaired utilization and convertibility of funds in currency
in which investment made
Seven-year guarantee that investor will not be affected by unfavorable changes
in taxes and export duties

BRAZIL

Accelerated depreciation rates available
No capital tax
Up to 25 percent income-tax credits on approved projects
80 percent reduction on duties and other taxes on imported equipment
Up to ten years' tax holiday for projects in development areas
Up to 90 percent reductions on duties for exporters of manufactured goods

CANADA

Oil companies that are at least 65 percent Canadian-owned can earn special
grants for exploration and development (ownership rate will increase 2 percent per year to eventual 75 percent target)
Great variety of regional industrial grants at both the federal and provincial
government levels (see Chapters 5 and 6)

CHILE

Equal treatment with local investors
Investor can sign contract establishing fixed over-all income tax at 49.5 percent
on taxable income
Free profit and capital remittance
No time limit on how long foreign investment can be maintained in Chile
Regional incentives
Import allowances

CHINA

Chinese government protects resources invested by foreigners
Reduction of income tax for first two or three profit-making years, particularly
for joint ventures using new technology
Encouragements given to foreigners for depositing in Bank of China
Tax refund of 40 percent to those reinvesting their profits in Chinese enter-
prises for a five-year period
Significant concessions available in free-trade zones

COLOMBIA

Double-taxation agreements
Free-trade zones

COSTA RICA

Equal treatment with local investors
Tax holidays
Up to 100 percent import-duty exemptions on machinery, equipment, and
fuels (except gasoline) used strictly for the industrial process
Capital assistance
Tariff protection
Export-promotion program

DENMARK

Equal treatment with local investors
Regional development incentives:
Grants
Subsidized loans
Unimpaired repatriation of profits

ECUADOR

Incentives given in accordance with the contribution made by enterprise to
national development. Incentives include:
Favorable interest rates
Tax concessions, especially on customs taxes
High-priority projects involving industrial and regional development may be
eligible for:
100 percent exemption from taxes other than income and sales taxes
100 percent exemption on duties on raw materials for products to be exported, new machinery, accessories, and spare parts
70 to 100 percent exoneration for import duties on raw materials not produced in Ecuador
100 percent deduction from income tax for capital increases in cash or
kind
7 to 15 percent tax credit for exports
Exoneration from income and sales taxes for up to ten years

EGYPT

Prohibition on confiscation and nationalization
Repatriation of capital and profits in foreign currency
Tax holiday—5 years (extendable to eight to ten years in certain cases)

Exemptions/deferments of customs duties on all or part of capital goods
Application of private-sector law on *all* projects
Four free-trade zones in country:
   Exemption from all customs procedures and duties for all goods entering or leaving zones
   Exemption from all taxes on commodities imported and exported (1 percent or less annual duty)

EUROPEAN ECONOMIC COMMUNITY

See individual member country

FEDERAL REPUBLIC OF GERMANY

West Berlin—Special advantages:
   Reductions in VAT and taxes on income and profits
   Depreciation allowances
   Risk guarantees
   Beneficial credit
   Terms for investment
Regional promotion program offers:
   Credits at low interest rates
   Direct subsidies to companies investing in industrial plant and equipment
   Subsidies for development of land, for infrastructure projects, etc.

FINLAND

Equal treatment with local investors
Regional incentives include:
   Loans
   Transportation subsidies
   Tax relief
   Grants—up to 40 percent of cost
   Start-up subsidies
   Aid in export promotion
   Support for product development

FRANCE

Purportedly equal treatment with nationals, but over 80 percent of incentives go to French-controlled firms
Present incentives generally reserved for regional development:
   Cash grants
   Long-term loans
   Accelerated tax depreciation
   Relief from local business tax and from transfer taxes
   Tax exemptions
   Subsidies for job training

GABON

Tax exemptions
Stabilization of taxes
(Other guarantees according to relative importance of contribution to national
    development)

GREECE

Tax-clearance certificates valid for one year may be issued to foreign personnel
Imported items necessary for equipping office exempt from:
    Import taxes   Turnover taxes
    Customs duties   Luxury taxes
    Stamp duties
Exemption from income tax for income derived from activities outside Greece
Government may allow stretch of shore and sea area for exclusive use by enter-
    prise (for fifteen years from commencement)
Further exemptions from tax are applied when majority of personnel hired are
    Greek
Further incentives given in industrial, handicraft, and mining industries for
    certain R & D
Regional incentives
Personal and property rights of aliens protected

GUATEMALA

Incentives given to total export industries only
Temporary exemption (up to one year) of custom duties, taxes, and fees on:
    Raw materials
    Semifinished goods
    Samples and engineering samples necessary to acquire world standards of
        production
    Stamp-tax exemption
Ten-year tax exemption on income from exports (unless subject to same taxes
    in home country)
Member of Central American Common Market (consequently tax incentives
    available)

HONG KONG

Equal treatment with local investors
No exchange controls or restrictions on remittance of capital or profits
    overseas
No discrimination between local residents and foreign nationals in holding
    title to land
No customs tariffs

INDIA

Two free-trade zones

INDONESIA

Tax holidays—up to a maximum of six years

IRELAND

Double-taxation treaties
New manufacturing companies not required to pay Irish income tax and corporation profits arising from exports
Allowances for:
Depreciation   Staff training
Scientific research   Patent rights
Shannon Industrial estate (300-acre customs-free industrial zone):
Duty-free items   Training
Grants for machinery Housing
All profits from exports exempted from Irish income tax till 1990
Profits freely repatriated

ISRAEL

2700 Israeli-made products can be imported to U.S. duty-free
Fifteen double-taxation treaties
Cash grants and low-interest loans up to 75 percent of investment in fixed assets
Subsidized infrastructure costs in special development zone
Up to 50 percent subsidy of R & D costs on approved export-oriented products
Developmental zones:
Low rentals
Grants
Low-interest mortgages
Low-cost industrial equipment and machinery leasing
Full exemption from income tax on profits earned during five-year period starting with first year of taxable income (possible extension to twelve years)
50 percent annual depreciation rate on new industry machinery and equipment
Training subsidy
No VAT on exported goods
Deferment of or exemption from customs and purchase taxes on imported material to be used in products destined for export markets

ITALY (SOUTHERN ITALY OR MEZZOGIORNO)

Low-interest rates for medium-term loans
Cash grants
Prefinancing at low interest rates
Contribution to investments by means of increased VAT deductions
Incentives through leasing operations
Tax holiday—ten-year term
Capital-equipment subsidy
Ten-year reductions on social security payments for newly employed workers
Grants to industry in Southern Italy of up to 40 percent of plant cost
Free feasibility studies and market surveys
Free search for suitable location and labor
Training of skilled personnel
Up to 80 percent of expenditures on R & D
Labor incentives of up to 73 dollars per month for each employee trained (subject to exchange-rate fluctuations)

IVORY COAST

Ten-year exemption on:
  Custom duties   Transaction tax
  Fiscal entry tax   Contractual tax
Other exemptions of varying lengths of time:
  Taxes on industry and commercial profits
  Property tax on buildings or property
  License tax (mine and quarry concessions)
  Material-extraction tax
Reductions for ten years in:
  Contractual taxes for exportation

JAPAN

100 percent foreign investment in new existing companies possible
Double-taxation treaties

KOREA

Some tax exemptions permitted for key industries
Various incentives currently being phased in by government

KUWAIT

No restrictions on repatriation of capital and profits

LUXEMBOURG

Unconditional capital subsidy
Loans at reduced interest rates
Loans in part can be underwritten with state guarantees
Land made available to investors for industrial purposes
Organizational studies promoted by state subsidies
Part or whole cost of worker's training or retraining subsidized
Income-tax reductions
No restrictions on importation of foreign capital
Tax credit granted for investment in fixed assets (except land and buildings)

MALAYSIA

Double-taxation agreements with certain countries
Investment-guarantee agreements with certain countries
Free-trade zones for certain industries
Pioneer-status companies are allowed tax-relief period for two years from first
    production day (the normal 40 percent company tax, 5 percent development
    tax, and excess-profits tax are waived)
Tax relief for additional years (maximum of eight years) for:
    Development areas
    Priority product or industry
    50 percent Malaysian ownership
    Capital expenditures in excess of a million dollars
Tax exemption periods up to eight years available for employment of Malay-
    sian labor
25 percent or more tax credit for approved companies not enjoying pioneer
    status
40 percent increased capital allowance
Up to 12 percent export allowance
Accelerated depreciation allowance of up to 60 percent for companies which
    export 20 percent (of value) of their total production
Tax deductions for overseas promotion
Special incentives for hotel construction
Up to ten years' tax relief for special locations
Special incentives for approved agricultural industries
Up to 100 percent accelerated depreciation allowance for establishment, mod-
    ernization, and expansion of industries between 1978 and 1983
Up to 25 percent reinvestment allowance

MEXICO

Fiscal incentives given in development areas
Tax credits
Capital, profits, and dividends may be readily transferred to and from Mexico

Chemical plants given special tax benefits and energy and feedstock discounts
up to 30 percent
Special benefits available to exporting firms

MOROCCO

Exemption from custom duties on imported capital goods
Partial or total exemption from income taxes for up to ten years
Reduction of the capital-registration tax to 0.5 percent
Exemption from the turnover tax and the business tax for up to ten years
Guaranteed transfer of dividends and repatriation of capital up to the amount
invested by foreign investors
2 percent rebate on medium- and long-term loans
Full exemption from production taxes on purchase or leasing of domestic or
imported equipment
Five-year exemption from the annual license tax
Up to 50 percent of costs financed by the government for mining ventures
investing more than 110,000 dollars or creating more than fifty jobs (subject
to exchange-rate fluctuations)

NETHERLANDS

Investment Account Act:
Bonuses on investment in buildings of up to 40 percent of individual's cost
Up to 10 percent bonus on investments in machinery and equipment
Bonuses are untaxed
Small businesses can receive tax-free cash payment instead of bonus
Cash grants up to 25 percent of fixed assets (to maximum level of 2 million
dollars)
Both state and regional bonuses can amount to between 35 to 40 percent of total
investment in fixed assets
Vocational-training subsidy provides approximately 80 dollars per trainee per
day for duration of training period
Low-interest loans granted (partly and wholly guaranteed by government)
Tax treaties with many countries
Fiscal incentives such as carry-back or carry-forward of losses, etc. —

NEW ZEALAND

25 percent depreciation allowance on plant and machinery for first year
Up to 20 percent export-manufacturing-investment allowance
Up to 20 percent regional-investment allowance for eleven priority regions
Up to 25 percent tax deduction for increased exports
Up to 11 percent tax rebate of f.o.b. sales value for exported goods
Up to 68 percent tax rebate for export promotion

Export-market-development grants and loans available
Elimination of double taxation

NIGERIA

Many incentives to boost agricultural production
Double-taxation agreements
Income-tax relief for pioneer industries
Relief from import duty
Tariff protection
Relief from excise duty

NORWAY

Equal treatment with local investors
Incentives in less developed regions
Tax treaties

PAKISTAN

No restriction on remittance of profits
Repatriation equal to original investment allowed
Reinvestment may be treated as investment for purposes of repatriation (including appreciation of any capital)
No rules concerning joint participation of Pakistani capital
Investment guarantees available for losses in exchange or against expropriation
Elimination of double taxation for certain countries
Up to five years' tax holiday available in certain areas
Tax credits of up to 15 percent for modernization
Exemption of dividend and capital-gains tax
Investment allowance and exemption of dividends available
Depreciation allowance
Tax rebate on income from exports
Sales-tax exemption on machinery and export of manufactured goods
Customs-duty exemption on machinery

PANAMA

Industries with entire production for export, eligible for:
100 percent exemption on import of:

Materials	Machinery
Semimanufactured products	Equipment for production
Containers	Spare parts
Packaging	Fuels and lubricants

100 percent exemption on:
  Duties
  Taxes
  Tariffs
  Income-tax payments on benefits from exports
  Export taxes
  Sales taxes
  Capital-gains taxes
Incentives for regional location, particularly within the Colon Free Trade Zone

PHILIPPINES

Freedom from expropriation without just compensation (expropriation only for
  public use, public welfare, national defense)
Repatriation of investment in currency originally expended
Preferential tax benefits in preferred areas
Incentives differ according to enterprises whether in nonpioneer or pioneer
  category.

Nonpioneer:

Deduction from taxable income
Accelerated depreciation of fixed assets
Carryover of first ten years' operating losses
Some exemptions from import tax of machinery equipment for the first
  seven years
Tax credits
Antidumping protection
Protection from government competition

Pioneer:

The previously identified incentives plus tax exemptions from all taxes ex-
  cept income tax:
    100 percent exemption—years one to five
    75 percent exemption—years six to eight
    50 percent exemption—years nine, ten, etc.
Postoperative tariff protection
Duties and taxes on importation of machinery and equipment limited to 5
  percent
Export incentives available if:
    60 percent Filipino-owned
    70 percent of total production is exported
    Firm located in export-processing zones

PORTUGAL

Low-interest loans and grants for building construction plus equipment and
machinery
Corporate and personal income-tax exemptions
Tax exemptions and special tax allowances on investments deemed helpful to
the nation
Tax forgiveness or moratorium on:
Land   Equipment
Capital improvements   Machinery
Tax exemption on:
Goods in transit
Raw materials used in manufacturing
Government-owned industrial park sites
Government-sponsored training for industrial employees
Reimbursement of wages paid and wage subsidies for new employees
Foreign investments *preferably concentrated* in:
Automobile-assembly plants Property development
Electronics   Tourism
Cosmetics   Wood pulp
Metal products   Textiles
Electrical machinery   Clothing
Pharmaceuticals   Petrochemicals
Paint
Double-taxation treaties—if individual does not work more than 183 days per
year in Portugal

SAUDI ARABIA

Equal treatment with local investors
Tax incentives   Financial/technical assistance
Tariff-protection guarantees   Freedom of capital flow
Inexpensive land, utilities, and water at industrial estates
Funding from Saudi Industrial Development Fund (up to 50 percent of ven-
ture's capital requirement at a 2 percent annual administrative fee)
Tax holiday for five to ten years
Customs exemptions for raw materials and capital goods to be used in manu-
facturing
Special incentives for petrochemical industry

SINGAPORE

Zero tax on company profits for five to ten years in pioneer industries
Up to 50 percent investment allowance for companies not meeting pioneer-
industry criteria

50 percent tax reduction for five years on profits derived from export sales or export services for companies which expand warehousing and servicing or international consultancy services

Accelerated depreciation allowances of up to 33⅓ percent for a period of three years for plant and equipment

Tax exemption on interest on approved foreign loans for purchase of productive equipment

Duty-free importation of equipment

Government advisory services

Government training schemes

Government capital assistance

Reduced tax on export profits from 4 to 40 percent and lasting up to fifteen years for exporting companies with nonpioneer status

Additional incentives for R & D activities

No restriction on the remittance of interest earned by nonresidents

Double-taxation agreements with various countries

No capital-gains tax

No turnover tax

No value-added tax

No surtax on imports

No development tax

A concessionary rate of 12 percent (instead of 36 percent) on property taxes for twenty years is available in areas designated for urban redevelopment

Investment guarantees with various countries

SOUTH AFRICA

Unlimited amounts may be remitted from abroad

Foreign investors are allowed to buy local currency at a 30 percent discount for certain purposes

Current incentives (which are presently under review by government):

Loans at low interest rates

Factory premises at subsidized rentals

Income-tax allowances (related to expenditure on wages and manufacturing plant)

Cash grants for moving costs

Railage rebates

Price preferences on purchases from certain public-sector bodies

Unimpaired repatriation of profits in many sectors

Housing for key, white personnel

Projects over 30 million rand evaluated for incentives according to locational disadvantages

Incentives in economic-development areas:

Allowances of up to 10 percent of costs of electricity and water

Up to 35 percent subsidy for employee housing during first year (10 percent during nine succeeding years)

Machinery investment and industrial-building allowance
20 to 40 percent allowance in wages paid to non-whites
30 percent of cost of manufacturing plant subsidized

SOVIET UNION

Special export arrangements available on a case-by-case basis

SPAIN

Special incentives offered in:
  Electronics
  Telecommunications
  Automobile accessories
  Chemical production and pharmaceuticals
  Industries located in preferential zones
  Steel mining
  Food processing
  Agriculture
  Shipbuilding
  Fishing
Incentives include:
  Assistance in plant location
  Reduction of up to 95 percent of the transfer tax and other taxes related to setting up business
  Freedom of depreciation during first five years (starting with first year of operation)
  Priority in obtaining official low-interest credits
  Government loans
  Subsidies (on a case-by-case basis)
  Accelerated depreciation rates
  Reduction of import duties for plant equipment not available in Spain
No restriction on right to transfer
Income-tax deductions of up to 15 percent
Tax exemptions if net worth of investment is increased
Alternate amortization system
Incentives for company mergers
Incentives to encourage:
  Energy savings
  Environmental protection
  Industrial research and development
  Employment
  Usage of parts or elements made in Spain or imported
Regional incentives

SUDAN

Tax reductions for up to fifteen years
Facilitated land acquisition
Protective tariffs
Customs exemption
Favorable electricity and freight rates
Full remittance of profits and capital

SWEDEN

Tax treaties
Generous depreciation on:
    Inventories (can be marked down 40 percent of purchase price or market
       value)
    Buildings
    Machinery and equipment
Area-development grants (location aid available for Gotland and Oland for up
    to two-thirds of total investment)
Low-interest relocation loans
Regional incentives:
    Up to 50 percent subsidy of building cost
    Low-interest relocation loans
    Subsidy for relocation of machinery

SWITZERLAND

Mountain region:
    Long-term loans
    Interest-free loans or preferential interest rates
Economic Development Programs cover two-thirds of Switzerland:
    Guarantee of investment credit
    Participation in exceptional cases in settlement of interest on guaranteed
      investment credit
    Tax relief with regard to direct federal tax
    (Specifics vary by canton)
Double-taxation treaties
Complete freedom of transfer of investment income and repatriation of capital

SWITZERLAND—SUBNATIONAL UNITS (CANTONS)

(Land offered at favorable rates by all cantons)
Zurich—Training of personnel subsidized to prevent unemployment and to
    provide jobs for formerly unemployed
    Holding companies benefit from a special tax system

Berne—10 to 15 percent contributed toward project costs in less developed areas

If project particularly beneficial to economy, canton may assume interest payment for six years

Investment-credit guarantees of up to 3 million francs

Salary supplements up to 20 percent offered during initial training of work force

Holding companies taxed favorably

Reserves for research and company transformation are free from taxation

Lucerne—First ten years, companies may be entitled to tax privileges

Uri—Same as Lucerne

Schwyz—Same as Lucerne—number of years not specified on tax privileges

Obwalden—Same as Lucerne

Nidwalden—Same as Lucerne

Glarus—Loans at low-interest rates

Subsidies for R & D and training of labor

Possible initial six-year tax exemption

Holding and domiciled companies taxed favorably

Zug—Holding and domiciled companies taxed favorably

Fribourg—New companies—total or partial exemption from both cantonal and communal tax—offered up to ten years

Favorable tax status for holding, domiciled, and service-sector companies

Some subsidies for research in particular fields

Solothurn—Industry promotional fund of 25 million Swiss francs

Possible purchase of land for sale or lease at favorable conditions

Loans granted at low interest rates

Bank credits and payment of all or partial interest for period

Newly established companies may be exempt from taxes for ten years

Basel—New companies offered tax privileges—up to seven years

Holding and domiciled companies benefit from a special tax status

Schaffhausen—Financing of some investments by special fund

New companies offered tax privileges for up to ten years

Lower tariffs for energy supply

Holding and domiciled companies benefit from a special tax status

Appenzell A. RH.—Important single tax redemption

Cantonal Economic Fund for Development provides interest-rate assistance

Appenzell I. RH—Newly established companies offered tax privileges for up to ten years

Holding companies benefit from a special tax status

St. Gall—Newly established companies are offered tax privileges up to ten years and are also offered reduced tariffs and fees

Holding and domiciled companies benefit from a special tax status

Grisons—Government may assume part of interest to be paid on investment credits

New companies offered tax privileges up to ten years

Holding and domiciled companies benefit from a special tax status

Aargau—Tax exemption possibilities in compensatory acquisitions, mergers, and separations

Taxation of corporate bodies standardized throughout canton

Thurgau—Newly established companies offered tax relief for five to ten years

Holding and domiciled companies benefit from a special tax status

Ticino—May contribute "A Fonds Perdu" which assists in:

Building costs

Technical equipment and training costs

Loans may be guaranteed by government

Holding and domiciled companies benefit from a special tax status

Vaud—Can grant loans to small and medium-size companies

Newly established companies are exempted totally or partially from taxes for up to ten years

Holding and domiciled companies benefit from a special tax status for up to ten years

Valais—Investors may be assisted "A Fonds Perdu" in land and building costs

Training of labor within companies may also be subsidized

Newly established firms offered tax exemption (partial or total) for up to ten years

Holding and domiciled companies benefit from a special tax status

Neuchatel—May assume all or part of development costs when land is acquired

Credit guaranteed

Partial payment of interest owed to banks

Loans at preferential terms

Newly established companies can be exempted from taxes for a period of up to ten years

Geneva—Land sold at attractive terms or long-term leases available

Holding and domiciled companies benefit from a special tax status

Jura—Capital available for developing large industrial zones at competitive prices

Partial tax exemption for up to ten years

New companies can receive guaranteed loans or the partial or total settlement of interest due on financial contracts

TAIWAN

Equal treatment with local investors

100 percent foreign ownership allowed

All net profits and interest earnings can be converted and remitted

After one year of business operations, up to 20 percent of the total invested capital may be repatriated each year

If investment is over 45 percent of total registered capital, it is protected against government expropriation or requisition for twenty years

Protection of patents, trademarks, copyrights

Five-year tax holiday
Accelerated depreciation of fixed assets
Other tax incentives for productive enterprises, such as 22 to 25 percent business income tax
Refund possible on import duties paid on raw materials, etc.
Tax incentives for:
  Importation of goods
  R & D
  Saving and promotion of the development of capital market
  Promotion of reasonable operations management of enterprises
  Acquisition of land for industrial use
Special incentives available in free-trade and high-technology zones

TANZANIA

Tax-free provisions
Guarantee against expropriation (provision for scheduled takeover in five to twenty years depending on nature of enterprise)
Variety of fiscal incentives
Import duty relief
Exclusive licenses

THAILAND

Tax holiday (some taxes totally, others partially, exempted)
Full exemption from corporate income tax (three to eight years)
Tax reductions during early years:
  Business taxes
  Import duties (up to 50 to 90 percent on necessary equipment and raw materials)
Special incentives to export-oriented firms or firms which locate in promotion zones outside Bangkok
Guarantees against:
  Nationalization
  Competition of new state enterprises
  State monopolies with similar products
  Price controls
  Government state imports with tax exempted
Exemption of up to five years on:
  Withholding tax
  Royalties
  Fees remitted abroad
Special bilateral tax and economic agreements provide exemptions from certain restrictions

TRINIDAD/TOBAGO

Double-taxation agreements
Tax holiday
Rebate on customs duty up to ten years
Tax exemption on dividends
20 percent initial allowance on capital expenditures after tax holiday
Export allowances
Carry forward of aggregate net losses for five years after end of tax-holiday
    period

TUNISIA

If manufacturing for export:
    Complete customs exemption
    Exemption from tax on corporate profits over a long period of time
    Free repatriation of capital profits
    Free currency conversion
Manufacturing for domestic market:
    Benefits of shorter duration than above
Incentives in less developed regions:
    Fiscal advantages if investment creates ten permanent jobs and is 30 percent
        self-financed

TURKEY

Virtually all fields, including agriculture and mining, are open to foreign in-
    vestors
Investment in tourism—no restrictions if facility has 400 beds with 60 percent
    foreign tourist accommodation
Petroleum—open field (35 percent of oil may be exported)
Nonguaranteed commercial debts liquidated if creditor prefers payment in
    Turkish currency
Exemption from custom duties and other import taxes on the required input for
    investments and production
Foreign investors may have up to 50 percent of own investment considered
    for tax rebate purposes
Interest rebating on medium- and long-term credits
Exporters of manufactured goods can retain 50 percent of export earnings for
    purchase of machinery, etc.
Exporters can leave abroad some of their foreign-currency earnings as reserve
    for business expenses

UNITED ARAB EMIRATES

Tax exemptions
Rent-free land for specified period of time
Financial support for projects with local majority ownership

UNITED KINGDOM

Equal treatment with local investors
Development areas and urban-enterprise zones:
   Grants   Training assistance
   Tax allowances Wage premiums

UNITED STATES

Federal government permits grants allocated to state and local governments to
   be used for incentives to foreign investors
Municipal, county, and state governments provide wide array of incentives
   (see Chapters 2 and 6)

URUGUAY

Guarantees for repatriation of profits and reimbursement of invested capital
Incentives available in duty-free zones
Credit assistance, tax exemptions, and concessions if investment is in the na-
   tional interest
Investment allowance for machinery and buildings
Capital tax allowance

VENEZUELA

Tax exonerations
50 to 100 percent tax exemption (50 percent for industries and 100 percent for
   agro-industries) for up to ten years in developmental areas
Two free-trade zones—Island of Margarita and peninsula of Paraguara
Exemption from income tax on interest earned on foreign loans for certain
   industries
Up to 30 percent tax rebate on f.o.b. value of the goods exported
Financial assistance for qualifying exporting companies
Up to 20 percent investment tax credit for investments in fixed assets in:
   Industry
   Agriculture
   Transportation
   Construction

YUGOSLAVIA

Less-developed regions:
   Tax incentives established by each region
   No tax liability if wages paid by the foreign company
   No upper limit to investment

ZAIRE

Proportional tax exemption
Up to five years' exemption from business tax on profits
New enterprises exempt from nonrecurrent tax on salaries paid to expatriates
until marketing of output produced begins
Exemption for up to five years of real estate tax
Exemption from customs import duties on:
New machines
Machinery
Equipment and tools required for new enterprise (or expansion or moderni-
zation)
Guarantee of fair reimbursement of outlay and profits
Mining enterprises are exempt from business tax on profits set aside as reserves
for restoration of mineral deposits

ZAMBIA

Priority classifications:
Use of domestic raw materials
Production of intermediate goods used by other industries
Creation of substantial permanent employment opportunities
Improvement of domestic industrial skills and technology
Promotion of industry in rural areas
Incentives for priority classifications:
Preferential receipt of important licenses
Rebates of import duties on intermediate and capital goods
Relief from sales and selected employment taxes
Partial exemption from income taxes
Enterprises using significant amount of foreign capital are not subject to
nationalization

INDEX

Rukeyser, Louis, 131
Rumania, 53
Rummel, R. J., 57, 58
Russia (see Soviet Union)

Saint-Gobain, 161
Saks Fifth Avenue, 9, 12
Salt Lake City, 102
San Diego, 25
San Francisco, foreign investment in
  commercial real estate in, 11
Sandoz, 139
Santa Fe International Corporation, 19,
  109, 138
Sardinia, 155
Saskatchewan, 99
Satra Corporation, 16
Saudi Arabia, 18, 109, 164
  investment in United States by, 11, 18
  investment incentives in, 203
  investment restrictions in, 185
Schultz, George, 142
Scotland, 111, 118
Screening of investments, 4, 89, 132, 133,
  142, 154
Seagrams, 87, 103, 139
Securities Industry Association, 26
Securities laws, 97
Security issues, 19, 30
Separatist movements, 47, 84
Servan-Schreiber, J.-J., 7
Service sector, 78
Severance pay, 116
Shareholders, 136, 169
Shell Oil, 18, 20, 54, 55
Sheraton Hotels, 157
Shipping facilities, 153
Siberian natural gas pipeline, 139
Sicily, 155
Simmonds, Kenneth, 60
Simon, William, 17
Singapore, 39, 46, 128, 130, 157
  investment incentives in, 203, 204
  investment restrictions in, 185
Site-location services, 158
Slave trade, 29
Small businesses, 25, 93, 132, 168, 169
Snail darter fish, 4
Social consequences of direct investment,
  23, 43, 60, 112
Social psychology skills, 71
Social-welfare policies, 163, 167
Socialism, 123
Socialist Party (France), 162

Société Lafarge-Emballage, 133
Somalia, 52, 164
Sony, 8, 113, 114
SOS soap pads, 9, 12
South Africa, 53, 68
  investment incentives in, 204, 205
  investment restrictions in, 185
South America, 70, 108
  investment incentives in, 191–194, 211
  investment restrictions in, 173, 175–
  177, 188, 189
South Carolina, foreign investment in, 13,
  15, 25, 114
South Korea (see Korea)
South Yemen, 52
Southeast Asia, 108, 129
  investment incentives in, 197, 199, 202,
  209
  investment restrictions in, 180–182,
  184, 186, 187
Sovereignty, 42, 56, 61, 77, 78, 80, 97,
  104, 107
Sovereignty-Association, 84, 97
Soviet bloc nations, 3, 5, 132, 165, 170
Soviet Union, 2, 7, 28, 31, 47, 77
  investment incentives in, 205
  investment restrictions in, 185
Spaak, Paul-Henri, 107
Spaceship earth, 122
Spain, 54, 111, 149
  investment incentives in, 205
  investment restrictions in, 185, 186
Spartanburg, South Carolina, 15, 25, 114
Sperry Corporation, 133, 134
Sri Lanka, 52
Staffing considerations, 71
Standard of living considerations, 130,
  164, 172
Standard Oil of Ohio, 9, 12, 109
Standard and Poor's, 78
Star, The, 9, 12
State governments (United States), 99,
  111–124, 138, 152, 158
  policies of, 67, 68, 104
State-owned enterprises, 3, 6, 24, 47, 65,
  99, 100, 102, 109, 144, 162, 164, 167,
  170
Steel industry, 16, 65
Stereotypes, 56, 62
Stock disclosure regulations, 138
Stock market (U.S.), 11, 13, 14, 87
Stock portfolios, 16
Stock transfers, 156
Stockholders, 136, 169
Stouffer Hotels, 9, 12